Korean Studies of the Henry M. Jackson
School of International Studies

James B. Palais, Editor

Korean Studies of the Henry M. Jackson
School of International Studies

*Over the Mountains Are Mountains: Korean Peasant Households
and Their Adaptations to Rapid Industrialization*
by Clark W. Sorenson

Cultural Nationalism in Colonial Korea, 1920–1925
by Michael Edson Robinson

Cultural Nationalism in Colonial Korea, 1920–1925

Michael Edson Robinson

University of Washington Press
Seattle and London

Library of Congress Cataloging-in-Publication Data

Robinson, Michael Edson.
  Cultural nationalism in colonial Korea, 1920–1925

(Korean studies of the Henry M. Jackson School of
International Studies)
  Bibliography: p.
  Includes index.

  1. Nationalism—Korea—History.   2. Intellectuals—Korea—History.   3. Korea—
Intellectual life.   4. Korea—History—Japanese occupation, 1910–1945.
I. Title. II. Series.
DS916.55.R63 1988   320.5'4'09519—dc19   88-18804
ISBN 0-295-96600-9

To June and Homer

Contents

Acknowledgments

I began to work on the research for this book in 1975 in preparation for my Ph.D. dissertation under the direction of Professor James B. Palais of the University of Washington. I owe a profound debt of gratitude to Professor Palais for his tireless support and encouragement and his invaluable scholarly criticism and advice at all stages of this project. I would also like to thank Professors Kenneth B. Pyle and Bruce Cumings for their assistance and encouragement during and after my graduate studies.

The research and preparation of this book was supported at various stages from the following sources: National Language Fellowship Grants, H.E.W. Fulbright-Hays Doctoral Dissertation Research Abroad Fellowship, Social Science Research Council, John Randolph Haynes and Dora Haynes Faculty Fellowship, and the International Cultural Society of Korea. While in Korea, I benefited from the guidance and support of Professor Kim Junyop at the Asiatic Research center of Korea University. In addition, discussions with Professor Lew Young-ick of Hallyon University provided me with insights that improved the manuscript. Professor Sin Yongha also helped me at critical times during my stays in Korea, and I must also acknowledge Kim Kunsu for opening his collection of colonial periodicals to my scrutiny. Finally, I owe a special debt to Professor Chong Chinsok for giving unselfishly of his time and expertise as I submerged myself in the often baffling world of Korean colonial publications.

I would also like to thank my colleagues at the University of Southern California Department of History In particular, I benefited from discussions and comments from Professors John E. Wills Jr. and Gordon M. Berger. Special thanks are also due the staff of the U.S.C. Department of History, especially Martha Rothermel who, without complaint, prepared the manuscript in its numerous incarnations.

In addition, I am grateful to the University of Washington Press for their interest in the manuscript. The labors and professional skill of my editor, Margery Lang, greatly enhanced the manuscript. I, of course, am responsible for any errors or omissions.

My greatest debt I save for last. I wish to thank my parents, Homer and June, for giving me the gift of learning and introducing me to the world of books. Their interest in teaching led me to the life of scholarship. And, finally, a special thanks to my wife, Ellen Brennan, for her patience, support, and love during both the dark and light moments.

Cultural Nationalism in Colonial Korea, 1920–1925

Introduction

On March First, 1919, the Korean nation awoke, it seemed, from a decade-long sleep. On that day hundreds of thousands of Koreans from all walks of life joined in demonstrations to declare Korea's natural right for independence from Japanese rule. Brilliantly organized and pacifist in intent, the March First demonstrations led to sustained rioting throughout the torrid Korean summer that year. The Japanese authorities were caught by surprise. Suddenly, the heretofore quiescent colonial population was in the streets vocally denouncing Japanese rule and they provoked a swift and brutal Japanese repression. Tens of thousands of people were arrested, many more injured, and, although statistics vary, deaths related to the rioting reached into the thousands.[1]

The March First movement marked an important watershed in the history of modern Korea. Korean nationalism had become a mass phenomenon, no longer the monopoly of Westernized intellectual elites. A decade of harsh Japanese rule had combined with the spread of literacy and communications to galvanize a widespread Korean national consciousness. Thus, a broad segment of the colonial population embraced enthusiastically the simple program of the movement, a program calling for immediate Korean independence based on Korea's right of self-determination.[2] Although the movement failed in its ultimate objective, nationalist leaders in the colony and abroad were excited by the evidence of mass support. Some believed that a new era had dawned, lifting suddenly the gloom of several decades of failure and offering a future bright with possibilities. Perhaps Korea had come of age politically. Suddenly, it seemed that the broad base of support, support the nationalist reform movement lacked before 1910 and that had not materialized to buttress any significant anti-Japanese movement, was now available for a nationalist drive for independence.

The demonstrations provoked a significant change in Japanese colonial policy. For nine years Japan had ruled the colony with unremitting repression. So harsh was the system created by the first governor general, Terauchi Masatake, that it came to be known as the

Military Dictatorship Government (Budan seiji). The first governor generals had created a colony that resembled a military camp. Nevertheless, the policy of suppression, backed by the feared military police, failed to anticipate the mass demonstrations of March 1919. Embarrassed by the scope of the demonstrations and by the amount of force required to subdue them, Tokyo moved decisively to modify its colonial policy.

Saitō Makoto, appointed governor general in the aftermath of the March First disturbances, brought with him a mandate to reform colonial governance. Within the first year of his administration, Saitō instituted a number of significant changes under a new colonial policy of cultural rule (bunka seiji). Designed to soften the appearance of repression while at the same time strengthening Japanese control, the Bunka seiji changed decisively the tone of Japanese rule. In retrospect, the cultural policy was a brilliant co-optative maneuver. Although the more extreme and offensive policies were masked by a number of cosmetic changes, Saitō and his new colonial police chief, Maruyama Tsurukichi, strengthened the police control apparatus.[3] The colonial police relied increasingly on informers and an efficient network of spies to prepare for potential challenges before the fact. Moreover, by expanding the acceptable arena of political and cultural activity, they provided an escape valve for tensions in the colony. The Saitō policy recognized new realities in colonial life and met the potential threat of expanded Korean political and publishing activity with flexibility, not dogmatic repression. In the years between 1919 and 1925, Saitō walked a tightrope between renewed repression and tolerance of political activity in the colony. The goal was to make Japanese rule acceptable not only to world opinion, but to gain legitimacy within the colony as well.

The cultural policy stimulated a renaissance of nationalist activity in the colony, of which the center was the new vernacular press. Two daily newspapers received permits in 1920. Suddenly, the Korean people had a voice, and although strictly censored, the press broadened instantly public awareness of political life in the colony. Intellectual journals and specialized magazines also received permits, some for publication of explicitly political material. These journals became the forum for intellectual debate within the nationalist movement. Furthermore, organizations mushroomed in the 1910–25 period. Youth groups, study circles, labor organizations, tenant groups, and project-specific interest organizations appeared on the scene, each competing for attention in the colonial press.

The new vernacular press strained the flexibility of the colonial authorities to the limit. Having allowed the new publications in the first place, the Japanese now faced the problem of controlling them. This responsibility fell on a new office within the colonial police system, the High Police (Kōtō keisatsu), whose task it was to oversee colonial publications. An elaborate system of prepublication censorship became the chief means of control.[4] The censorship system was designed to eliminate dangerous thought or overtly subversive articles, but in the early years of Cultural Rule the censor's gaze was often myopic. A clear policy of what was acceptable and what was unacceptable had not yet emerged, and the Korean press grew faster than the censorship staff. As a consequence, the period between 1920 and 1924 represented a relatively open period for Korean intellectuals. By 1924, however, the Japanese had begun to tighten their controls; instances of erasure, sales ban, and publication suspension, both temporary and permanent, increased as the colonial censor moved to expunge dangerous ideas from the press in the name of public order and security.

Nevertheless, between 1920 and 1925, nationalists in the colony were relatively free to discuss social, cultural, and, within limits, political issues, but there was a new urgency to the discussion. Two decades of reform proposals, historical and cultural introspection, discourses on Western political philosophy and social organization, and inquiry into the nature of Korean national identity had neither maintained nor regained Korean independence. The times demanded, it seemed, practical political programs and action.

In 1920, the Korean nationalist movement stood at a crossroad. The nationalist movement that had developed in exile after 1910 was divided by personal and ideological disputes. Domestically, the March First movement had demonstrated the potential for mass action, but it had failed to attract foreign intervention for Korean independence. The March First movement had stimulated the creation of a government in exile, the Shanghai Provisional Government, yet within months, the exile movement had returned to the internecine factional disputes that had characterized the exile movement before 1919.[5] Many nationalists in exile, disillusioned with the movement abroad, returned in the aftermath of the March First movement with the hope that some practical achievements might be possible in the changed political climate of the colony.

As might be expected, nationalists were not in agreement over what action was necessary; in fact, the ensuing debate among nationalists also revealed differing perceptions of what basic problems faced the movement. Therefore, between 1920 and 1925, the nationalist movement split along ideological lines, between moderate nationalist leaders who advocated gradualist reformist solutions to the problem of independence and a younger, more radical group who advocated social revolution and overt resistance to Japanese imperialism.

The moderate nationalist group was united by several movements that emerged at this time and that came to be known collectively as the cultural movement (Munhwa undong).[6] Supporters of the cultural movement believed that a gradual program of education and economic development was necessary to lay the basis for future national independence. Moreover, they advocated working within the political limits of the colony to take advantage of the post-March First reforms. The ideology behind the cultural movement appealed to reason and presented itself as a realistic alternative to conflict with the powerful Government General of Korea (GGK). In addition, the cultural movement, in many ways, represented a distillation of Korean nationalist thought since 1900, emphasizing as it did education, national consciousness-raising, and capitalist development. In short, this movement was based on the assumption that national development had to proceed further before Korea would be ready and able to maintain her political independence as a modern nation-state.

The moderates were challenged by radical nationalists. "Radicals" describes loosely a group of nationalist intellectuals that came to prominence after 1919. The political universe of this group was shaped by the widespread fascination with social revolutionary thought after the Russian revolution. Nurtured in the political hothouses of Tokyo, Peking, and Shanghai, Korean students abroad had thrown themselves into the intellectual ferment of contending doctrines. Like their Chinese and Japanese counterparts in the post-World War I era, Korean students searched amidst the whirl of ideas— political democracy, bolshevism, social democracy, syndicalism, guild socialism, anarchism, Fabianism, and national socialism—for a solution to the Korean national problem. Returning to Korea, these young intellectuals, some of whom established contact with the Korean Communist movement in exile, injected these ideas into the controversy over what was to be done. Consequently, they began to challenge gradualism and cultural development only, offering instead more radical solutions for the dual problem of Japanese imperialism and Korean independence.

The ideological splitting of the Korean nationalist movement in the

1920s is not unique. Other nationalist movements after World War I, in China and Vietnam, for instance, reveal similar patterns. The study of the Korean case reveals how general patterns of foreign imperialism in conjunction with the Russian revolution and Marxist thought provided the basis for schism within a national liberation movement. Therefore, by examining the schism in the Korean movement we can link the Korean experience to broader historical trends in East Asia in the 1920s.

Examination of the ideological split in Korean nationalism in the 1920s yields rich rewards. The debate revealed that the issue of national identity, often treated as a foregone conclusion after 1919, was still a matter of controversy. Differences over the locus of national identity and the future form of an independent Korea led inexorably to varying stances on political tactics. There was no doubt that Korean nationalism was a mass phenomenon after the March First demonstrations; however, moderate and radical nationalists each moved to ĸ mobilize this force around significantly different visions as to what and whom constituted the core of the Korean nation. The debate certainly demonstrated that in these terms Korean nationalism was no monolith.

Studying this debate provides new insights into the development of the Korean Left. Clearly, many radical intellectuals were studying Marxist classics as well as Lenin's ideas about national liberation movements in the colonial world. The application of these ideas to the Korean situation brought radicals into direct conflict with moderate nationalists over what constituted the nation itself and what political tactics would insure its liberation from imperialist rule.

An understanding of the fundamental ideas that underlay the nationalist schism helps explain the course of united front politics after 1927. The united front organization, the Sin'ganhoe (1927–31), attempted to bridge the widening gulf in the nationalist movement between moderates and the radical camp, which, by then, was led by the beleaguered Korean Communist party. The united front, however, never became a force for national liberation because from its very beginnings it was only tolerated by the Japanese because of the self-limiting gradualism of its titular moderate leadership. Thus, it provided little cover for Communists working within it and ultimately self-destructed in 1931.

The importance of this debate cannot be overemphasized. It began a process that ultimately divided the Korean nationalist movement and enervated the drive for independence for the remainder of the colonial period. The debate marked the challenge by the Left of the heretofore dominant ideological orientation of the nationalist leadership. Furthermore, the division of the movement can also be linked to the evolution of Japanese control policy, which tolerated the moderate cultural nationalist line while it repressed vigorously the moderates' bitter critics on the Left. Understanding the rift makes it easier to comprehend the failure of the Korean nationalist movement to overthrow Japanese rule by placing responsibility upon both the debilitating effects of ideological schism within the movement as well as upon efficient Japanese repression from without.

Nationalism and Korean Intellectuals

Nationalism is an extraordinarily broad and inclusive concept, and it has been much used and abused in historical writing. Indeed, virtually all accounts of modern Korean history are linked to some degree with this general concept. In history, nationalism has been used to describe everything from individual patriotism and sentiment to mass political phenomena. Furthermore, political scientists and sociologists have built theory around the concept of nationalism to describe and predict broad currents of political and social development.

In the most general sense, nationalism is interpreted in one of three ways. Perhaps its most general use focuses on sentiment. Man's longing for inclusion in the broader society of his fellows, the intense identification of the patriot with the nation-state, and the willingness of people to commit themselves to political action on the basis of this emotion are all examples of nationalism conceived as sentiment. Theorists have argued variously that this sentiment is inborn, linked to ethnic and cultural attachments, or can be artificially induced. Thus, nationalism as sentiment or emotional attachment to a broader political identity has been used to describe a wide range of phenomena. In this sense, xenophobic reaction to outsiders, traditionalist reform movements, progressive political parties, and anticolonialism are all forms of nationalism. The only important criterion seems to be that some form of collective identification, often culturally defined, be manifest.[7]

Nationalism also is the central concept behind a wide body of scholarship that focuses on political and social development.[8] This literature describes nationalism as a process that is more or less predictable, given certain conditions. Variables such as language, cultural ties, religion, territorial boundaries, communications, economic development, and ethnic stratification are examined in this literature and are correlated with the emergence of nation-states. In combination with broader historical analysis, the political and sociological theories of nationalism are often combined to explain the even more general concept of modernization.[9] Thus, nationalism is often linked closely to the diffusion of modernization. As forms of political and economic organization that originated in Western Europe spread outward in the eighteenth and nineteenth centuries, they bore with them the idea of nationalism as both an ideology and a political system. Therefore, nationalism in the non-Western world became linked to the broad and complex phenomenon of political and economic change as well as to new currents of thought.

The third general use of nationalism is in reference to ideology. In this sense, nationalism describes the creation of an ideology that serves to celebrate and emphasize the nation as the preeminent collective identity of a people. Similarly, ideology serves as the basis for political programs conceived to either strengthen and maintain an existing state as the correct focus for national loyalties, as the basis for regaining independence and political autonomy, or even for the creation of a new political entity altogether.

Broadly defined, nationalism as an ideological phenomenon includes diverse assumptions. At its core is the belief that the nation-state is the ultimate and natural political expression for group identity. Nationalist ideologues thus assume the responsibility for defining the collective identity in terms of national symbols, shared cultural values, religion, and historical experience. In addition, they articulate political programs upon which the collectivity so defined may move toward the goal of creating a nation-state, either by remaking an existing state, overthrowing the existing state, or creating a separatist movement to establish a separate state with a new identity from the old.[10]

Since this study will focus on nationalist ideology during the colonial period in Korea, it is necessary to have a more precise definition in mind. We shall define nationalism as an ideological movement, the search for and articulation of national identity that is combined with the creation of programs for the maintenance or attainment of self-government and independence on behalf of a group, some of whose members conceive it to constitute an actual or potential nation like others.[11] This definition includes important elements of the broader concept of nationalism discussed above. It focuses on the creation and nurturing of national identity, and it highlights the creation of specific political programs to spread this collective sentiment and mobilize it for political action.

Because this study focuses on ideology and intellectual leadership of a nationalist movement, this definition, highlighting as it does the role of intellectual leadership, seems eminently suitable. Intellectuals are at the core of many theories of nationalism. Indeed, the role of the intellectual appears close to being a necessary factor in all nationalist movements, because they assume the responsibility for defining the nation and attaching symbolic value to it.[12] Intellectuals also reside at the heart of new educational and literacy movements, the major means for spreading national consciousness. Finally, intellectuals often become the leadership of emerging nationalist movements, they define the political agenda, and create programs with which to fulfill their goals.

Many studies of modern Korean history have relied extensively on nationalism as a major interpretative focus. In fact, this focus has been so strong, in both English and Korean language histories of this period, that modern Korean history becomes, in effect, coincidental with the growth of Korean nationalism.[13] By applying the broadest possible sense of nationalism, historians of modern Korea have included a diverse array of events under this comfortable blanket. Beginning in the late nineteenth century, Koreans responded to the growing threat to national sovereignty in a variety of ways. Conservative officials sought to revitalize the traditional regime; a major peasant rebellion (Tonghak) emerged, in part, in reaction to foreign encroachment; peasant guerrilla bands (*Ŭibyŏng* [*Righteous Armies*]) led by local elites fought against foreign troops; and progressive intellectuals examined new institutions and ideas taken from the Western model of the nation-state as a base for reform. Whether conservative or progressive, elitist or mass-based, as long as these phenomena sought to bolster national exclusivity, independence, or autonomy, they can be entered under the general rubric of nationalism.

This study focuses on one aspect of Korean nationalism, the ideological struggle among nationalist intellectuals of the early twentieth century. These modern intellectuals continued a legacy that had its roots in the progressive reform movement of the 1880s. Heavily influenced by Western ideas and institutions, they dominated the leadership of the Korean nationalist movement after 1900. In terms of the fundamental desire for independence, these intellectuals agreed with conservatives who wished to maintain the old system as well as the mass strain of Korea nationalism that had risen in reaction to increasing foreign presence in Korea and had violently rebelled against

Japanese encroachment after 1905. They were separated, however, from their elite brethren as well as the masses by their conception of what needed to be done to maintain and, later, to regain national independence. The problem was not simply how to throw out the foreigners; it was, rather, how to transform Korean society to create the fundamental strength requisite of a modern nation-state, the nation-state represented by the Western model.

This study shows that among Korean intellectuals nationalism was not a fixed idea but was subject to a rich variety of differing interpretations. Beginning in the 1880s, intellectuals began to examine alternatives to the traditional political system and its ideological underpinnings. They were motivated by the belief that traditional methods of reform were wholly inadequate in the vastly changed international situation in the 1880s. The Western intrusion into China after 1840, the Meiji Restoration in Japan, and the opening in 1876 of Korea to foreign commerce and diplomatic relations provided incentives for a complete re-examination of Korean politics, social system, and international diplomacy. Therefore, progressive Korean intellectuals combined their desire for political autonomy with a radically new set of ideas about the form, structure, and purpose of the state and the state's relationship to the people.

There was little consensus in the beginning over what was to be done. In turn, reformers proposed to revitalize the traditional system, first through selective reform and adaptation of new military technology and government institutions, and later they proposed the complete overhaul of the political system from the top down. If nationalism is love of nation, however defined, and a desire to maintain political autonomy for the nation, then all programs and efforts to maintain the traditional state were examples of nationalism. Thus, in the face of internal and external crises, the obdurate Confucian elite who insisted that maintaining the purity of state orthodoxy would revitalize the traditional system were nationalists. Yet, by so labeling the traditional elite, how shall we differentiate them from those whose "patriotism" was directed toward different goals?

The concept of the nation-state came to Korea in its Western form in the late nineteenth century. Its initial introduction was based on the intrusion of Western military and economic power in East Asia at the beginning of the nineteenth century that forever altered the East Asian world order. Suddenly, Korea was forced to deal with an increasingly hostile international environment in which centuries-old political assumptions and diplomatic usages had become bankrupt. More important, the passing of the traditional East Asian world order challenged the core political identity of the traditional elite.

The gradual collapse of the East Asian world order forced the Koreans to redefine their position vis-à-vis China, whose increasingly obvious weakness threatened Korea's reliance on it for protection in international affairs. The severing of the special relationship with China also challenged intellectual assumptions about state power, monarchical legitimacy, elite political identity, and the means of maintaining state power. Indeed, the ability of the Western nation-states to subdue China and impose their own ideas of international relations on East Asia eventually stimulated Korean intellectuals to inquire into the sources of Western power. This inquiry began, as it did in China and Japan, with military technology, but soon spread to a detailed examination of political institutions, ideology, social systems, and core values that underlay the power of the West. In doing so, traditional institutions and ideas came under intense scrutiny. Ultimately, this inquiry produced an intellectual crisis in Korea, as it had earlier in China and Japan. As the traditional system failed repeatedly in its attempts to cope with the changed international environment, it became increasingly clear to some that fundamental changes were necessary. The power and wealth of the Western nation-states became a model to be emulated for survival, even at the cost of transforming the traditional state and society. In intellectual terms, then, the roots of Korean nationalist ideology as it developed during the colonial period lay buried in this dilemma and was, as its origins, a concern of intellectuals.

Thus, the early Korean nationalists emerged in responding to the intellectual crisis of late nineteenth-century Korea. They were the first to accept the model of the nation-state and attempt to apply it to Korean society. In so doing, they faced squarely the problem of altering the traditional order, almost always in the face of opposition of the political and social elite. Their burden was a heavy one: redefining the Korean political order on the basis of nationalism required changing the basis of legitimacy for the state, the relationship between the state and the Korean masses, and an inquiry into the relevance of the entire cultural and political tradition to the creation of a new collective identity based on the nation. In short, nationalistic goals required fundamental cultural and sociopolitical changes.[14]

Nationalist intellectuals took upon themselves the dual role of redefining the basis for group identity, that is, the creation of a new national identity, and the creation of a political program of institutional reform to maintain and strengthen political independence for the collectivity, now defined in national terms. This activity presupposed political consciousness and an awareness of the internal and external crisis that faced Korea after 1876. At its beginnings, therefore, an important aspect of Korean nationalism was this elite, intellectual movement. This is not to say Korean nationalism was simply a movement of intellectuals. As we will see in chapter 1, the common man was also part of the initial stirrings of Korean nationalism. The initial xenophobic reaction of Korean peasants to the presence of outsiders gradually transformed into a heightened sense of national identification and political consciousness. After the turn of the century, economic changes, increased literacy and education, and the shock of Japanese colonial rule conspired to bring the elite and mass strains of Korean nationalism together.

Increased literacy and education after 1900 spread nationalism to wider circles of Korean society, and by 1920, nationalism was a mass phenomenon. As the focus of this study is nationalist ideology and the nature of intellectual controversy within the broader context of colonial Korea, it is important to understand the roots of this conflict in the intellectual origins of Korean nationalism and the key role played by intellectuals in its development. Yet the development of widespread national consciousness did not mean that mass action toward the goal of overthrowing Japanese rule was forthcoming automatically. The intellectual leadership of the Korean nationalist movement still faced the task of creating a program and organization with which to harness this force. Indeed, the discussion of the nature of the nationalism in the early twentieth century had long been replaced by a debate over how to save the Korean nation and, after 1910, how to regain national sovereignty.

The idea of nationalism had come a long way since 1900, and to appreciate the context of the ideological debates within the nationalist movement between 1920 and 1925, it will be necessary to discuss the intellectual origins and development of Korean nationalism since the late nineteenth century. This is the focus of chapter 1. Thereafter, we will consider the ideological debates within the Korean nationalist movement. Chapters 2, 3, and 4 will discuss the rise of cultural nationalism, its concrete expression in the cultural movement, and the radical critique in turn. Finally, in chapter 5, we will examine the implications of this debate for Korean nationalism in general.

Modern Korean Nationalism

Korean nationalism was born in the fifty years that preceded the fall of the Yi dynasty and the advent of Japanese rule after 1910. Initially, nationalism in Korea was a response to an international threat to the traditional political and social order of the Yi dynasty. At one level, the Yi dynasty elite sought to preserve Korean political autonomy and cultural integrity by revitalizing the traditional system. By the 1880s, however, a new progressive elite had emerged opposing this approach. The progressives also wished to preserve Korean political autonomy, but their vision as to what constituted the nation and what means were necessary to accomplish this goal was profoundly different. It was from this beginning that the modern nationalist intellectual elite emerged.

By the late nineteenth century, a second strain of Korean nationalism emerged on the level of the common man. The opening of Korea in 1876 brought foreign economic and political penetration. Ultimately, the increased presence of foreign traders, missionaries, and even military troops provided a target for growing peasant discontent. The antiforeign slogans and program of the 1894 Tonghak Rebellion signaled the nascence of mass nationalism in Korea, directed both at the corruption and incompetence of the Yi political system and the growing foreign cancer that threatened Korean society.

Modern Korean nationalism was formed by a joining of these two impulses over a period of several decades. Moreover, as the strength of the nationalist impulse on both levels increased, the conception of what was being defended changed. The idea of the nation-state drawn from the Western model came to dominate the statements of nationalist reformers after the 1880s. According to such men, the preservation of Korean independence hinged on fundamentally altering the political and social system, and in this endeavor they were pitted as much against their own conservative Korean brethren as against the threat from the outside. At the level of the masses, antiforeign, patriotic sentiment continued to increase at the end of the Yi dynasty. Ultimately, Japanese colonial rule and the dramatic economic and

14

social changes accruing by the first decades of the twentieth century combined to produce a pervasive consciousness of anti-Japanese sentiment ripe for mobilization by nationalist elites.

After 1910, Korean nationalism was dedicated to regaining independence. The fall of the Yi dynasty discredited the traditional system and its political elite. The new nationalist intelligentsia that emerged to claim leadership of the independence struggle needed to redefine the nation, provide new symbols to galvanize nationalist consciousness among the masses, and devise a political program with broad support that would solve the problem of Korean independence. From the beginning, nationalist intellectuals were divided as to what should be done, and by the second decade of Japanese rule, the nationalist movement had reached a turning point. Anti-Japanese sentiment was running high, but no single program nor any single group of leaders had emerged that seemed able to channel nationalist energies into a drive to unseat the Japanese.

The debate over this dilemma is the subject at hand. However, a general survey of the rise of Korean nationalism is first necessary to provide the general context of the issues that united as well as those that divided the nationalist leadership in the 1920s.

The Yi Dynasty and the Nineteenth-Century Crisis

By the middle of the nineteenth century the Yi dynasty had marked over four and a half centuries of rule on the Korean peninsula. The dynasty ruled a well-defined territory that encompassed the entire Korean peninsula; three-quarters of this territory had been under continuous Korean control since the Silla unification in the later eighth century. The population of Korea (between eight and ten million in the 1870s) was linguistically and culturally homogeneous as a result of this long experience of political autonomy and centralized rule. The dynasty ruled through a centralized bureaucratic state adapted and refined from Chinese institutions. The Yi monarch's authority was, in theory, absolute; his authority was augmented by Confucian ideology, a state orthodoxy that supported a stratified social structure. In addition, this orthodoxy legitimated an aristocratic elite's monopoly of bureaucratic service and, by extension, its political and economic power.[1]

The Yi monarchs derived their legitimacy from the simple fact that there had been kings in Korea since the earliest recorded history. The founder of the Yi dynasty had assumed the right to rule through military force, but his dynastic pretensions were supported by careful use of traditional monarchical symbols, ritual investiture by the Chinese emperor, and the skillful use of Confucian political ideology. It must be noted, however, that the Yi monarch enjoyed none of the transcendent power or prestige of the Chinese emperor. In ritual terms, the Yi monarch was subordinated to the Chinese emperor, recognized as supreme ruler in his own land, but of lower status. To support the creation of a new dynasty, the Yi founder had petitioned the Chinese emperor for a name for the new dynasty and had requested investiture as monarch. Successful in his attempts for recognition, the founder laid the basis for Chinese-Korean relations that would endure for five centuries.[2] By acknowledging Korea's ritual subordination and accepting Chinese centrality in a universal world order, the founder solved, for the most part, the problem of Chinese military threat while legitimating his own rule. Although the Chinese never interfered with the authority of the Korean monarch, "his legitimizing role did set limits on the aura of transcendence that surrounded the Korean throne."[3]

The China-Korea relationship after 1392 was structured by the ritual of the Ming tributary system that required regular visits by envoys from subordinate nations. The Yi dynasty was allowed more numerous visits as a major tributary. Although the Ming tributary system lapsed after a century or so, Korea maintained its ritual position, even after the rise of the Manchus in the seventeenth century. The Koreans simply maintained the relationship with a different ritual suzerain. By and large, the adherence to the rules and rituals of their tributary relationship served them well. Ritual, however, could not protect them from invasion. The Ming intervention during the disastrous Hideyoshi invasions of the late sixteenth century was inspired more by motives of self-defense than a desire to protect their tributary. Furthermore, loyalty to the Ming after the rise of Manchu power in the early 1600s provoked two nearly fatal incursions by the Manchus.

The principal reason for dynastic stability lay in the unique Korean political and social system. The Yi monarch ruled through a centralized bureaucratic system that was staffed by the yangban elite.[4] The yangban had many of the attributes of an aristocracy; it maintained itself through the legal and de facto inherited status privileges, landholding, officeholding, and utilization of Confucian orthodoxy for the legitimation of status and economic interests. And as James Palais has observed, "king and aristocrat were both mutually antagonistic and mutually supporting; each was dependent on the other for the continuation of his place in the political and social structure."[5] This situation placed the power of the yangban and monarch in a rough state of equilibrium and, again following Palais's argument, "although the state of equilibrium might shift from one pole to another—from relatively strong monarch to aristocratic-bureaucratic domination of the throne—the balance of forces was never destroyed."[6] This situation impeded the development of centralized monarchical power as well as political decentralization or the growth of feudalism in Korea. Thus, a power balance between monarch and aristocrats expressed through a partially centralized state bureaucracy characterized the Yi political system.

The Korean masses over which the Yi monarch and yangban class ruled were neither linked closely to the central government nor were they a source of legitimacy for government authority. And incomplete centralization of government authority prevented deep penetration into the predominantly rural society.[7] Peasant mistrust and avoidance of officials also hampered efficient control of the population.

The population was not, however, separated from governance or internally divided by racial, linguistic, or cultural cleavages. A millennium of stable borders and little in-migration had homogenized the population, and the long rule of the Yi dynasty had continued this process.[8] Indeed, Korea never suffered the debilitating interethnic conflict that often characterized the collapse of traditional bureaucratic empires during the nineteenth century or multiethnic colonies in the postcolonial era. The Korean masses were thus unified and culturally homogeneous, sharing a well-developed folk culture closely tied to their long history as a tightly knit agrarian society—a fact that eased the process of developing a strong national consciousness in the twentieth century. The long tenure of the Yi dynasty and its elite's adherence to Confucian orthodoxy altered societal values. By the nineteenth century, the Korean masses, although carriers of the shamanistic folk tradition, had begun to emulate elite values with regard to family law, ancestor worship, and interpersonal relations to a certain extent.[9]

The Korean elite, on the other hand, while sharing this general sense of ethnic solidarity, were separated from the masses by their participation in the wide East Asian cosmopolitan culture, which required a familiarity with Chinese writing, literature, political philosophy, and social thought. The Korean elite based the education of their children on the Confucian classics, Chinese poetry, and writing skills in classical Chinese. The civil service examinations, successful participation in which was an important step in gaining government position, required long and tedious preparation, a process beyond the reach of most commoners. The great houses of the Yi yangban followed meticulously formal Confucian family ritual, and relations between yangban families and individuals were governed by strict adherence to rules of etiquette strongly influenced by Chinese norms. In short, the Korean elite self-consciously participated in a cosmopolitan cultural universe. It owed, in part, its very status to their monopoly on formal education. Yet its East Asian cosmopolitanism was based on a foreign language and foreign intellectual tradition; although it was selectively indigenized, this elite tradition separated the ruling class of the Yi dynasty from the remainder of the population, a fact of considerable significance for the development of Korean nationalism at a later date.

Although ignored in the initial thrust of Western intrusion in East Asia, by 1860 the Yi dynasty was well aware of the momentous changes in the international environment. Growing internal difficulties such as peasant rebellion, corruption, mismanagement in government, and imbalance of aristocratic power had already weakened the central government. In addition, Catholicism and the new Eastern Learning (Tonghak) religious movement challenged state orthodoxy. In the midst of this crisis a minor, known to history by his posthumous title, Kojong, ascended the throne in 1864. His father, Yi Ha'ŭng, became the de facto regent and assumed the title Grand Prince (Taewŏngun). The Taewŏngun embarked on a major series of reforms to bolster the power of the throne. He met foreign overtures for trade and diplomatic relations by reaffirming the traditional isolationist policy and reinvigorating military defense. He attacked aristocratic power through major institutional reforms, vigorously persecuted heretics, and repressed rebellion.

In the end, the Taewŏngun's reform program failed. Although successful initially in reasserting isolation in foreign policy, this success was due primarily to the weakness of the early foreign thrust. By 1874 and the majority of Kojong, Korea was faced with persistent and ultimately successful Japanese demands for a commercial treaty and recognition of the Meiji Restoration. In the domestic sphere, although he was successful in eliminating some sources of unrest, the Taewŏngun failed to redress the original balance of social and political forces that weakened the monarchy.[10] The failure to assert monarchical authority under Kojong and the reversion to the original status quo significantly affected Korea's ability to cope with the increasingly dangerous international situation. In the crucial last decades of the nineteenth century the kingdom vacillated: the attempt to concentrate power had failed, and, concurrently, confidence in the validity and ability of the system to reform itself was eroded significantly.[11] After 1876, the dynasty lacked purpose and direction, even the will, to react creatively to the pressures it faced.

In 1876, two years after Kojong's majority, Korea was brought into the new international system with the signing of the Kanghwa Treaty with Japan. Treaties with the major Western powers followed in the early 1880s. Although by treaty Korea became an independent actor in the new international system, her leaders continued to view these arrangements as secondary to the primary relationship with China. Treaties simply recognized foreign demands, and multiple treaty arrangements balanced foreign powers against each other, thus preserving Korean autonomy.[12] In the twenty years subsequent to the opening in 1876, the Yi dynasty attempted to participate in the Western state system and retain as well its unique Confucian relationship with China. And the fiction of Chinese stewardship and protection in international affairs provided incentives to avoid troublesome internal reforms. The Chinese defeat in the Sino-Japanese War in 1895, however, shattered the illusion of Chinese protection. Yet, in the last fifteen years of Yi rule, the dynasty continued to seek special relationships with her more powerful neighbors, first Russia, then Japan. The result was continued erosion of Korean sovereignty.

Reform, Rebellion, and Korean Nationalism

After 1876, the dynasty took tentative steps to strengthen itself in the face of Korea's changing position in the international environment.[13] Initial reforms aimed at bolstering the Korean military, training foreign experts, and importing new technology were predicated on maintaining the dynasty in its present form, thus encouraging the support of conservatives. But as the threat deepened in the 1880s, new forces rose that questioned the traditional political system itself. Basing their ideas on the model of Japan's successful modernization program, the progressives of the 1880s began to advocate wholesale changes that anticipated the rise of modern Korean nationalism. Interest in national independence, conceived in terms of the Western nation-state system, took hold among a portion of the Korean political elite.

The self-strengthening program focused on importing Western military technology and training personnel in its operation and construction. A new office, the Office for the Management of State Affairs (T'ongni'gimu amun), was created to coordinate a diverse set of activities with regard to foreign relations with China and other neighbors, border defense, technology imports, foreign-language study, and shipbuilding. In addition, the government recruited and sent students and artisans to study Western military technology at the new Chinese Tientsin Arsenal in 1882. Finally Kojong organized an inspection mission to Japan to gather information on modern government institutions, factories, and foreign trade. The mission was secretly organized to avoid public outcry by conservatives.

The self-strengthening initiatives eventually provoked a backlash by conservative officials and literati. They attacked officials who promoted self-strengthening for undermining the basis of the state by advocating heterodox doctrines and they deluged the king with memorials that warned of moral ruin and affirmed isolationism. The conservative reaction forced the reform-minded officials to defend themselves on ideological grounds. The dynasty's credibility as protector of Confucian values was at stake, but only a serious crackdown on memorialists, including banishment and execution for some, ended the conservative protest.[14]

Ultimately, the self-strengthening program failed because of a lack of serious financial commitment by the dynasty. Although the ideological commitment was apparent, government resources, already stretched to the limit, were unavailable for many proposed projects. Students returned from training abroad to find no place to apply their new skills. The T'ongni'gimu amun became a new focal point for factional intrigue, and although Korea was now tied to the "unequal" treaty system with the signing of treaties with the United States, Britain, France, and Germany, the feeling of insecurity with regard to foreign relations continued.

A mutiny by disgruntled troops in the poorly paid Korean army precipitated a major foreign crisis in July of 1882. China and Japan sent troops to Korea to help stabilize the situation. Using the old rationale of "special interests" in Korea, the Chinese sought to counter what they saw as a growing threat of Japanese intrusion. Acting swiftly, the Chinese put down the military rebels and restored Kojong to power. To prevent open conflict with Japanese troops, they opened negotiations and mediated Japanese demands for reparations in the Treaty of Chemulp'o between Korea and Japan. The 1882 mutiny provoked the first serious Chinese intervention into Korean internal affairs, and for the next decade the government was closely monitored by the Chinese. While the Chinese were protecting their own interests, their heavy-handed policy served to stimulate a nationalist reaction in ● Korea.[15]

Continued Chinese interference in Korean affairs was viewed with alarm by a small group of modernizers known variously as the Enlightenment party (Kaehwadang) or Progressive party (Chinbodang).[16] The enlightenment group included young officials and some of the first Koreans to travel and study abroad. Led by Kim Okkyun and Pak Yŏnghyo, the progressives wanted to transform fundamentally Korean governance and society. Although encouraged by self-strengthening efforts, this group sought more than simple material or technological imports grafted on to the body of traditional wisdom.[17] The progressives looked to Japan for inspiration; for ● example, Kim Okkyun had studied with Fukuzawa Yukichi, a foremost popularizer of Western thought in Japan. Although favored by the king and occupying minor posts in government, the progressives were frustrated by the slow pace of change and by the increasingly obstructionist power of the consort Min clan. The intrusion of Chinese troops and waning of Japanese influence after the 1882 incident turned frustration into despair and desperation.

By 1884, Kim Okkyun and his followers determined that change within the traditional system was impossible. They resolved to seize control of government with the help of the Japanese legation troops, promulgate their reform program by royal edict, and eliminate high officials who obstructed reform. On December fourth they seized the king and assassinated six prominent conservative officials. Intending to work through the monarch, the leaders planned, but had no time to implement, a wide program of social and political reforms.[18] Without popular support, military backing, or foreign recognition, the failure of the coup was a foregone conclusion. Moreover, Kim's reliance on Japanese support undermined his patriotic justification for the coup itself.

Reaction to the coup was swift and final. In three days the progressives were in flight along with the Japanese legation. Chinese troops controlled Seoul, and the government was reassembled with minor changes. Yet, as it was later labeled, the Kapsin Coup was more than a defeat for Kim and his followers. It left a bitter legacy of continued Japanese-Chinese rivalry on the peninsula. More serious, perhaps, was the coup's role in bankrupting the general cause of reform in Korea. The bloody tactics of the coup besmirched the image of reform in the eyes of officials and the public alike. It also alienated

Kojong, heretofore sympathetic, from the progressive cause. Finally, the flight of progressives and the execution and imprisonment of supporters removed from the scene some of the most able young officials in the Korean government. More indirectly, the failure of the coup and unofficial connivance of local Japanese officials discredited Japan as a model for reform.[19] In the end, the reassertion of Chinese influence after 1884 slowed the pace of change in Korea, encouraged conservatives, and inhibited wider Korean contact with the outside world.

The conflict between self-strengtheners and progressives that culminated in the Kapsin Coup anticipated the emergence of modern nationalism in Korea. Although the progressive leaders were not prolific writers and their reform philosophy must be inferred from cryptic sources, it was clear that they embraced a fundamentally new conception of what was necessary to make Korea into a modern nation. The progressives linked clearly the concepts of national sovereignty and dignity with social leveling, equitable taxation and land reform, and the creation of streamlined and responsive governmental institutions. The indignities of continued tributary ritual and attitudes towards China and the Chinese insistence on "special interests" enraged the progressives. Their belief that the Korean nation could be re-made within the traditional system, or failing that, reform could be imposed from the top down given sufficient access to the authority of the monarch, marked their ultimate failure. And their reliance on Japanese military support obfuscated their commitment to Korean autonomy. Was conservative reliance on Chinese support to maintain the traditional system any more obnoxious than relying on foreign troops in the service of new ideas?

Within the progressive program, however, lay the origins of modern Korean nationalism. Reacting to international crisis with the hope of building a strong, independent nation, the progressives looked toward the Japanese model of the Meiji Restoration and beyond to the secrets of Western power. Their approach toward reform was totalistic: they believed that the piecemeal adoption of selected Western technology and institutions could not save the Yi state and that the real crisis lay in the fundamental underpinnings of the traditional system. Yet the forces that supported the traditional state were strong enough to deflect fundamental social and political reforms, even at the expense of continued erosion of sovereignty in international relations.

A full decade of worsening international conditions and growing internal problems would lapse before another strong reform movement would emerge in Korea in 1894, this time in the form of a popular peasant uprising known as the Tonghak Rebellion.[20]

The Tonghak religious movement had begun in the 1860s as a reaction to the influence of Christianity and Western ideas in Korea. It's founder, Ch'oe Cheu, and his successors created a syncretic religion combining Confucianism, Buddhism, Taoism, and practices of lower-class popular religion. In spite of its affirmation of traditional ideas and insistence that they upheld orthodox Confucian precepts and maintained loyalty to the king, the dynasty persecuted the Tonghak as heresy. Nevertheless, its spiritual appeal and unique organization fueled its growth in the 1870s and 1880s.

The rise of the Tonghak religion occurred at a time of increasing rural poverty and repression. Therefore, the situation was already ripe for rebellion in 1893 when the Tonghak church organized a petition drive to legalize their religion. Rebuffed by local officials and the throne, the initial Tonghak drive transformed into a demand for wide-scale reforms to address the issues of local governmental corruption, yangban privileges, rural poverty, and the growing foreign presence in Korea.[21] The Tonghak mobilized a large peasant army and were dispersed only with great difficulty by government troops augmented by Japanese forces sent to Korea during the crisis, sparking, ultimately, the Sino-Japanese War of 1895.

The Tonghak Rebellion figures prominently in most treatments of Korean nationalism. Although the faith was a syncretic mixture of religious elements that included some elements of Christianity, its very name, Tonghak—literally translated "Eastern Learning"—celebrated the movement's Korean roots in opposition to Sŏhak ("Western Learning"). And even though the reform program of the rebellion emphasized loyalty to the monarch and traditional system, it raised issues of social equality and economic equity that were unique in the history of Korean peasant rebellions. Moreover, the explicit antiforeign statements of the Tonghak rebels emphasized their patriotism, introducing a unique nationalistic flavor to the movement.

Tonghak nationalism might be characterized as conservative antiforeignism, but the "fusion of patriotic motives with the religious, social and economic incentives of the peasant rebels was unique."[22] It represented a mass reaction to broad changes in rural life brought about by the intrusion of capitalism in the form of Japanese rice brokers, Chinese merchants, and Western traders. It also signaled mass dissatisfaction with the Korean government's seeming inability to stave off foreign political and economic encroachment.[23] In later years the patriotic antiforeign sentiment of the Tonghaks was revived by the Righteous Army movements (Ŭibyŏng, 1905, 1907–11) against the Japanese.

The legacy of the rebellion continued with the revival of the Tonghak religious organization in the Ch'ŏndogyo (Church of the Heavenly Way) after 1900. Indeed, the base of the Tonghak faith expanded beyond the rural peasantry as many middle-class nationalist intellectuals joined its ranks, attracted by its uniquely Korean theology. During the colonial period, the Ch'ŏndogyo played an important role in the nationalist movement through publishing and education.

Rocked by internal and external threats, the dynasty vacillated. In the years after the Sino-Japanese War, a new movement for fundamental reform emerged, grounded on a widespread questioning of the efficacy of the traditional political system to save the nation from total collapse. In intellectual terms, the flowering of modern Korean nationalism can be dated from this period.

The Independence Club

During the Sino-Japanese War the Japanese used their renewed ascendancy to impose a series of radical political and social reforms on Korea. The Kabo Reforms of 1894 and 1895 were pushed by pro-Japanese Korean officials, but again, the taint of foreign sponsorship and conservative foot-dragging vitiated the impact of the reform program. The reforms addressed significant social and political institutions. A cabinet system of government, social leveling, manumission of slaves, reform of the civil service examination, the outlawing of Confucian social practices such as early marriage, even minor sumptuary regulations were included in the Kabo legislation.[24] With the exception of the abolition of slavery and the examination system, the Kabo legislation was ignored. Conservative officials fought to preserve their power, and there was a wide public outcry over insensitive social legislation such as the notorious "topknot" decree, an order banning the traditional male hair style. Ultimately, the weakening of Japanese power due to the Triple Intervention in the aftermath of the Sino-Japanese War and the resurgence of conservatives around the king doomed the Kabo program to failure.[25]

The Triple Intervention by Russia, Germany, and France was a serious blow to Japanese interests in East Asia, and it provided a respite for the Korean court as well. Although the Chinese defeat removed their influence from the peninsula, the mentality of dependence continued as the dynasty continued to seek patrons. In the years following the war the dynasty signed concession agreements with various Western powers for the exploitation of natural resources and railroad development. Rather than support Korean independence, the tactic of playing one foreign power off against another simply continued the erosion of Korean sovereignty. A low point was reached in 1896 when Kojong, fearing for his safety after the brutal assassination of Queen Min at the hands of the Japanese, took up residence in the Russian legation.

The events of 1895 and 1896 laid the groundwork for the rise of a unique reform movement in Korean history, the organization of the Independence Club in 1896. The Independence Club revived interest by the modernizing elite in the cause of reform. Unlike the progressives of a decade earlier, however, the club sought no outside patron for their cause. The way to national strength lay in manipulating national symbols to encourage patriotic public support for the government as well as reforming the political system along the lines of the Western model of the nation-state.

Returning from a ten-year stay in the United States, now a medical doctor, Sŏ Chaep'il (Sŏ is also known by his Anglicized name, Philip • Jaisohn) established the club to propagate new ideas and encourage public involvement in Korean political affairs. Reform-minded officials and intellectuals rallied to Sŏ's cause, among whom were members of the old Progressive party, such as Yun Ch'iho. The abject state of affairs alarmed the club members, and they embarked on a campaign to rally support for the cause of true Korean independence both within government and among the general public. Sŏ had begun with the idea of publishing a newspaper in the Korean vernacular to encourage patriotism and political participation, and to spread Western knowledge. Soon, however, the club's activities expanded to discussions of political and social reform as well as educational activities.[26]

Initially, the club had some success attracting moderate officials to its activities. In its first year the club promoted symbolic projects that everyone could support, such as the building and renaming of a meeting hall, Independence Hall, on the site of the old Chinese embassy. It also coordinated the erection of Independence Arch on the site of the gate that had been used for centuries by Chinese envoys. In 1897, the club spearheaded a movement to have Kojong declare himself emperor (*hwangje*) and to rename the kingdom the Empire of Korea (Taehan cheguk). This would elevate the monarch from the

Chinese-imposed title as king (*wang*) and remove the old name the Kingdom of Korea (Chosŏn wangguk) granted by the Chinese at the beginning of the dynasty. The use of patriotic symbols was obviously popular at court, and the club gained the financial support of the king in its early period.

Other programs of the Independence Club, however, were not so popular. The club's publication, *The Independent* (*Tongnip sinmun*), was regarded with suspicion by some officials. The newspaper deliberately used the vernacular script, *han'gŭl*, to make it accessible to the Korean masses. Although *han'gŭl* had been invented in 1443, classical Chinese had continued as the official court written language as well as the literary language of the yangban. From the beginning, the vernacular script itself was controversial, opposed by conservative officials as vulgar and demeaning.[27] Its use by Buddhists, novelists, and women sustained its development until the Independence Club embraced vernacular use as a patriotic issue. Publishing in *han'gŭl*, indeed, the very existence of a private forum for political discussion was unprecedented. In addition, the radical tone of the newspaper caught the attention of conservatives who, in spite of its patriotic content, viewed the newspaper as a vehicle of heterodoxy. Supporting the dynasty was fine, but public discussion of state policy was the monopoly of the elite.

The club also flirted with official disapproval by denouncing foreign influence at court and the signing of concessions. It advocated indigenous exploitation of national resources, and supported technical education to develop Korean expertise in railroad construction and mining. They also worried about the court's tendency to depend on powerful foreign patrons to insure political autonomy. The club's advocacy of an independent foreign policy was not a repeat of the shrill xenophobia and isolationism of previous decades. Its critique was grounded on a cosmopolitanism that sought to join, not exclude, the modern world of nation-states. Club leaders stressed the importance of learning from the outside world and applying the new learning to projects that would strengthen the state in international affairs.

Even more controversial was Sŏ Chaep'il's interest in representative political institutions. Sŏ attacked the large number of sinecures in government and advocated the wholesale dismissal of two-thirds of the officialdom. Editorials in the *Independent* also discussed the role of the people in representative governments in the West.[28] The concepts of a constitutional monarchy and a transition to representative government lurked beneath this important theme in the club's writings. Although the club adopted the language of social contract, its demands for inclusion in the privy council and advocacy of a limited franchise revealed its essential elitism. The national assembly was conceived as a body of "wise and erudite men," not a body that represented a cross-section of the nation.[29]

In its first year, the club had already demonstrated its interest in popular participation in government through the unprecedented use of public rallies at which government policy and issues facing the nation were debated. In some of the early debates, the arrival in sedan chairs of dignified officials wearing the full regalia of their rank added an ironic note to the assemblage of students, intellectuals, and members of the general public. Debate topics ranged from the efficacy of street lighting in reducing crime to more significant political issues, such as representative government. In the last year of the club's existence, street rallies attended by thousands provoked official ire and their growing conviction that the club's ultimate aim was the destruction of the monarchy itself.[30]

The ideology and tactics of the Independence Club signaled the advent of modern nationalism in Korea. The belief that Korea constituted a nation among others in a world system of nation-states was explicit in the club's program of action. The attack against the traditional mentality of *sadae* (to serve the Great [China]) in relations with outside powers (as in the granting of concessions) and the club's promotion of national symbols to express Korea's independence as a nation-state underscored this fundamental conviction. More important, the club introduced the issue of the relationship between the state and the people to the political agenda of the late 1890s. Inherent in Sŏ Chaep'il's understanding of the Western nation-state model was the idea that the power of these nations was not derived simply from economic and technological strength. Korea had to instill in its people an identification with the state, and the state had to learn to encourage patriotism as a source of strength.[31] The compilation of a national history, the use of the vernacular language, both as a symbol of national identity and as a communication device, and advocacy of participation in government through elective officials and public rallies, characterized the club's nationalism.

A major failing of the club was its elitism. Although it embraced national symbols and called for broad patriotic support, the scope of its activities never expanded beyond participation by a small minority of progressive intellectuals. Their understanding of the importance of mass support was clear, but aside from a few public rallies, the club had little time, if inclination—if we are to judge by its emphasis on elite participation in its proposal for a national assembly—to develop a truly mass following. Thus, the club's nationalism remained elitist and separate, in organizational terms, from the Korean masses.

It is no mystery why the king disbanded the Independence Club after barely two years of existence. Although interested in augmenting his prestige and power through the use of national symbols, the king was still dependent on officials who owed their power to the traditional political system. In the end, Kojong opted to uphold the theory of royal authority, however limited it was in reality, rather than risk opening the political system to public participation. The club's disbandment ended the reform movement of 1896–98, but it had a dramatic effect on the intellectual climate of Korea. In its short existence, it spearheaded the cause of intellectual inquiry into the fundamental sources of Western power and introduced important issues such as the role of the people in legitimating state power and the importance and potential power of public participation in government. And in the years following the exile of Sŏ Chaep'il and the club's ultimate demise, its depiction of the "national" crisis facing Korea served as inspiration to a broad cultural and intellectual movement known as the Korean enlightenment.

The Korean Enlightenment

The origins of the broad intellectual and educational movement known as the Korean enlightenment can be traced to the progressive movement of the 1880s.[32] There was a rapid expansion of interest in the outside world among intellectual circles in Korea in the last decade of the Yi dynasty. This interest manifested itself in the creation of study societies, publications, and the establishment of schools specializing in Western subjects, the "new learning." The growing sense of national crisis coupled with important changes in the educational system, the advent of a public press, and increasing foreign travel for students and intellectuals broadened the movement. And nationalistic themes were central to the intellectual activity of the period.

In the years after the demise of the Independence Club, the enlightenment became a truly nationwide movement, spurred on by the growth of the Korean language press. Early newspapers in Korea were generally in-house publications for officialdom. The *Independent,* however, had created a precedent for the development of a popular press. The *Independent* was followed by the publication of the *Hwangsŏng sinmun* (*Capitol Daily*). Published in a mixed-script of Chinese and Korean in lots of 2,000, the *Hwangsŏng sinmun* appealed to upper-class intellectuals. Between 1898 and 1910, the *Hwangsŏng sinmun* was an important forum of ideas and reform, and some of the most important enlightenment writers such as Chang Chiyŏn (1864– 1921), Sin Ch'aeho (1880–1936) and Pak Ŭnsik (1849–1926) participated on its editorial board. Another important newspaper of this period was the *Taehan maeil sinbo* (*Korea Daily News*). Published between 1904 and 1910, the *Taehan maeil sinbo* became the first truly mass publication in Korea. It was published in lots of 10,000 and distributed nationally.[33]

Small specialized magazines augmented the growth of the Korean press after 1900. These magazines focused on discussions of Western thought, translations of Western classical literature and political philosophy, and treatises on educational reform. They were the by-product of the growth of national and provincial organizations devoted to spreading Western thought and educational reform. The nationwide Korea Self-Strengthening Society (Taehan cha'ganghoe) and smaller provincial study societies all published journals that provided important fora for the discussion of enlightenment issues and created a loose countrywide network for the growing nationalist intelligentsia.[34]

The Korean enlightenment signaled the expansion of a modern Korean intelligentsia. The newspapers, journals, and organizations of the enlightenment were led by a group of older intellectuals whose traditional education and later interest in Western thought put them in a transitional position, a foot in each tradition. These older intellectuals were joined by younger men, many trained abroad or in the new schools in Korea, who saw their future not in terms of the old system of advancement through the traditional civil service exams and mastery of Confucian learning, but in the study of Western thought. Their loyalties lay not in supporting the old system but in the creation of a modern Korean nation. Consequently, the Korean enlightenment witnessed a debate between patriots of contrasting views about the importance of the Korean intellectual tradition as well as the future form of Korean politics and society. As in China in the 1890s, older reformist intellectuals attempted to reconcile the tradition with the Western tradition, while many younger intellectuals attacked the tradition as an obstacle to the maintenance of national autonomy.

Changes in the Korean education system supported the expansion of enlightenment activity and political activism of the Korean intelligentsia. Early government educational reforms such as the establishment of technical and foreign language schools heralded a boom in schools that specialized in the "new learning." Western missionary schools established after 1890 became another source of Western learning and were more popular for their modern curricula than for theological training. After 1900, there was a boom in private, Korean-run, schools; the boom expanded as more and more students returned from study abroad, mostly from Japan. In spite of stiffening regulations and the hostility of the Japanese-dominated Ministry of Education in the last years of the dynasty, there were 2,131 private schools in Korea in November of 1909.[35]

The new schools represented more than a desire for new learning. Behind their establishment lay a new philosophy of education. In addition to its focus on Western technology and science, this philosophy was also concerned with inculcating new values in the Korean people. Pak Ŭnsik, classically educated and committed to Confucianism even in the cause of reform, stressed the importance of instilling in students a new sense of cultural and social responsibility as a prerequisite to creating new citizens (*sinmin*). The new citizens would have an appreciation of science as well as a deep understanding of the Korean cultural and historical experience. It was important to galvanize identification with the nation or the fruits of the new education would be wasted.[36] The new schools also spearheaded the reexamination of the tradition. Enlightenment thinkers wanted to draw from the past, but they did not want to keep social customs and attitudes that would inhibit progress toward the development of a more dynamic society.

The intellectual developments of the Korean enlightenment can be divided into two broad categories of inquiry: the discussion of Western political theory and social development, and the re-examination of the Korean tradition.

Although interest in the political and social thought of the West had begun in Korea in the 1880s, after 1900 this body of knowledge was studied increasingly to unearth its relationship to the power and wealth of the Western nations. Sŏ Chaep'il had learned at first hand in the United States about democratic institutions, but direct experience with Western government and society was still rare in Korea. By 1900, Japanese and Chinese scholars had built an impressive body of writing about the West, and it was primarily from these secondary sources that Korean intellectuals built their own ideas. Works in the Chinese language were accessible directly to all Korean scholars, and the writings of transitional Chinese intellectuals such as K'ang Yu-wei, Liang Ch'i-ch'ao, and Yen Fu found avid Korean readers.[37] The majority of Korean students studying abroad went to Japan, and here they encountered numerous Japanese translations of Western political theory, social thought, and history.

Thus, Korean intellectuals absorbed Western thought primarily through the filter of Japan and China. Understandably, they shared with their Japanese and Chinese cohorts a similar motivation, a desire to understand the basis for Western wealth and power, and, by implication, to search in this different tradition for ideas and institutions that could help strengthen their own societies.

Korean intellectuals focused on Western science and the philosophy of science as a central keystone to Western technological superiority. Empiricism was not new to East Asia, but the Western enthusiasm for man's mastery over nature excited Korean intellectuals. Repeatedly, articles in the new vernacular press stressed the centrality of the Western faith in science and progress. This was no mere sop to importing and learning how to manipulate foreign technology, but a concern for the fundamental attitudes that lay behind the development of this technology. Science and Western positivism challenged basic assumptions in the Korean tradition about the ability and desirability of man to understand and alter society and his environment.

The inquiry into science led quickly into discussion of Western concepts of progress and social development. The idea that societies developed along a line of increased sophistication and complexity challenged the traditional assumption of a past utopia inherent in Confucian dogma. The idea that change and progress were desirable, indeed inevitable, seemed linked inextricably to Western dynamism. Furthermore, the ideas of progress and evolution were promoted by Koreans' study of Social Darwinism, then in vogue in China. Chang Chiyŏn's translation of Liang Ch'i-ch'ao's work on Spencer, and other translations of Darwin and Huxley, in Japanese and Chinese, had a tremendous influence on Korean intellectuals after 1900.[38] They seized the ideas of social evolution, struggle, and the survival of the fittest to explain the contemporary prostration of Korean society. They reasoned that Korean society was not inherently weak or unfit for incorporation in the world system of nations, it had just been diverted from the mainstream of evolution. Indeed, the acceptance of Social Darwinist concepts underscored the urgency of the enlightenment reform program. Korea had to work harder to develop politi-

cally, socially, and technologically if she was to survive in a world
• dominated by struggle and competition. Furthermore, the intense
discussion of Social Darwinist concepts indicated that Koreans implicitly accepted the nation-state as the highest form of social and political
evolution, thus intensifying nationalism in Korea.

Koreans also examined Western liberalism in translation. Pak
Ŭnsik, for example, studied Rousseau and Locke and attempted to
reconcile these new ideas with the Confucian tradition by pointing out
their similarities.[39] Yet for the most part, there was no concerted
attempt to reinterpret Confucianism in light of its commonalities with
Western thought as did Liang Ch'i-ch'ao.[40] Central to the examination of the Western liberal tradition was a concern for the relationship
between the state and the people and the role of the individual in
society. The idea of a social contract highlighted the weak connection,
in the minds of enlightenment thinkers, between the traditional state
and the Korean masses. Thus, democratic institutions such as elec-
tions, representative bodies, free speech, and a popular press were
viewed less as guarantees against state domination of free individuals
than as important sources of encouraging mass identification with the
state, and thus a source of state power.[41]

The role of the individual in Western society fascinated Korean
intellectuals. The concept of free individuals, joined socially but
preserving their autonomy, was in direct conflict with traditional
views about man and society. In Korea, the individual gained expression as part of the collective; he was enmeshed in a web of social
relationships, and he gained identity and purpose in playing out his
prescribed roles within the group, whether it be family, lineage,
school, or occupation. In contrast, Western individualism presupposed inherent rights, autonomy, and freedom for the individual.

Koreans approached the Western concept of individualism from a
frankly instrumentalist point of view. They de-emphasized the fundamental doctrine of human rights and focused on individual freedom as
a source of dynamism and vitality. Intellectuals linked directly Western creativity and initiative with individual freedom; and, conversely,
they identified the strong collective orientation of traditional Korean
society as a source of stagnation. In iconoclastic writing on the Korean
tradition, intellectuals criticized the Confucian family system for its
role in repressing individual talent and initiative. Thus, liberating
individuals from the web of Confucian social norms became a first
step toward creating a source of creative dynamism.

The discussion on individualism was linked with the concepts of human will and activism. Interested in the Western notion of progress, the Social Darwinist concepts of struggle, and individual liberty, Korean intellectuals soon focused on the issue of human will and activism. Although the potential for activism within the Confucian tradition existed in the personal struggle needed to overcome evil and realize the good nature within oneself, formalism and collective values had overridden activism.[42] Koreans, however, did not focus on a potential for activism within the Confucian tradition. As we shall see, their critical judgment of the passivity of the tradition proved this.

This study of Western thought led Koreans to consider what had to be done to reshape their society in order to survive. Although they had isolated core values in Western society that underpinned its strength, Korean intellectuals continued to be deeply influenced by their own tradition of social reform. Confucian thought stressed the primacy of upholding proper values in society. Leaders functioned as exemplars of proper conduct and primary values that underlay social harmony in society. If leaders were virtuous and proper values were understood and followed by the masses, then society would be harmonized. Therefore, it was incumbent on the traditional ruler to educate the people to proper conduct and the maintenance of Confucian values. Disorder or unrest in society were a primary indication that rulers or the people had lost the proper way. Therefore, traditional reform took the form of rectifying improper conduct, rooting out heterodoxy, and removing the basic causes of disorder. When enlightenment thinkers turned to the problem of social reform in the early twentieth century, they focused on the job of understanding the value system of the West, learning how this system supported state power, and, finally, instilling these ideas in the population at large. Thus, to some intellectuals, the fundamental task at hand was education. This would be the means to rid Korean society of its traditional intellectual baggage that inhibited change. In short, changing fundamental values was a prerequisite to social change.[43]

A critical re-examination of the Korean tradition characterized the second major category of enlightenment writing. The continued failure of the traditional system to right itself and the steady erosion of Korean political autonomy encouraged this iconoclastic view. The critique of the tradition fell into three broad categories: the attack on political and cultural subservience to China, a critique of Confucian social ethics, and the discussion of native Korean folk culture.

The furor over *sadae* relations with China has already been discussed. By 1900, the importance of independence and the use of national symbolism reflecting theoretical Korean equality with other nations was a fact. Nevertheless, the issue of *sadae* continued during the Korean enlightenment as intellectuals examined the broader and, in their view, more insidious issue of cultural dependence on China. Looking into the elite tradition, the cultural debt to China was obvious and inescapable. Yet intellectuals worried that the dependence on Chinese culture and philosophy had obscured, or, even worse, denigrated indigenous Korean culture.[44] Thus, beginning with the Independence Club, *sadae*, formerly a neutral term connoting the nature of Korea's status vis-à-vis China, took on an increasingly pejorative tone. *Sadae, sadaejuŭi* (the doctrine of *sadae*), and *sadae ŭisik* (a *sadae* mentality or consciousness) became synonymous with dependence, subservience, lackeyism, or toadyism in the eyes of nationalists. Nationalists hurled the charge of *sadae* at conservative officials who rejected new ideas as heterodoxy and defended Confucian orthodoxy as the basis of traditional society.[45] By 1900, the use of classical Chinese as the official form of written communication was linked to the issue of cultural dependence.

The *sadae* issue resided at the core of the movement to expand the use of the Korean vernacular. Use of the native Korean script became a cause célèbre among nationalists, an affirmation of Korean cultural identity. In the words of Chu Sigyŏng, father of the vernacular movement, using *han'gŭl* was a means "to seek the end of aristocratic cultural slavery to Chinese culture."[46] The vernacular movement attacked, then, both the utilitarian problem of education and illiteracy in Korea as well as the more insidious problem of cultural subservience.

Concern over the issue of cultural subservience stimulated a renaissance in historical writing after 1900. Nationalist historians, disgusted with the traditional Korean sinocentric historical tradition, began to exhume a national past. Histories by Pak Ŭnsik and Sin Ch'aeho written at this time rejected Confucian historiography that cast Korean history in the light of the Chinese experience.[47] Traditional histories judged its heroes and villains on a scale of Confucian morality; and Korean history had become a story of its gradual sinification. Sin and Pak sought to write a truly national history, the story of the origins and struggle for survival of the Korean nation. Sin in particular elucidated the role of history in the creation of national consciousness and patriotism. He worried that a nation with no strong sense of its past would lose its spiritual base and, given such conditions, the same nation would have very little hope for the future.[48]

Confucian social customs became another favorite target of nationalist iconoclasts in this period. With their new interest in the individual and in Western liberalism, some intellectuals criticized Confucian concepts of filial piety, social harmony, and social relations as ideas that systematically repressed the individual. Thus, ancestor worship, obligation to parents and elders, subordination of women, the banning of remarriage for widows, formalism, and elaborate protocols of etiquette were attacked as authoritarian and destructive to individual initiative and free will.[49] The attack on Confucian social norms was undoubtedly spurred on by the conversion of many Korean intellectuals to Christianity. Indeed, Sŏ Chaep'il and Yun Ch'iho, both Christian converts, had initiated the discussion of Confucian social norms in *Independent* editorials, and many prominent intellectuals of the enlightenment attended Christian schools. The influence of Christianity on nationalist intellectuals, however, has not been systematically studied.[50] Yet the enlightenment owes a considerable debt to Christian schools; moreover, prominent Christian nationalists linked in their own minds Western social and political institutions with Christianity. The March First movement's emphasis on women's equality and pacifism were two later outgrowths of this Christian influence.

The re-examination of traditional Korean folk culture was a third feature of enlightenment iconoclasm. Although the elite Confucian tradition had seeped down in Korean society and regulated family ritual, most notably with regard to ancestor worship, peasant society remained strongly influenced by coexistent indigenous folk beliefs and norms. Korean folk culture, with its shamanistic tradition, was a rich mixture of customs and beliefs tied together with ritual, dance, music, and art. Although this folk tradition provided a rich repository of unique symbols of nationalist identity, modern nationalists attacked its elements of superstition and fatalism as antiscientific and fatalistic. Belief in the power of the shaman eroded the spread of modern Western science, and dependence on fortunetellers and geomancy encouraged fatalism and passivity.[51] Once again, enlightenment thinkers were quick to point out Korea's failings, contrasting their own tradition with their understanding of what was modern, progressive, and scientific. Although early iconoclasts attacked the folk tradition, there was a revival of interest in folk culture during the colonial period as nationalists sought to strengthen national identity through the study of native customs and traditions.[52]

The contradiction between enlightenment rationality and the desire to exploit irrational folk beliefs as a source of national identity highlighted a major dilemma for nationalist intellectuals. Nationalist sentiment, at its core, is an emotional state. Early Korean modernizers, however, in their enthusiasm for things Western, were reluctant to seize upon an irrational, superstitious tradition to bolster group identification. Such attitudes served to isolate intellectuals from the masses; during the 1920s, this issue became important as nationalists fought over means to mobilize nationalist sentiment for the independence struggle.

The political crisis of the late nineteenth century merged with the growing intellectual crisis after 1900 to spawn the Korean enlightenment. And nationalistic concerns resided at the core of intellectual ferment. If Korea was indeed a nation like others, and this fact was accepted then by most, and the traditional political system was incapable of maintaining political autonomy, what, then, constituted the Korean nation? What aspects of the Korean historical, cultural, political, and social experience could provide national solidarity in combination with elements drawn from the models of nation-states who threatened Korea's very existence? The search for national identity was perplexing because Koreans had survived political threats and invasion before and had maintained their independence. Furthermore, Koreans had a solid sense of ethnic solidarity, cultivated over centuries. The fact remained that traditional identity and political system no longer seemed able to maintain independence, and new models challenged the efficacy of the old.

The issue of national identity opened a Pandora's box for Korean intellectuals. The language movement, new histories, discussion of national spirit, and investigation of the cultural tradition were evidence of this search. The questions of who are we, and why should we strive to maintain our autonomy as a people became a central theme in Korean nationalism.

This search was not without its problems. Korea's cultural alliance with China brought up questions of subservience and dependence. The urge to celebrate cultural uniqueness and autonomy clashed with the modern interpretation of *sadae*. This put nationalist ideologues in the ambivalent position of rejecting many aspects of Korea's long and successful political and cultural tradition. Furthermore, truly indigenous culture, such as the folk tradition, fell under suspicion because it lay outside modern science and Western rationalism. Yet was not the act of criticizing indigenous folk culture on the basis of outside standards another example of subservience? In spite of these contradictions, nationalists led in the process of creating a national identity in the face of the growing national political crisis after 1900. The intellectual ferment of the enlightenment developed without significant support from the failing dynasty. Although the dynasty continued after 1900 to sponsor selective reforms, there was little effort to open the political system, nor was there an attempt to seek popular support among the Korean masses. The nationalists of the enlightenment period found themselves facing a hostile elite in high government circles as well as the growing influence of Japanese advisers within the government. Thus, isolated from political power, nationalists continued to work in education and journalism in the hope of galvanizing patriotism and continued to clamor for significant reforms on the part of the crumbling traditional regime.

Fall into Colonial Status

Japan's victory over Russia in the Russo-Japanese War of 1904–5 paved the way for the ultimate annexation of Korea. During and immediately after the war, Japan secured international recognition for its preeminent interest in Korea through the Anglo-Japanese alliance (1904) and the Taft-Katsura agreement (1905) with the United States. With the defeat of Russia no outside power opposed Japan's plans to ultimately annex Korea. In 1905, Japan assumed responsibility for Korean foreign affairs by signing a protectorate agreement with the Korean government. Increasingly thereafter, the Japanese assumed control of Korean internal affairs through the creation of the Japanese Residency General. Japanese vice-ministers monitored all governmental functions, and Resident General Itō Hirobumi controlled a large police and regular military force to insure the pacification of Korea.[53]

In 1907, the Japanese forced Kojong to abdicate in the aftermath of the monarch's attempt to appeal for outside intervention through a secret mission to the world court at The Hague. Installing Kojong's son as emperor, the Japanese continued to tighten their grip. The resident general disbanded the Korean army in 1907, and in the next three years laid the framework, backed by military force, to control organizational life, publications, and education in the colony to be. All preparations were carried out with scrupulous attention to foreign opinion. In addition, the resident general worked with pro-Japanese organizations such as the Ilchinhoe and the expanding Japanese press in Korea to pacify public opinion and encourage support for Japanese "reforms." By 1910, the groundwork was ready for formal annexation. On August 22, 1910, the signing of the Korean-Japanese Treaty of Annexation ended the five hundred and eighteen-year rule of the Yi dynasty.

The inexorable Japanese advance stimulated broad Korean reaction. Government officials opposed the erosion of their power by the Residency General, intellectuals protested in the Korean press, and guerrilla bands, the Righteous Armies (*Ŭibyŏng*) led by the local Confucian elite and ex-officers and soldiers of the disbanded Yi army, attacked Japanese facilities and residents in the countryside. The 1905 protectorate agreement was greeted with shock and dismay by the anti-Japanese officialdom. Some Korean officials, such as Min Yŏnghwan, committed suicide rather than serve under the Japanese. Several collaborating officials were assassinated and others were attacked, their houses burned. The initial *Ŭibyŏng* disturbances in the wake of the protectorate were put down by the Japanese only to reemerge in 1907 after the disbanding of the Korean army. From 1907 to 1911 the Japanese army and police force waged, with great difficulty, a bloody struggle against these guerrilla bands. No match for the modern Japanese army, the *Ŭibyŏng* were subdued eventually. They did, however, demonstrate the power of nationalist sentiment. Considerable local peasant support, whether mobilized by the traditional conservative elite or professional soldiers, was mobilized in this movement to regain national sovereignty.

Resistance by intellectuals continued unabated throughout the protectorate period. National organizations, local study societies, and journals and newspapers fought Japanese rule through propaganda and appeals to the general population to resist. The major Korean newspaper to oppose Japanese policy was the *Korea Daily News* (*Taehan maeil sinbo*). The *Korea Daily News* avoided overt censorship because of the extraterritorial privileges of its English editor, Ernest Bethell. Eventually, however, the Japanese gained control over the media by passing strict publication laws (1907, 1908, 1909) in preparation for annexation.[54] In 1907, Korean organizations were restricted by the new Peace Preservation Law; after this, only pro-Japanese organizations avoided strict governmental scrutiny. In the educational arena, the 1908 Private School Ordinance established strict registration requirements for establishing new schools, and this began the slow constriction of the private school boom that had begun a decade earlier.[55]

The denouément of the Korean kingdom transformed the nationalist movement from a reformist to an independence movement. In one fell swoop, the *ancien régime* was gone, the Japanese provided stipends to the royal and major yangban families, rewarded key collaborationist officials with peerages, and replaced the traditional government with a modern, centralized, authoritarian, colonial regime. The fall of the dynasty crushed enlightenment intellectuals' hopes that changes could be fostered to provide a base for continued political autonomy. And conservative patriotic resistance in the form of guerrilla warfare was crushed by superior Japanese military force.

Yet the Japanese began their occupation in a Korea much changed from 1900. A decade of educational growth had expanded the politically conscious, nationalist intelligentsia. Moreover, the brutality of Japanese pacification after 1907 had begun to awaken the peasantry to the realities of foreign rule. These developments laid the basis for the joining of two streams of Korean nationalism, intellectual inquiry and leadership with mass sentiment. As anti-Japanese sentiment deepened throughout society, the issue became how to harness this growing force to the cause of regaining independence. The nature of Japanese rule between 1910 and 1920 stimulated the growth of national consciousness while repressing its political expression. Therefore, intellectual leadership continued to advocate enlightenment programs of education and nationalist consciousness-raising, unable to create, for the first ten years of colonial rule, a broader political movement.

Building on the base laid during the protectorate period, the Japanese created a powerful colonial state in Korea after 1910. The governor-generals, with only one exception, were high ranking officers in the Japanese military, highlighting the strategic importance of the colony to the Japanese. An impressive array of legal-bureaucratic and coercive power was at the disposal of the governor-general. He commanded a large military force and gendarmerie that was eventually augmented by large numbers of Korean policemen. Although the police system was modified over time, it continued to expand its power and reach into Korean society throughout the colonial period. By 1945, almost every facet of life in the colony felt the presence of the feared colonial police.[56]

The Japanese colonial state penetrated Korean society more thoroughly than had any previous traditional government. With over forty years of experience in centralizing and directing their own society since the Meiji Restoration, the Japanese applied their experience and twentieth-century technology to the task of organizing, mobilizing, and controlling the development of Korea to meet their own economic and political goals. Koreans remained outside of the policymaking process and, except for lower level appointments toward the end of the colony, administration. Thus, the creation of the colonial state, its power and reach, imposed Japanese administrative and legal forms on Korean society, and the singlemindedness and comprehensive quality of colonial rule transformed Korea in a generation of rule.

Official colonial policy assumed, in theory, the eventual cultural, linguistic, and political assimilation of Korea. The first Governor-General Terauchi Masatake noted the close proximity, shared culture, and ethnic origins shared by Japan and Korea as proof of the possibility of eventual assimilation.[57] Yet the ideology of assimilation presupposed Japanese superiority and the eventual effacement of a separate Korean cultural identity. Moreover, political assimilation was assumed to be a separate process, and there was no indication of willingness to create "equal" Korean citizens of the Japanese Empire.

Inequality between colonizers and the colonized was supported by a legal system of dual standards. The Japanese regulated education, publishing, organizational life, criminal sentencing, and even company ownership with two sets of laws, one for Japanese residents and another for Koreans.[58] Educational policy considered advanced training unsuitable for colonial subjects and stressed primary Japanese language and vocational skills, thus supporting an economic policy that required a skilled work force.[59] Segregated schools highlighted differences between ruler and ruled. The Japanese suppressed Korean vernacular newspapers, and carefully regulated the few vernacular journals and books that were published. Even after the 1920 press liberalization, Korean publications suffered different treatment in terms of legal permits, censorship, and even distribution regulations.[60] In short, Japanese colonization might have been unique in world colonial experience from the standpoint of close Japanese-Korean cultural and racial ties, but the legal, administrative, and economic policies in Korea left no doubt as to the status of ruler and ruled in the colony.

After 1910, the Japanese moved decisively to lay the economic base for exploiting their new colony. One of the first important programs of the Government General of Korea (hereafter GGK) was a comprehensive cadastral survey. Designed to fix a consistent tax base and rationalize ownership patterns, the land survey between 1910 and 1918 touched virtually all Koreans in some way. Public and royal lands were brought under GGK control and sold. There was, however, continuity in landholding patterns with most Korean landlords retaining their hold on land.[61] Low interest government loans for land improvement, reclamation, and irrigation paved the way for increases in rice production. With a fixed land tax and rent system based on a percentage of the harvest, usually 50 percent, and rising productivity, landlord income increased steadily. Tenants assumed many of the risks, had no control over prices, and soon found themselves in a progressive spiral of debt, a situation that worsened as the colonial period dragged on.[62]

Many nationalists chose exile over living under Japanese rule. The repression of the *Ŭibyŏng*, closure of Korean newspapers, and ban on political activity put many under risk of imprisonment for continued resistance. For most exiles the situation within Korea appeared hopeless. Congregating primarily in Vladivostok, Manchuria, and Shanghai, Korean nationalists formed diverse organizations to prepare • for an independence struggle. As the first decade of colonial rule wore on, however, the unified purpose of the exile movement was hampered by difficult communications with the colony and with each other, lack of financial resources, and growing ideological differences. A full spectrum of political predilections appeared as different groups devised plans to overthrow the Japanese.

Within Korea, nationalist intellectuals struggled under increasing repression to continue projects begun in the enlightenment period. Terauchi viewed all cultural and educational activity with considerable suspicion. The press and education system in the colony were to encourage the development of good citizens of the empire, not to promote the growth of Korean cultural or national identity. Terauchi attended to intellectual opposition in the colony with the same thoroughness with which armed insurrection had been repressed. In 1911, using charges of a conspiracy to assassinate the governor general, the police arrested over 700 Koreans and charged 123 Christian leaders with sedition. After a year of brutal interrogation and a highly publicized trial, 105 were sentenced and imprisoned from five to ten years. Behind this sweep was the GGK's intention to serve notice to nationalist leaders who used church organizations as a base of operations.[63] The Japanese were also concerned about the activities of the nationalist New People's Association (Sinminhoe). The Sinminhoe organized by Yi Kap, An Ch'angho, and Yi Tonghwi in 1908, had gone underground after 1910 and was trying to continue its work to promote Korean industry, education, and the creation of a cadre of young nationalist leaders.[64]

After the 105 conspiracy trial, intellectuals were on notice that the

Japanese meant to deal harshly with all forms of resistance. The 1910–20 decade is often referred to as the "dark period" (*amhŭkki*) in histories of the colony, an apt depiction given the pervasiveness of Japanese repression. In spite of the repression and the bewildering array of changes that unsettled Korean life, there were some hopeful intellectual developments. A surprising number of small academic journals, religious publications, and youth magazines survived. Responsibility for continuing the vernacular movement as well as some network of intellectual communication fell on these publications.[65] In addition, more Koreans sought education in the new colonial school system as well as abroad. The nationalist movement assumed a very low profile in the 1910–20 decade; nationalism as an idea, however, flourished as social and economic change combined with growing anti-Japanese sentiment to actually increase the potential for political action.

A decade of colonial rule stimulated Korean social mobilization. Rapid railroad and road construction after 1910 linked larger areas of the hinterland to urban centers. Rail junctions transformed sleepy villages such as Taejŏn and Iri into important urban centers.[66] In addition, the creation of new administrative centers spurred on urban development. Since 1876, the penetration of capitalism had already transformed the Korean economy and colonial economic policy further stimulated market growth. Koreans were progressively tied to larger market networks, and the advent of rail and road transport stimulated physical mobility. By 1919, more Koreans lived in cities, and the vast majority residing in rural villages had direct access to new market centers and, by extension, the outside world.

Increased physical mobility was complemented by continued expansion of education and literacy. Since 1880, new government, private, and mission schools had augmented the traditional education system. After 1910, the Japanese added to this expanded system a centralized education system of elementary and secondary schools. Although the best colonial facilities were for Japanese residents, Korean elementary and technical secondary schools were established in all provinces. Thus, education became available to a wider segment of the population. Graduates of the new schools, literate in Japanese as well as Korean, entered colonial society with heightened awareness of the world beyond the village or county seat. This new awareness made acceptance of the reality of life in the colony as an educated Korean all the more difficult.

Accounts of the repression between 1910 and 1919 stress its

successes. In terms of state building, economic reforms, and the imposition of Japanese law, the Japanese were spectacularly success-ful. The heavy-handed control measures, however, failed to achieve acceptance of Japanese rule. By 1919 Korea resembled an enormous pressure cooker. Broad structural changes engendered by colonial development had mobilized a significant portion of the population. Increased communication, rising educational levels, spread of basic literacy, and urbanization stimulated political consciousness. Concur-rently, the systematic exclusion of Koreans from public life alienated the expanding intelligentsia. Japanese rule destroyed the traditional political system and began to transform the society upon which it was based.

Korean intellectuals, however, took scant comfort in Japanese-directed reforms and world events increased intellectual tension. The Russian revolution accelerated interest in socialism and Marxism among Korean students abroad and in the colony. These radical ideologies, legitimated by the rise of the Bolsheviks in Russia, brought a new dimension to nationalist ideology and the end of World War I and the ringing pronouncements of self-determination emanating from the Versailles conference emboldened more conventional nation-alists. In addition, daily discrimination at all levels of Korean society produced a deep well of common resentment against Japanese rule. The powerful negative symbol of Japanese rule and their discrimina-tory development program and repressive cultural policy united to create eventually intolerable pressures that burst forth in the March First demonstrations of 1919. The disaster for the Japanese of the March First movement proved the failure of their initial colonial policy, and for Korea it signaled the maturity of the nationalist movement.

The March First Movement is treated as the greatest event in the history of pre-World War II Korean nationalism, and the details of the movement are well known.[67] The movement was organized by a moderate leadership concentrated in religious organizations. Chris-tian, Ch'ŏndogyo, and Buddhist leaders worked closely with students in Japan. They also influenced greatly the pacifist ideology of the movement. Wilsonian idealism, in particular the well-publicized doc-trine of self-determination, provided the original inspiration for the demonstration. With the backdrop of the Versailles conference, nationalist leaders conceived a massive, peaceful demonstration of Korean desire for independence, hoping for Allied intervention on their behalf.

The demonstration was a spectacular success. Staged to coincide with the funeral of ex-Emperor Kojong on March 3, 1919, a simultaneous nationwide demonstration was organized, and a declaration of independence was prepared. At the last minute, the date was changed to the first because of the danger of Japanese discovery. On March first, people gathered in public parks, schoolyards, and market commons to hear a reading of the declaration; following this, demonstrators proceeded to march through the streets shouting *"manse"* (long live Korea) in a massive show of solidarity and patriotism—for once, the two streams of Korean nationalism were joined. In the following weeks, the demonstrations spread and perhaps as many as one million people joined the rallies at their height.[68]

The Japanese reaction bordered on hysteria. Colonial police met peaceful demonstrators with violence that in turn sparked reprisals and rioting. In the months following March First, the Japanese arrested thousands of Koreans, seized printing presses, searched homes, closed schools, and eventually brought more troops to the colony. The movement failed to unseat the Japanese, and Western intervention was never forthcoming. It did, however, galvanize Korean will to resist and demonstrated, not in the least to Korean leaders themselves, the depth of public support and the tangible possibilities of mass organization. Moreover, the demonstrations provoked a Japanese reappraisal of colonial policy that produced welcomed changes for life in the colony. Ironically, within this triumph lay the seeds of a more successful Japanese approach to long-term control.

The party government of Hara Kei watched the crisis in Korea with considerable concern. Eventually, Hara's own liberal tendencies and spirit of compromise affected his instructions to the newly appointed governor general. Under the softer label of "harmony between Japan and Korea" (*nissen yūwa*), Hara instructed the new administration to take necessary measures to align colonial rule with "the progress of the times."[69] Hara's government itself had inaugurated party rule in Japan, and it was clear that the heretofore heavy-handed policy in Korea was not in keeping with Hara's style. He worried, in addition, about world opinion and was sensitive to charges of Japanese brutality and unenlightened colonial rule. Nevertheless, there was no slackening of Japanese will to rule Korea and the task of the new colonial administration was to remove the more obnoxious features of colonial rule while binding Korea more tightly to Japan.

Hara entrusted this job to Admiral Saitō Makoto. An urbane, well-traveled diplomat, Saitō enjoyed the backing of Hara's civilian government as well as a reputation within the Japanese military establishment. As second in command, Saitō brought with him Mizuno Rentarō, former home minister (1916–18) as director-general of political affairs. In 1920, Saitō drafted Maruyama Tsurukichi, a young and brilliant civil servant who had become an expert on colonial police affairs in the course of a world tour of Western colonies, as head of the colonial police. With this new brain trust, Saitō began the job of revamping Japanese colonial policy.

The overall objectives in Korea remained unchanged; however, naked coercion was replaced by a softer but even more effective policy of manipulation and co-optation. Saitō redressed major Korean grievances with regard to discriminatory laws. Whipping for minor offenses, a Yi dynasty practice retained for punishment (Koreans only) of misdemeanors, was abolished. Saitō also modified unpopular laws regulating traditional burial practices as well as police interference with peasant markets and slaughtering. The dual pay scale for Korean and Japanese civil servants was also readjusted. In legal matters, Saitō chose to concentrate on areas where Korean cultural sensibilities could be mollified without diluting colonial authority.

Saitō also reformed cosmetically the colonial police system. A civilian police force replaced the military gendarmerie; civilian uniforms without swords replaced the old military dress both for policemen and colonial officials. Saitō announced his intention to expand educational opportunity for Koreans with an ambitious goal of one primary school in every district (*myŏn*) and the opening of more secondary schools. Along with these important reforms the administration announced a new press policy. It offered permits for vernacular newspapers, and allowed journals and magazines to carry content on political and social affairs.

The conciliation policy strove to remold world opinion about Japanese rule as well as court favor with important opinion leaders in the colony. The urbane Saitō utilized his fluent English in a series of meetings with foreign missionaries, many of whom had been ardent critics of colonial policy. Saitō also opened negotiations with prominent Koreans by creating an advisory council to assist the GGK in policy formation on cultural matters. Prospective publishers came for meetings with the GGK to discuss guidelines and the mechanics of permits and censorship. Thus, the Japanese created an aura of change and moderation by appearing open and sensitive to the needs and opinions of important residents in the colony.

The conciliation policy was implemented through the dual strategy of mollifying public opinion through selected legal reforms and cosmetic changes in the police force and by currying favor with the elite by removing restrictions on publishing and organizational life. Yet behind the facade of conciliation, the cultural policy (*Bunka seiji*), as Saitō's reforms came to be known, was buttressed by a tightening of the Japanese control apparatus. Just as he changed the appearance of the police, Saitō increased their numbers. While educational goals remained an announced "target" of one school per district in four years, within five months the GGK had placed a police box in every district. Furthermore, Maruyama organized a new bureau, the High Police (Kōtō keisatsu), to oversee organizations, publications, and a strengthened surveillance apparatus. In short, the cultural policy dealt decisively with the tone and appearance of colonial rule, while concurrently, it strengthened Japan's hold over Korean society.[70]

Nevertheless, Saitō had made significant concessions by providing expanded opportunities for organization and publishing. And between 1920 and 1925, an atmosphere of experiment prevailed in the colony as Koreans tested the new boundaries and as colonial administrators contemplated the limits of their tolerance. In addition, the dramatic changes in the atmosphere in the colony stimulated a profound change in the Korean nationalist movement, in exile and at home. The March First movement aroused the exile movement. In April of 1919, exiled leaders established the Shanghai Provisional Government (SPG) to bring unity to the far-flung exile movement. Nationalists were drawn to the government in exile and began to debate diplomatic, propaganda, and military programs to achieve independence. Contact was made with nationalists in the colony to elicit financial support. During the summer, an air of expectation and progress pervaded the rooms of the new government in exile.

By 1920, nationalists in the colony began to take advantage of the new rules; two Korean vernacular papers, the *East Asia Daily (Tonga ilbo)* and *Korea Daily (Chosŏn ilbo)* and intellectual journals such as *Creation (Kaebyŏk)* received permits to publish on political affairs and current events. After 1920 there was a renaissance of organizational activity. Study societies, youth groups, farmer's associations, labor cooperatives, and women's groups appeared and efforts were made to link the new organizations into nationwide networks. In opportunities for intellectual organization and expression, the early 1920s could not have contrasted more with the era of military rule.

In spite of the excitement, the fundamental reality of Japanese rule remained unchanged. By the end of 1920 much of the impetus of

March First had dissipated. The SPG foundered on ideological and tactical disputes. The heady idealism of possible Western intervention on Korea's behalf crumbled with the realization that the principle of self-determination was not to be applied to Asia. Indeed, there was a growing disillusionment with the West in the post-World War I period. Concurrently, after 1919, there were signs of dissension within the nationalist leadership. The Russian revolution of 1917 had stimulated increased interest in social revolutionary ideas. Exiled nationalists in the Russian Far East and China formed groups in common cause with Russian Communists against the Japanese. In the following years, the Korean socialist movement continued to grow, spurred by support from the Soviet Union for national liberation movements. These developments had a decisive effect on the intellectual leadership of the Korean nationalist movement in the colony. Nationalist intellectuals since the time of the Independence Club had been in rough agreement on the issues of national development and had been following, for the most part, a model based on Western capitalist democracies. After 1917, however, radical nationalists began to challenge this line, offering more radical solutions to the problem of national liberation.

These differences emerged in high relief in the period after the Saitō reforms, as radicals attacked the moderate cultural nationalist movement with increasing ferocity. The cultural movement was an attempt to build on the success of the March First demonstrations, and it represented, in many ways, the mainstream of nationalist thought that had developed since 1900. The radical attack and ensuing debate among the nationalist leadership decisively split the nationalist leadership with important future consequences to the movement as a whole.

Before discussing the ideological split, however, we must first turn our attention to the ideological origins and political development of cultural nationalism as it appeared after 1919.

CHAPTER 2

The Rise of Cultural Nationalism

The Nationalist Renaissance

If 1910–19 had been a dark period for the Korean nationalist movement, 1920–25 was, in contrast, a true renaissance. The events of March 1919 seemed to augur a host of opportunities, and exiled nationalists redoubled their efforts to organize a unified movement. The formation of the Shanghai Provisional Government (SPG) in the fall of 1919 provided the first umbrella organization for the exile movement. With much difficulty, contending strategies and personal differences were overcome temporarily and in its early existence the SPG attracted major exile leaders under its banner. Older leaders such as Yi Sŭngman (Syngman Rhee), An Ch'angho, and Yi Tonghwi accepted posts, some in absentia, in the new exile government. They soon were working with a large group of younger patriots attracted to the SPG from Tokyo and Korea.[1]

In spite of internal squabbling, the SPG created an aura of hope in its first year. It established communication with the colony to report on the international situation and solicit funds. It published a newspaper, the *Independence News,* and pushed forward diplomatic activity in Paris and the United States. The SPG, however, foundered early on the shoals of ideological and tactical differences among its members. The major splits occurred among three factions led by Syngman Rhee, An Ch'angho, and Yi Tonghwi. The Rhee faction wanted to continue diplomatic representation abroad; they were opposed by gradualists clustered around An Ch'angho as well as radicals led by Yi Tonghwi. In general, radicals opposed both the diplomatists and gradualists and argued for an immediate formation of an armed force to fight for independence. Many of the radicals were veterans of struggles in Manchuria and the Soviet Far East against the Japanese. For one, Yi Tonghwi represented an important leftist faction and had a long exile experience in Manchuria and Russia; moreover he was the organizer of the first Korean Communist party in 1920.[2]

The failure of the diplomatic strategy in the immediate aftermath of the March First movement also drove a wedge between SPG leaders. Syngman Rhee continued to act unilaterally abroad in the name of the SPG even after he had been censured for acting as "president" without authorization.[3] With no help forthcoming from the victorious Allied powers at Versailles and a similar failure at the Washington Conference (1920–21) to gain support for the cause of independence, serious difficulties rose over future tactics. By 1921, the SPG was in serious trouble. Japanese security had been tightened, making linkage with the colony progressively more difficult.[4] Financial resources for the government were seriously deficient. And the left wing of the movement was increasingly unwilling to cooperate with moderates and their gradualist tactics. Besides, Soviet support for underground activity and propaganda spurred interest in a social revolutionary movement. Despite the failure of the SPG, exile activity increased on a broad front. Rival leftist groups competed for Soviet patronage, and the moderates continued to organize Korean communities abroad. The Korean communities in the United States (6,000), Manchuria (600,000), and the Soviet Far East (400,000) continued to support the operations of various exile nationalist factions. Although intense, exile nationalist activity remained fragmented; efforts to reorganize a united effort in the 1920s, for example the National Representatives Conference of 1923, failed repeatedly.[5]

Within the colony, the nationalist movement revived after a ten-year period of repression. Emerging from the cowed quiescence of the 1910–19 period, nationalists took advantage of the expanded limits for organization and publishing announced by Saitō in his cultural policy. Opportunities in the colony attracted returning students from Japan as well as exiles in the United States and China and in the 1910–25 period, intellectual and political life in the colony was transformed as Koreans discussed new ideas, considered the future, and debated programs at group meetings, and, more broadly, in the forum of the new nationalist press.

The domestic nationalist revival was most obvious in organizational life. From 1910 to 1919, the Japanese had strictly circumscribed organizations. Only religious and highly specialized cultural-academic groups had been permitted, and all had been monitored carefully. With the cultural policy "thaw" came a mushrooming of organizations. In 1920, there were 985 organizations of all types registered with the colonial police.[6] These were local youth groups, religious organizations, educational study groups, academic societies, and social clubs. By September 1922, the number of organizations had swelled to 5,728; the breakdown by type of organization was as follows:

Political and intellectual	48
Labor	204
Youth	1,185
Church youth	639
Religious	1,742
Tenant	26
Children's	40
Academic	203
Industrial	470
Health	6
Anti-drinking/smoking	193
Self-improvement	235
Recreation/social	348
Women's	56
Savings and purchasing cooperatives	53
Other	280
Total	5,728[7]

The organizational boom was a direct result of nationalist efforts within the new guidelines of the cultural policy. The vast majority of these groups restricted their activities to "safe" social or enlighten-ment projects. Yet even a cursory glance at their publicized goals reveals that group activities were almost always conceived as nation-alist self-strengthening projects.[8] Japanese officials, however, were concerned about the explosive potential inherent in labor and tenant organizations as well as the enthusiasm of youth groups for political activity. In August of 1920, Governor General Saitō already was making plans to "avert this tendency toward radicalization" and to use the "opportunity" represented by the presence of so many new organizations to steer them "toward a proper view of assimilation [*nissen dōka*]."[9]

In addition to the rapid growth of organizations there was a significant structural change in their interrelations. With increased operational freedom similar groups began to coalesce into national federations and leagues. This trend was most obvious in the formation of a national linkage of youth groups. In June of 1920, 600 groups joined together to form the Korean Youth League (Chosŏn ch'ŏngn-yŏn yŏnhaphoe).[10] Other leagues and federations emerged in the early 1920s and, particularly in the youth movement and labor groups, competition between moderate and leftist nationalists for control became quite intense. The organizational boom of the 1920s fulfilled the promise of the earlier growth of nationalist organizations between 1896 and 1910. A decade of colonial rule, expanded education, urban growth, and development of communications had only increased the Koreans' capacity for organization.

The Expansion of the Vernacular Press

The cultural policy also permitted a vast expansion of vernacular publications. Without changing the legal structure that regulated publication, the Japanese began issuing permits under the newspaper (1907) and publication (1909) laws. The legal framework required prepublication inspection of daily newspaper galleys, and all magazines and books had to be submitted to the censor prior to distribution. The Publications Department (Toshoka) of the Government General had been responsible for censorship up until 1920; Toshoka officials followed a general set of censorship guidelines very similar to that used in Japan proper. In the colony, standards stiffened, gradually becoming more inclusive, and police gave certain categories special attention: defamation of the emperor or imperial institutions, military matters, radical ideology, Korean-Japanese relations, and Korean nationalism.[11]

Publication in the colony was restricted, therefore, by the censorship standards and the absolute power of the Government General to issue permits. In the 1910–19 period, the Japanese choked off Korean vernacular publications by simply refusing permission to publish. With the cultural policy, a decision was made to relax the permit • system. In 1920, the Japanese issued 409 permits under the Publication Law (magazines and books); the number of permits tripled to 1,240 by 1925.[12] In 1920, the Japanese also issued permits to two Korean newspapers. Regulated by the Newspaper Law, the daily press enjoyed permission to print articles on current affairs (*jiji*); this included discussion of politics, social problems, and international events, a privilege granted to six magazines in the early 1920s as well.[13] Growing from a virtual zero base in 1920, combined circulation of the vernacular press reached 103,027 by 1929.[14]

Almost immediately, the censors felt the pressure of the rapidly expanding press and censorship matters were transferred to the newly created High Police Office. As this office was responsible for information on and control of subversive activities in the colony—thought crimes, illegal organization, and illegal political activity—the job of monitoring the press and enforcing censorship standards fell naturally on the High Police. They had wide latitude to interpret publication standards, and it is clear that the whole issue of censorship was handled quite subjectively. A close interpretation of the existing code would have required action on a daily basis against the new press, and few magazines would have stayed alive. In fact, the police, under guidelines set down by Saitō, interpreted the standards liberally in the first years of the cultural policy era. They reserved their most potent weapons—seizure, suspension, fines, and jail terms—for only very serious infractions. The most common form of censorship was erasure, and although mechanically effective, this often provoked wider interest in items so treated.

An atmosphere of trial and error pervaded the publishing world between 1920 and 1925 as Koreans pushed to the limits, and the censors attempted to hold the line, often taking a wait-and-see attitude. The police strived to head off problems with prepublication warnings and negotiations with publishers. In the case of the daily newspapers, however, where censorship inspection was simultaneous with distribution, they often were forced to act with deliberate speed, usually unsuccessfully, to repress and recover offensive editions after the fact.[15] Statistics on seizures indicates that in the 1920–24 period censorship standards were administered fairly loosely. After 1924, however, the police tightened control on the printed word because of concern for the rise of social revolutionary ideology in the colonial press.[16]

Two nationalist newspapers emerged in 1920, each serving in the resuscitation of the Korean nationalist movement. For the next twenty years, the *East Asia Daily* (*Tonga ilbo*) and the *Korea Daily* (*Chosŏn ilbo*) served as the major foci of political and social life in the colony. The papers attracted many of the best and brightest Korean intellectuals to their editorial boards and reporting staffs. Here was one honorable career within the colony for politically conscious and patriotic Korean youth. Moreover, youth was the watchword on the new papers. For example the founder and president of the *Tonga ilbo*, Kim Sŏngsu, was barely thirty years old in 1920, and the majority of the writers were in their twenties.[17]

The new papers also represented a leap forward in journalistic sophistication from the precolonial Korean press. Each was well-financed, supported by the sale of public stock, and, after rocky beginnings, soon became profitable commercial ventures in its own right.[18] Distributed in the tens of thousands, their circulation dwarfed the comparatively meager distribution of their precolonial antecedents, *The Independent* and the *Korea Daily News*. Modern Korean culture flourished within the new press. The papers featured serialized novels, short stories, essays on social problems, international news, political cartoons; in short, daily reading of either newspaper was de rigueur for any informed citizen of the colony. Moreover, advertisements for the latest consumer items, patent medicines, and other commercial services provide a vivid glimpse into the daily life of the rapidly growing urban culture.

Politically, the new press arrogated to itself both the civilizing task of spreading advanced ideas in the colony and the role of spokesman for the nation. The inaugural edition of the *Tonga ilbo,* for example, announced the paper's intention to "represent the masses" (*minjung*), promote democracy, and encourage the spread of culturalism (*munhwajuŭi*).[19] Within the first year of publication, the editors were emboldened to replace "masses" with "nation" (*minjok*); and they continually walked the narrow line between promoting social reform for the Korean people and outright advocacy of independence. One can almost hear the Japanese censors gnashing their teeth. The *Tonga ilbo*'s original statement of purpose asserted its belief in human equality and the necessity of recognizing the political rights of all nations in the Far East, a barely veiled reference to the doctrine of self-determination of nations that had incited the idealism of the March First leaders the year before.[20]

The burgeoning of journals and specialized magazines after 1920 added depth and breadth to intellectual life. In addition to the wider range of subject matter, there was a significant change in the character of periodical journals. Early Korean magazines were almost exclusively small, privately financed organ journals that spoke for the ideas of various associations and intellectual societies. The *Honam Study Society Monthly* (*Honam hakhoe wŏlbo*), published by *Tonga ilbo* founder Kim Sŏngsu's father, and Chang Chiyŏn's *The Korean Self-Strengthening Society Monthly* (*Taehan cha'ganghoe wŏlbo*) were examples of this early journalistic trend.[21] These magazines were published only intermittently and were limited in distribution.

During the 1910–19 period, a small number of intellectual journals sustained the development of vernacular publishing that had taken off between 1900 and 1910. Of the thirty-three magazines published during this period sixteen were religious publications. Two magazines of the Terauchi years did have a significant influence on later journalism. The titles of both are best translated as *Youth*, in Korean: *Sonyŏn* (1908–1911) and *Ch'ŏngch'un* (1914–1918). Both magazines were published by the brilliant and precocious Ch'oe Namsŏn (1890–1957).[22] Featuring articles on Western science, social thought, translations of Western literature, and biographies of famous patriots, from both Korean and world history, these magazines kept alive the enlightenment consciousness that had dominated intellectual life in Korea before 1910. Only nineteen himself, Ch'oe aimed the message of *Sonyŏn,* published as the organ of the Youth Student Association (Ch'ŏngnyŏn hag'uhoe), at the future leaders of Korea. The enlightenment content of *Sonyŏn* was suffused with patriotic undertones. Biographies of world leaders and the revival of Korean historical studies carried a clear message to Korean youth. Ch'oe, himself, was responsible for reviving the indigenous Korean poetic form of *sijo.*[23] Indeed, *Sonyŏn* continued the precolonial discussion of spritual revival and the importance of developing a strong national identity that had been championed by Ch'oe's elders, Sin Ch'aeho and Chang Chiyŏn.

Also published by Ch'oe Namsŏn, *Ch'ŏngch'un* continued the theme of new education and enlightenment; in addition, there was a more strident iconoclastic tone to its content. Not content to simply foster the new learning, authors in *Ch'ŏngch'un* began to lash out at obstacles to progress within the Korean tradition itself. *Ch'ŏngch'un* provided a forum for a new generation of Korean intellectuals who came of age in the early colonial period. Less affected by the tortuous debates of the 1880s and 1890s over saving the tradition while borrowing from the West, young intellectuals like Ch'oe and Yi Kwangsu published bitter attacks against the "feudal" nature of the political tradition and the "tyranny" of the Confucian social system.[24] Moreover, Yi Kwangsu, whose ideas will be treated at some length below, became one of the first to champion the liberation of women in the pages of *Ch'ŏngch'un,* a theme sustained in journals after 1920.

Building on experience gained between 1910 and 1919, and given permission to expand their content area, magazines and journals matured in the 1920s. In contrast to issue-specific, privately financed, and narrowly distributed intellectual magazines, the so-called *tong'in chapchi,* of the 1900–20 period, the 1920s produced the first true integrated, wide-circulation journals, called *chŏnghap chapchi.*[25] The *chŏnghap chapchi* were of wider appeal, covered current affairs as well as intellectual subjects, and might be compared to Western intellectual monthlies. The emergence of these magazines was a direct result of the decision to grant the coveted "current affairs" permit to six monthlies in the early 1920s. This opened the way for the creation of political journals that provided a forum for discussion of current social and political topics in the colony. Six magazines were given current affairs permits: *Creation* (*Kaebyŏk*), *New Life* (*Sinsaenghwal*), *Eastern Light* (*Tongmyŏng*), *New World* (*Sinch'ŏnji*), *Light of Korea* (*Chosŏn chigwang*), and a pro-Japanese magazine *Co-prosperity* (*Kong'yŏng*).[26] The names of these new journals themselves evoked the aspirations and enthusiasm of their youthful editorial boards.

If the new newspapers were the heartbeat of the nationalist renaissance after 1920, the intellectual journals were its soul. Just as the March First movement marked the advent of mass nationalism in Korea, the emergence of the major intellectual journals of the 1920s signaled the maturation of a new generation of nationalist intellectuals. Any study of intellectual life and nationalist ideology in colonial Korea must begin with an examination of their content.

Creation and the Nationalist Cultural Revival

The journal *Creation* (*Kaebyŏk*) rose from among the many new magazines appearing after 1919 to become the major intellectual forum of the 1920s. Lasting for seventy-two issues (1920–26), *Kaebyŏk* was also one of the longest-lived journals of the decade.[27] *Kaebyŏk* was the brainchild of young leaders in the native Korean religious movement, the Ch'ŏndogyo. The Ch'ŏndogyo had emerged from the mid-nineteenth century Tonghak movement as the modern church of the original Tonghak teaching. It had long been involved in the independence movement, advocating the formation of a modern elite, reconstruction of national life, and social equality.[28] The Ch'ŏndogyo had also played an important role in the March First movement. Their religious status allowed them relative organizational freedom, and their syncretic religious philosophy, a mixture of native religious beliefs, was popular among modern intellectuals.

The Ch'ŏndogyo connection provided *Kaebyŏk* with a sound financial and organizational base. In September of 1919, with many of the church elders in prison in the aftermath of the March First movement, younger church members organized the Ch'ŏndogyo Youth Association (Ch'ŏndogyo ch'ŏngnyŏnhoe) to promote educational and cultural projects. To propagate church doctrine as it related to social reform and the new culture, the Ch'ŏndogyo also established a publishing house, the Kaebyŏksa, in order to bring out a series of specialized magazines.[29] In the spring of 1920, they received permission to publish an intellectual journal, and having arranged financial backing from wealthy church members, the first issue of *Kaebyŏk* appeared on June 25, 1920.[30]

The first issue invited articles on a wide spectrum of topics. Although the magazine featured articles on Ch'ŏndogyo doctrine in its early issues, it was generally ecumenical in its editorial selections; it included pieces on social reform, literary criticism, history, economics, and translations of Western literature. It also encouraged original short stories and poetry. Although it restricted its content to intellectual and cultural issues, the censor twice delayed publication of the inaugural edition.[31] This was only the first of many encounters with the censor, yet *Kaebyŏk* continued to thrive. In its early years, its content reflected a broad intellectual coalition that formed around the issues of social reform, cultural development, and the reinvigoration of the Korean national spirit. In this sense, *Kaebyŏk* can be compared to the influential Chinese journal *New Youth* (*Hsin ch'ing nien*, 1915–22). The original coalition that formed around *Kaebyŏk* was inspired by a general interest in reforming the thought and behavior of youth; and both magazines had to temper their political content in response to restrictive publishing climates.[32] Moreover, both quickly became centers for contending political philosophies as the initial cultural line came under attack by radicals, who insisted cultural transformation should not delay political action.[33] By October 1921, *Kaebyŏk* had received a current affairs permit; this allowed the editors to expand into political subjects. The strong financial backing, inclusive intellectual tone, and, finally, current affairs status combined to solidify *Kaebyŏk*'s stature as the premier journal of its day.

The editorial line of social regeneration attracted writers from a new generation of Korean intellectuals. Born in the 1890s, these men came of age in the last years of the old dynasty, and for the most part were products of the new schools. Many of these writers also had studied in Japan, usually financing their studies with their own resources, but some went to Japan through the limited Government General scholarship program. Few Koreans managed entrance to the imperial universities; however, prestigious private institutions such as Waseda, Keiō, and Meiji universities had contingents of Koreans. Waseda University alone produced many Korean graduates who later became prominent in colonial intellectual circles. Ch'oe Namsŏn, Kim Sŏngsu, Yi Kwangsu, Chang Tŏksu, Hyŏn Sangyun, all important members of journalistic, literary, or academic circles, were either graduates of or students at Waseda. School ties reinforced intellectual connections, and although more research on personal connections between colonial intellectuals needs to be done, the general patterns are clear. General tracking of school and employment patterns of active writers in the 1920s will, more often than not, reveal common educational roots, in Korean schools as students and instructors, links to Japanese private universities, and professional ties to various newspapers and political organizations.

Kim Sŏngsu, Yi Kwangsu, and Chang Tŏksu provide good examples. Kim Sŏngsu (1891–1955) attended Waseda between 1908 and 1914. Returning to Korea, he took over and managed several schools that later became an integrated private educational conglomerate, including a private college, the precursor of the present-day Korea University. Kim also organized and obtained funding from his wealthy family for the *Tonga ilbo*. In the world of business, Kim invested in the textile industry and ultimately became one of colonial Korea's most successful industrialists. Chang Tŏksu (1895–1947) followed Kim at Waseda, and after graduation and his involvement in Korean exile politics in Tokyo and Shanghai, he returned to Korea, taught in one of Kim's schools and eventually became editor of the *Tonga ilbo*. Likewise, Yi Kwangsu (1892– ?) also attended Waseda and his studies were supported financially by Kim Sŏngsu. Subsequently, he became an activist in the exile movement, a prominent literary figure, essayist, and journalist, also serving at one time as editor of Kim's newspaper.[34] The personal, educational, and professional enmeshment of Kim, Chang, and Yi, here in highly abridged form, illustrates the close world of the Korean intelligentsia of the 1920s. It also helps to illumine the origins and progression of political factions. In this case each individual can also be linked to the moderate cultural nationalist line that emerged in the 1920–22 period. Each played separate roles in this movement, Kim as an organizer and financial backer, Yi as an ideologue, and Chang as a youth leader and journalist.

Kaebyŏk served as a focal point for the development of a post-March First intellectual movement that stressed cultural and social development of Korean society. In a sense, the political failure of March First simply channeled energies toward enlightenment projects on a mass scale as an alternative to independence. Combined with this enlightenment consciousness was a desire to pull Korean society into the mainstream of world thought. This made reform, including a systematic break from the tradition, and cosmopolitanism the watchwords of the early issues of *Kaebyŏk*.[35]

Upon closer examination, the theme of social and political unity also pervaded the early issues of *Kaebyŏk*. The conviction that Korean society was being torn asunder by new economic and social divisions emerged repeatedly, and authors attempted to grapple with various solutions to this problem. At its roots, the perception of increasing social strife was justified because colonial economic development had begun to transform Korean society. There was a sense that if a way to harmonize and unify society was found, the ultimate horror of social revolution, pitting Korean against Korean, could be avoided. Therefore, in the sampling of moderate nationalist writings presented below, we find an attempt to blend traditional values that strengthened social solidarity with a program of national development in which differences would be temporarily set aside for the greater good of national unity. Ultimately, a rough consensus emerged that stressed national unity, education, and economic development in the service of remolding Korean society.

The inaugural editorial of June 25, 1920, stressed reform and cosmopolitanism. Announcing that the world was awakening to new demands of people on all continents, the editors emphasized *Kaebyŏk*'s role as the "people's voice."[36] By choosing the name *Creation,* the editors placed themselves in what they believed was a "world trend of reconstruction [*kaejo*]"; it was incumbent on Korean society to step away from its past and merge with the evolution of a new world culture.[37] Above all, this culture would be one that promoted peace and harmony and affirmed the natural rights of all nations, great and small. Indeed, the inaugural edition rang with the infectious post-World War I idealism, grounded in Wilsonian self-determination, that had swept East Asia after World War I. This line was, no doubt, a product of hope and idealism as well as the search for a lofty, attractive slogan acceptable to the Japanese censors.

The lead editorial of the second issue set forth three fundamental problems facing humanity. These problems centered on occupational (class), sex, and racial inequality.[39] In analyzing the development of these major inequalities in world history, the editors traced the amelioration of class division (described in the article as the "labor problem"—*nodong munje*) through the rise of democratic politics in the West. In a similar vein, they contrasted the position of women in Western society with contemporary Korea. In both cases, they asserted that Korea must strive to harmonize conflict in the future by understanding the development of more advanced societies; Korea was, they asserted, "an infant," but she would inevitably have to progress in the same general direction as the West.[39] And by understanding and following world trends, evils inherent in traditional Korea would be smashed.

Moving toward a general analysis of racial inequality and ignoring the specific situation of Korea under Japanese rule, this editorial noted hopeful trends in post-World War I world politics. Although the world was filled with inequality, injustice, and oppression characterized by the domination of "superior peoples" (*udŭng injong*, i.e., white, European) over "inferior peoples" (*yŏldŭng injong*, i.e., other races), the major powers had recognized this problem; efforts at Versailles and other world peace conferences were signs that racial injustice would fade as world peace was sustained.[40] Implicit in this analysis of the post-World War I world was the hope that through sustained cultural and social reform Korea, too, could be prepared to take her place in a just international society.

This belief underpinned a significant portion of *Kaebyŏk*'s early content. Whereas the *Kaebyŏk* editors could sketch the goals, it was up to individual contributors to fill in the details. What emerged between 1920 and 1922 was a search for a means to achieve no less than the transformation of Korean society. There was a general perception that Korea stood on the brink of change, to step back would be to admit defeat forever. One essayist concluded that "old and new ideas (value systems) were colliding"; and although the process of change and the contradictions it produced were natural, it was incumbent on modern Koreans to direct change along "progressive lines."[41]

No less a nationalist than Pak Yŏnghyo, a survivor of the progressive movement in the 1880s, concurred. To Pak, Korean society was filled with contradictions as remnants of traditional society struggled to hold back progress. In musing about the significance of *Creation*'s debut, Pak concluded that Korean society needed to create a new path (*to*) with regard to the development of both human and natural resources. This task was paramount if Korea was to overcome past mistakes.[42] Central to Pak's plan was a fundamental reordering of values; replacing evil traditional values with progressive concepts of justice, truth, and freedom was just as important as material progress.

Pak Sajik, Ch'ŏndogyo activist and youth leader, continued the emphasis on instilling new values in society in a July 1920 article, "The Problem of Cultivation (*suyang*) in Korean Society."[43] Pak focused on the fissures in Korean society between rich and poor, strong and weak, educated and illiterate, and he perceptively ascribed this problem to the growing complexity of modern life caused by economic change. Pak's solution, however, was to ameliorate these divisions by harmonizing (*chohwa t'ong'il*) conflicting values. If all individuals cultivated modern values of democracy, justice, and truth, society would maintain unity.[44] Pak's Ch'ŏndogyo theological training that taught the central tenets of "god in all men" (*innaech'ŏn*) and "treating man as one treats god" (*sain yŏch'ŏn*) helps explain his emphasis on propagating a new morality to solve the problem of social inequity. Moreover, there were strong Confucian overtones in the call for cultivating men's minds as a prerequisite to reform. Thus, Pak mixed a hard analysis of structural causes for social disharmony with a solution based on Ch'ŏndogyo morality and Confucian cultivation.

Hyŏn Sangyun (1893–?) continued the theme of moral regeneration within the context of a bitter attack on the Korean tradition. The task at hand was to overhaul the entire Korean tradition, its thought, customs, teachings, even its economic system. According to Hyŏn, all was rotten (*pup'ye*) and deficient (*malhyŏp*).[45] As a solution Hyŏn also advocated character reform as an initial step toward societal "rebirth," believing that only by reforming individuals would broad social renovation succeed. Although Hyŏn placed value on the individual, he was no advocate of untrammeled individualism; the individual had to harmonize his own needs and desires in accordance with the needs of the group. In doing so, Hyŏn revealed his continued commitment to Confucian values such as righteousness (*ŭi*) and virtue (*tŏk*) even as he derided other traditional values.[46] Hyŏn had been imprisoned in 1919 as one of the thirty-three signers of the March First Independence Declaration. After his release in 1921, he became prominent in academic circles and authored an influential *History of Korean Confucianism* (*Han'guk yuhaksa*). Although his writing was tempered by a strong academic and philosophical bent, Hyŏn contributed his prestige to the cause of spiritual reform in the 1920–22 period.

While still editor of the *Tonga ilbo*, Chang Tŏksu contributed an article to *Kaebyŏk* that added to the emerging spiritual regeneration thesis. Chang believed that "new relations of production produced a new spirit in society."[47] People with a modern spirit cannot live in an old society; the task at hand, according to Chang, was to encourage spiritual changes by "absorbing" and internalizing new ideas and values. He believed that it was necessary to cultivate reason, self-awareness, truth, and above all a "critical, scientific spirit" in order to break from the past. This critical spirit had to be tempered, however, with a commitment to consensus: "If we are to build a new culture that is uniquely our own, we must understand a life of freedom and equality. Living a life mired in blind acceptance and without a critical spirit, it is impossible to build a true consensus in society. Without true consensus in society (unity of values) how can we have true free-dom?"[48] Chang's curious ambivalence between a "critical spirit," an individualistic value, and a desire for consensus underscored the general interest in spiritual regeneration.

The writers discussed above were enthusiastic modernizers and iconoclasts. Yet they returned time and again to the theme of harmony and consensus in society. Aware of the growing complexity of modern society, they seemed driven to delineate some core value or ideal that could serve as an integrative force, a force that could fill the gap left by the increasing inability, in their view, of traditional values to bind society together. Implicit to the entire argument was a desire to mold and channel nationalist consciousness toward the goal of strengthening Korean society. Although they seemed to be saying that political independence was presently unobtainable, cultural, social, and economic self-strengthening was certainly an acceptable secondary goal.

To begin the process of rebuilding Korea a general program began to emerge at this time. Yi Tonhwa (1884– ?), editor-in-chief of *Kaebyŏk,* close associate of the third Ch'ŏndogyo leader Son Pyŏng-ghŭi, and director of the Ch'ŏndogyo Youth Department for the Study of Doctrine, recommended action on a broad front. Education was a priority, first as a means to develop a new leadership, and second to promote common learning among the masses.[49] Education was the means of unifying thought (*sasang t'ongil*) as a counterbalance to the inevitable specialization caused by continued economic develop-ment.[50] Yi believed that if a strong "common mind" (*kongnoe*) was maintained, then various parts of society would not drift into oppo-sition to each other; Yi revealed how his Ch'ŏndogyo predilections affected his view of the political and social cleavages in society:

> There is a common morality that is not based on individuals; this common morality is based, rather, on the conditions of life in a nation or all of humanity. If morality is based on all of human life, then applying this morality cannot be limited to individuals or one family—a new humanism is the basis of world morality. Just as it supports the idea of equality between men and women,

it also is a common bond between laborers and capitalists, the
powerful and the weak, the high and the low. Without a sense of
common morality, we cannot fall in step with modern life.[51]

Yi Tonhwa's view of building a new culture was not limited to
morality lectures. He went on to urge economic development as a key
to future strength. Recognizing the importance of agricultural development, he urged the creation of cooperatives to improve the plight of
farmers and attacked rural landlords for their conservatism and lack
of interest in their fellow man.[52] Yi believed, however, that the future
of Korea's economic development lay in her cities. Here was the key
link between the leaders of the future, the pioneers (sŏn'gakja), and
the means for development. This link was expressed in his concept of
"urban-centered (development)" (tosi chungsimjuŭi); cities were the
center of modern life, and values, skills, and economic arrangements
in the cities must diffuse eventually to all parts of Korea.[53]

Yi's model for development was the West, but he worried that
development along these lines would bring increased division and
conflict. Thus, he echoed the call of others to develop moral unity
based on universal values. National interests had to precede individual
interests if Korea was to overcome its present problems. Yi also
focused directly on the issue of intellectual leadership. As interpreters
of modern culture, urban intellectuals were exemplars of the new
publicly minded citizen, and they were also responsible for directing
educational and cultural movements.

Yi Tonhwa's discussion of the urban core echoes ideas presented
two months before by Yi Kwangsu. Yi Kwangsu had joined the
discussion of cultural rebuilding in a series of articles published in
Kaebyŏk directly upon his return from Shanghai in the spring of
1921.[54] In this series, Yi echoed the concerns of other culturalists by
advocating education, unity of values, and the dismantling of obstacles to progress in the Korean tradition. Supported by his reputation as a literary pioneer and political activist, Yi called on Korean
youth to form the vanguard of a movement to reconstruct Korea.[55]

In an essay entitled "The Core Class and Society," Yi went beyond
the general abstractions about the clash between old and new with a
forceful theory of change linked closely to intellectual leadership.[56] He
posited that all societies possessed a "core class" (chungch'u kyegŭp),
and the rise and fall of societies throughout history could be traced to
its vitality.[57] Moreover, revolution implied the toppling and replacement of one core class by another. In traditional Korea the yangban

had occupied the central position in society, but with the growing senescence and decay of the yangban, Korean society had lost its vital leadership. The core class had to understand and represent the ideals and values of society, and if society outgrew its leaders, a new core must emerge to lead. Turning his attention to contemporary Korea, Yi determined that the new core leadership would emerge from among the intellectuals (*chisikja*) and "men of property" (*yusanja*).[58] These were precisely the men who understood the spirit and ideals of modernity and would provide direction for social and cultural development.

The task at hand, therefore, was to encourage the emergence of the new core class in Korea through education and organization. Yi felt that this process might take another generation to accomplish, but the means were presently at hand, only a beginning need be made. Although the new core class was as yet too small, their numbers could be increased geometrically by organizing cultivation leagues (*suyang tongmaeng*) and education leagues (*suhak tongmaeng*).[59] Yi envisaged the process of cultural change led by an elite vanguard. He mused that China now possessed a fine constitution, but there was no stable leadership class to represent and implement its laws. Even with the world cry for equality, it was still necessary to have an elite leadership to direct the course of society. Yi's elitism was also evident in his admiration for Lenin's Bolsheviks and he cited their example in calling for the formation of a tightly organized and ideologically disciplined leadership.[60]

Yi's article brought together important elements of the discussion on cultural reform and rebirth. These were: unity of values, consensus (at least at the leadership level), the attack on traditional class leadership and thought, and the insistence on education as a first step toward action. He also expressed concretely a point that others only implied, that development would be led by the middle class. Korea's future, therefore, would develop along the lines of Western democratic societies.

It must be remembered that authors writing in *Kaebyŏk* between 1920 and 1922 were under censorship. Consequently much of the discourse is devoid of direct reference to the colonial situation. Censorship encouraged abstraction and possibly diluted the political import of many essays. Nevertheless, the overall line shared by a substantial number of writers can also be interpreted as a genuine attempt to activate nationalist programs within the new limits set by the Saitō regime. In addition, the tone of the cultural rebirth thesis continued many themes of the earlier progressive movement and the subsequent enlightenment. A modernizing intellectual elite who understood the core values of the modern world must direct the course of change in Korea. There was also a subtle acceptance of Korea's contemporary plight. One can almost hear echoes of the turn-of-the-century Social Darwinist interpretation of social evolution and the cry for self-strengthening in a competitive world of struggle.

Linked to the enlightenment roots of the cultural rebirth thesis was a desire to forge a solid unified nationalist program to continue the gains made in the March First movement. In addition, the call for harmony and consensus reflected widespread confusion among intellectuals over the many different doctrines contending for attention throughout East Asia after World War I. In this sense, the material presented in the early *Kaebyŏk* issues echoed the intellectual struggle of May Fourth China. And at least for a substantial portion of concerned nationalists in colonial Korea, the future seemed to lay in cultural self-strengthening and the development, in their words, of a middle-class leadership. And from this assumption sprang the broad nationalist cultural movement of 1922–25.[61]

Yi Kwangsu and the "Minjok Kaejoron"

The discussion of a cultural movement as a springboard to independence culminated in the publication of Yi Kwangsu's "Treatise on the Reconstruction of the Nation" ("Minjok kaejoron"; hereafter, *Kaejoron*) in May 1922.[62] In this long article, Yi forged a plan for a coordinated national movement to rebuild and reinvigorate Korean society. In doing so, he distilled and elucidated ideas and goals long associated with moderate nationalist intellectuals. His unique contribution to the self-strengthening thesis lay in his bold call for action within the colonial system. In short, Yi presented the case for gradualists, both at home and abroad, who believed continued national development had to precede political independence. Therefore, the *Kaejoron* crystallized the debate between gradualists and activists who promoted violent overthrow of Japanese rule, an argument that had already emerged in the exile movement and came to dominate discussion within the colony after 1922.

Yi Kwangsu had attained considerable stature by the early 1920s as a nationalist activist. His early life and education laid the basis for his later emergence as a leading intellectual of his generation. Born in 1892 in P'yŏng'an Province, Yi received his early education at a local village school (*sodang*). Orphaned at the age of ten, Yi was raised by relatives, who provided for his education and also enrolled him in the Tonghak faith. Through his family's Tonghak (after 1905, Ch'ŏndogyo) connection, he received an Ilchinhoe scholarship to study at the Meiji Gakuen in 1905. Returning home only once in 1907, Yi remained in Japan until his graduation in 1910.[63] After 1910, Yi began his literary career by writing his first novel, *Mujŏng (Hardheartedness)*, while teaching at the Osan school. After an extended trip to Shanghai and the Soviet Far East in 1913–14, Yi returned to Japan to continue his education at Waseda University with the financial backing of Kim Sŏngsu.[64] Graduating in philosophy at Waseda in 1918, Yi threw himself into nationalist politics, first as a student organizer in Tokyo, and, after the March First movement, in the Shanghai exile government. After two years in Shanghai, Yi returned to Korea in 1921 to resume his career as a teacher, writer, and journalist.

Throughout his youth and young adulthood, Yi participated in major nationalist organizations and contributed directly to the burgeoning literary and journalistic movements after 1905. According to his own memoir, Yi's political awakening began with the controversy surrounding the Ilchinhoe, Yi's scholarship source, after it came out in support of the 1905 Protectorate. The Ilchinhoe had formerly been linked to the Progressive Society (Chinbohoe), both groups using the Tonghak organizational networks to further their programs.[65] In 1907, Yi worked with Ch'oe Namsŏn on the magazine *Sonyŏn* publishing his first essays at the age of sixteen. After annexation, Yi leaped to prominence with the publication of *Mujŏng*.[66] Between 1910 and 1920, Yi and Ch'oe dominated the movement to create a modern Korean literature. His first novel laid the base for the ⚬ emergence of a vernacular prose literature and its content excited the imaginations and reformist zeal of his generation by championing the modern values of individualism and free will in a struggle against the confining influences of the Confucian tradition.[67]

Yi's political activities paralleled his literary and journalistic efforts. *Sonyŏn* was the organ of the Youth Student Association (Ch'ŏngnyŏn hag'uhoe), the youth arm of An Ch'angho's secret New People's Association (Sinminhoe, 1907). Yi had already heard An speak in Tokyo, and his work for *Sonyŏn* and the Ch'ŏngnyŏn hag'uhoe began a relationship with An and his ideas that would last until An's death in 1938.[68] With his return to Tokyo in 1915, Yi became active in student politics. He continued to write for publications in Korea and emerged as an ardent iconoclast and modernizer in a series of articles for another of Ch'oe Namson's magazines, *Ch'ŏngch'un*, in 1918.

Yi stepped to the fore of nationalist politics in February 1919 as author of the Tokyo Korean Student Declaration, an independence declaration endorsed by Korean student groups in Tokyo. The declaration was sent to members of the Japanese Diet, Government General of Korea officials, and the press on February 8, 1919, and sparked a round of consultations between domestic and exiled nationalists in preparation for the March First demonstrations.[69] After March First, Yi went to Shanghai to participate in the formation of the SPG.

Yi worked in the SPG for two years. In that time, he edited the SPG organ, *The Independent* (*Tongnip sinmun*), and participated in the heated debates over government organization and tactics. He soon became solidly identified with the gradualist faction led by An Ch'angho. An's faction advocated close ties with the domestic nationalist movement and long-term national development in preparation for future independence. The gradualists opposed Syngman Rhee's petition movement to gain foreign diplomatic intercession on Korea's behalf; they also opposed radicals who advocated armed struggle against the Japanese.[70] By 1922, Yi found himself embroiled in the increasingly bitter factional disputes that eventually broke the early unity of the SPG.

Frustrated with exile nationalist politics, Yi decided to return to Korea in the spring of 1921. He explained his decision to return:

> I think it was the autumn of 1919 when I heard about the Corps for the Advancement of Scholars (Hŭngsadan) from An Ch'angho. The principles of the Corps and the behavior of An Ch'angho impressed me very deeply. After hearing about the principles—I was convinced that the independence of our nation could not be attained through a radical movement, but only through cultivating the strength of the nation. The only way to cultivate the strength of the nation was through strengthening individuals and organizing them. Without this kind of collective strength, it would not be possible to realize independence. Even if independence were attained through the assistance of other nations, this could not be sustained for long. When I realized this, there was no choice but for me to return to Korea, where most of the Korean people were living. I concluded that a revolutionary movement in a sovereign nation is easier abroad, but a similar movement for a people without sovereignty is easier within the country. I saw actual examples from India and China—but the

situation for Korea was different. The Japanese controlled all military and police power. If we consider the Indian independence movement, it was centered inside the country since the rise of Gandhi; and it has used mainly legal means. It has emerged uniformly throughout the country by seizing opportunities to organize itself within the law. Most of our independence leaders have left the country. This was exactly the thing that would throw Korea into the hands of the Japanese—Korea seemed to be devoid ♦ of independence leaders—strengthening Korea itself seemed to be the proper path to take, not traveling around looking for the strength of others.[71]

This passage from Yi's "Confessions" revealed the nature of his disillusionment with exile politics and hinted at the program that would emerge from his pen a year later. His realistic appraisal of Japanese military strength and his admiration for the tactics and accomplishments of the Indian nationalist movement caused Yi to set his sights on work within the colony. The mention of An's Hŭngsadan was also significant. Yi saw within the Hŭngsadan a model for the creation of a new nationalist leadership devoid of the factional and personal differences that had enervated the exile movement up to that time.

Yi returned to Korea and made an instant sensation as an essayist in the colonial press. The prestige accrued as a literary figure, Tokyo student activist, and member of the SPG stimulated a wide readership for Yi's essays that appeared in *Kaebyŏk* after his return. By the appearance of the *Kaejoron* in May 1922, Yi had touched on all the major issues dominating the colonial press. He lashed out at the ✗ Korean tradition as an obstacle to progress, became a champion of individualism and free will, criticized early nationalist reformers for failing to maintain Korean independence, and encouraged capitalist economic development as the basis for the rise of a middle-class leadership. Finally, he brought these ideas together in his controversial essay which gave the name to the subsequent reconstruction movement (*kaejo undong*).[72]

Yi conceived the *Kaejoron* as no less than a master plan for the future of the Korean nationalist movement. It is dedicated to the pioneers in the nationalist struggle and to Korean youth, its future leadership, and Yi included in his preface the hope "that my colleagues abroad will eventually agree with this plan to which I devote my life."[73] Yi's plan, therefore, tied his analysis of past mistakes with a plan for future unity and progress toward national goals. In addition to this lofty goal, Yi also asserted that his plan would help Korea to come in step with larger world trends. Yi pointed to the post-World War I efforts to create international institutions to insure peace and cooperation among nations. He viewed these new bodies as "institutions that would remake the world—from a world of competition for survival to a world of mutual support."[74]

Yi began his treatise with a discussion of the meaning of reconstruction (*kaejo*). He felt that historical change could be divided into natural and "human-directed" change. A certain amount of slow, natural change was inevitable over time; what interested Yi, however, was man's ability to affect his environment and direct change according to his own will. Thus, a consciousness of change was a prime attribute of civilized man, and no society could prosper without this realization. Yi implied here that although Korean society had changed dramatically in the last fifty years, it still lacked a consciousness of change, and, therefore, the will to affect its direction.

Yi continued with a biting critique of Korean reform efforts to date. Interspersing a general discussion of the relationship between reform ideology and the importance of creating institutional mechanisms to implement these ideas, Yi castigated Korean reformers of the nineteenth and twentieth centuries. Yi cited Chǒng Yag'yong, an early nineteenth-century scholar associated with the Practical Learning School (Silhak), as an example of how difficult it was to translate good ideas into concrete action. Chǒng's lack of institutional or political connections prevented the implementation of his reform proposals.[75] Kim Okkyun and the progressives of the 1880s were able to seize power, but their program failed because they lacked a mass base or the support of traditional elites. The Independence Club, according to Yi, had the right idea of spreading enlightenment and national consciousness, but they attempted to gain political power too soon and suffered defeat at the hands of political reactionaries.

Yi believed that new ideas were important, but a spiritual awakening must accompany these ideas before they could be translated into action. To Yi, therefore, reconstruction was something more basic than any specific political ideology; indeed, it was a suprapolitical ideal:

> Finally it must be made clear that the movement for reconstructing the nation has no relation to a particular doctrine, nor is it a religious or political movement. It also attaches no allegiance to capitalism, socialism, democracy, independence or international-

ism. *The essence of reconstruction is found in the national* •
*character and life. Its goals are rooted in moral and practical
enlightenment* [italics added]. It is untainted by politics—all must
apply themselves to their own political and religious philosophies,
but they must join together for the overall goal of recon- •
struction.[76]

With this definition of *kaejo* Yi began part 2 of his essay by discussing reconstruction as "a moral/ethical issue" (*todŏkchŏk ilgŏt*).[77]
He believed that the national character (*minjoksŏng*) was embodied in
a nation's morals, and national character was distilled from this moral
base. Accordingly, Yi linked the success of England to its national
character, which he believed was embodied in the English respect for
freedom and justice. The historical development of its national
character had brought England into the twentieth century with a
respect for law, rationality, and a stable political system that enjoyed
the trust of its citizenry. England's national character was also
reflected in its benign colonial policy. England ruled its colonies with
respect for native culture, preferring to "administrate" not "sub-
jugate" its colonial subjects.[78] Ignoring the implications of this statement, he continued by asserting that England's success at home and
abroad was a result of their "national spirit" of freedom and realism.
    According to Yi, and reflecting a strong Confucian holdover in his
thought, national leaders of enlightenment and integrity engendered
the people's trust. Without this trust no national reform could be •
undertaken. Leaders, themselves, required personal integrity, faith,
commitment, trust, and valor; if a society's leaders were corrupt, how
could the people follow?[79] Yi pointed to the enlightened leadership of
Meiji Japan, and he asserted that the success of the Meiji oligarchs was
a direct consequence of the trust and respect they engendered in the
people.[80] Part of Korea's failure in the late nineteenth century had
been because the traditional yangban leadership was not trusted by the
people.
    Thus, national reconstruction should begin with recruiting a lead-
ership that combined integrity, understanding of the modern world,
and, above all, a commitment to action. For Korea, this leadership •
would rise from a core class of enlightened men, men who understood
the needs of the nation, were committed to the task of reconstruction,
and who possessed the values and skills to carry out their ideas.[81] And,
as Yi later explained, these men would rise from among the intellectuals and bourgeoisie of contemporary Korea.

Reconstruction involved reforming the nation's inner character as well as its outer material manifestations. Therefore, Yi devoted considerable space to an analysis of the good and bad points of Korean society's inner nature. To its credit, Korea had always respected humaneness (*in*) in men. Yi believed that many "modern" values such as self-respect, generosity, and justice were in accord with the traditional idea of humaneness.[82] In addition, traditional Koreans valued autonomy and valor, and throughout its history Korea had maintained good relations with powerful Chinese dynasties (T'ang, Ming, Ch'ing—he omitted mention of Koryŏ submission to the Mongol Yüan dynasty) without submitting to foreign domination. When foreigners criticized Korea's military weakness, Yi asserted that maintaining political autonomy without resort to warfare represented a vital strength in Korean society, an element of pacifism that augured well for the future. Yi asserted that at least Korea had no tradition of militarism or imperialism.[83] Yi's historical analysis overemphasized autonomy, but his point was to emphasize the positive values that had forged Korean identity in the face of great geopolitical and cultural obstacles.

Turning to weaknesses in the national character, Yi focused on those traits that militated against progress. Yi felt that in the past Koreans had valued ceremony (*yeŭi*) to an extreme, which led to sterile formalism and an emphasis of form over content in individual and political life.[84] Additionally, venerating ceremony led to situational ethics that inhibited respect for truth and the principle of law. Exclusivity and veneration of "face" also inhibited unity and trust. Accordingly, this tendency factionalized associational life and made organization difficult.[85] In a different vein, Yi considered the traditional favoritism of "abstract" philosophy over empirical, scientific thought as another weakness. This caused Koreans to place a low value on scientific and technological development. Finally, Yi bemoaned the lack of attention devoted to commercial and economic development; traditional bias against commerce and the creation of wealth had inhibited the development of Korean industry.[86]

Yi believed that the weaknesses in the Korean national character could not be overcome quickly. Therefore, national reconstruction was to be a long and gradual process of individual cultivation, mass education, and economic development. He warned that reconstruction had to avoid politics as well:

> The goal of national reconstruction cannot take on a political coloration. Political power is a fleeting phenomenon, but national

reconstruction is a task that will take at the very least fifty or a hundred years. Political organizations cannot manage stability because of shifts in the political climate—if the Independence Club had stuck to its long-range projects of education, developing industry, and promoting the vitality of the people and had not interfered in politics, it would not have been repressed by the politicians.[87]

Gradual accumulation was more permanent than a windfall, and leaders had to repress their instincts for "self-aggrandizement" and "martyrdom" by working in the trenches on projects of low visibility but concrete long-term results.[88]

Thus, the first task of reconstruction was to recruit and train leaders. By beginning with the minds of leaders, Yi felt confident that the subsequent organizational spread of reconstruction would be centered on proper values. One could not reform character through ideas alone, one had to internalize and thoroughly routinize ideas in practice before results would show. Yi set down a ten-step plan for implementing reconstruction. The plan involved commitment to the ideal of reconstruction, creating a plan for reforming individual character, forming groups and discussing reconstruction with the masses, winning support of the people, allowing leaders to rise and to spread ideas outward in a "contagion" of reform.[89] This abstract program never explicitly outlined the central ideas that would spread like a contagion, it simply reasserted the concept of individual character reformation, the emergence of enlightened leaders, and tight organization for propagandizing the central values of reconstruction.

The ten-step plan was explicitly elitist. True leaders were those enlightened individuals who understood the current need for reconstruction and who possessed the proper values and commitment to action. The process of spreading ideas was tutorial, stressing mentor-disciple relations in the early stages of leadership formation as leaders indoctrinated recruits to the movement. Although individual cultivation was central to his conception of the new citizen, Yi stressed commitment to the central value of reconstruction over the promotion of individualism: "In Korea today the cant of freedom and equal rights is too literally interpreted. The essential fact of leadership and following is ignored. We cannot progress this way. A president and the lowly patrolman have equal rights, but the patrolman still must follow orders. Organization needs followers as well as leaders."[90] Here, individualism was restricted by the idea of service (followership) to those who understood the true meaning of freedom, presumably leaders who could handle freedom "responsibly."

The core leadership for reconstruction would emerge from among the intellectuals in Korean society and would be augmented by the skills and talents of the emerging middle class:

> In this way, ten or twenty years from now the numbers of enlightened leaders will have increased to several thousands. The middle class which must handle the various specialized tasks in society will be augmented by the influx of these new leaders who have both confidence and ability. These men who will gradually expunge society of its old ways and will shake society out of hibernation. In several generations the vital spirit of the middle class will transform society. In fifty or a hundred years the process of reconstruction will thus be advanced. In this way, the historically unprecedented process of reconstructing Korea will be
> • accomplished. Revolution and restoration can be realized with the emergence of the new middle class.[91]

This important passage fused Yi's major concern, the creation of an enlightened, committed intellectual leadership, with the vitality of Korea's still nascent middle class. And over time, the expansion of this alliance would trigger the "revolution" of reconstruction. Yi was not alone in his enthusiasm for the progressivity of the new middle class. The nationalist press had already featured pieces on the "new business class." One such paean to business-class virtues in the *Tonga ilbo* asserted that "their rise will destroy class distinctions and bring social equality, rationality, and the pursuit of scientific knowledge."[92] Yi agreed that the expansion of business and the rise of a middle class was important, but his discussion of leadership in the *Kaejoron* made it clear that intellectuals should dominate the leadership of the reconstruction movement.

Yi closed the *Kaejoron* with a long discussion of organization and propaganda. Only strong organizations could sustain reform beyond the lifetime of any individual. Ideas, not leaders, must be the focus of organizational life. One prototype of the type of organization Yi had in mind was An Changho's Youth Student Association (Ch'ŏngnyŏn hag'uhoe, 1907–10). This group had emphasized rigorous selection criteria for its members, stressed moral and physical training, and avoided politics. It had also, according to Yi, provided for a strong financial base. Such an organization was strong enough to sustain a long-term project such as reconstruction.[93] Yi was also fascinated with the example of the American temperance movement, and he used this example to explain the power of organization to sustain and institutionalize an ideal:

> One strong organization has a great potential power for propa- •
> ganda, more powerful than hundreds or thousands of newspapers
> and magazines. One good example of the propaganda power of
> organization is the Temperance Movement in the United States.
> Starting only fifty-seven years ago with the idea of one minister,
> the anti-drinking movement grew one member at a time until it
> was able to sway over half of their countrymen's support to pass
> a prohibition amendment to the United States constitution. The
> reason that no such phenomenon has emerged in Korea is that we
> have been ignorant of how to use the technique of propaganda
> wedded to strong organization.[94]

Yi proceeded to delineate a host of projects that could be carried forth by strong organizations directed by the new reconstructionist elite. These programs emphasized specialized education for the new elite and basic literacy and morals education for the masses. He envisaged a gradual coalescence of the many existing cultural organizations into a vast league of reconstruction. There was no lack of activity, it just needed to be united around the common consensus embodied in Yi's overarching program of reconstruction. In the end, the unification of the diverse cultural and educational programs would create an enormous force for propaganda and activism. Yi saw this force bridging the gap between the core leadership, the repository of modern, nationalistic values, and the Korean masses. Yi viewed the masses as an untrained army to be infused with a new spirit of activism and mobilized for reconstruction under the tutorial leadership of the new elite.[95]

The Social and Political Implications of Cultural Nationalism

The *Kaejoron* was the most forceful and direct ideological expression of what might be properly called the cultural nationalist movement (referred to in the contemporary press as the cultural movement, *munhwa undong*). The discussion of cultural nationalism was centered, as we have seen, in *Kaebyŏk*, but the thesis found expression in other journals such as Ch'oe Namson's *Eastern Light* (*Tongmyŏng*) as well as the daily press. Cultural nationalism can be seen as both an

* outgrowth of earlier Korean nationalist thought and as a practical response to the changed political situation in Korea after 1920.

The cultural nationalist ideologues of the early 1920s continued to discuss themes raised during the post-1900 enlightenment but without explicitly linking these ideas to political demands for removal of foreign interference from Korean affairs. There was a continued fascination with viewing the future of Korea as following a Western model of development. Modernization for these writers meant evolution of capitalism and, with qualification, a liberal democratic political system. And they spent considerable time trying to analyze how traditional thought and institutions had deflected Korean evolution away from this path.

The cultural nationalist thesis differed significantly from the precolonial enlightenment in obvious ways. Without the traditional political system to blame, political failure to regain independence fell squarely on the nationalist movement. Moreover, the weakness and vacillation of the failed dynasty in its last years had undermined its potential as a symbol of national unity. In addition, the Japanese colonial state was busy directing the course of economic modernization, and economic benefits accrued, however unevenly distributed, could not become political capital for nationalist leaders directly. The Saitō reforms had given nationalists room to maneuver. And moderates of the cultural nationalist persuasion seized this opportunity to act within the prescribed limits.

The evolutionary gradualist approach toward social change fit well
* within these limits. Cultural nationalists viewed the Korean masses as ignorant of the new values necessary for the creation of a modern
* nation. Hence, they advocated education and enlightenment to nurture new values and skills while shaping mass nationalist sentiment to lay the basis for future independence. The means were conservative, but the goals of the cultural nationalist program were revolutionary. They advocated the creation of a strong middle class, mass literacy, and political participation. Indeed, Korea in the 1920s was still overwhelmingly agrarian and lacked any tradition of mass political participation; perhaps more significant, Korea was still held fast under the yoke of Japanese colonial rule.

The cultural nationalist program was explicitly elitist. Change was to emanate downward from an elite leadership and spread in concentric waves of educational enlightenment and organization. In particular, Yi Kwangsu emphasized the primacy of intellectual leadership. Thus, a small, well-educated (often in Japan) group of enlightened middle-class intellectuals formed the core class of the future, the class most qualified to lead. The elitism and emphasis on transforming values as a prerequisite to change highlighted the traditionalist flavor of the cultural nationalist style. Although the ideological content was different, the emphasis on values, moral exemplars, and cultivation all evoked the style and role of the traditional Confucian literati.

Harmony and nonviolence also characterized the cultural thesis. There was a coherent emphasis on finding ways to avoid conflict in a developing society such as Korea. Aware that economic development had exacerbated class conflict, cultural nationalists attempted to find new ways to mediate splits within Korean society. They attempted to promote nationalism (in the case of Yi Kwangsu, *kaejojuŭi*) as the main integrating value that could mediate conflicting interests. Although in retrospect this seemed terribly naïve, the search for a value with which to harmonize society resonated with their traditionalist approach to reform. Moreover, their analysis of Western political thought consistently stressed its consensual aspects. Time and again, they attributed Western social stability to consensus and free compliance with law and social solidarity based on shared values.

The economic program contained within the writings of the cultural nationalists was exceedingly vague. Yet it was clear that they favored the expansion of Korean capitalism and the concomitant growth of a large homogeneous middle class on the model of the United States and England (Japan was also cited in this regard). Entrepreneurs and managers in the modern economic sector were viewed as an important source of leadership. And a movement to mobilize national sentiment to encourage the development of native industries became one of the largest projects of the cultural nationalist program. In the end, however, the cultural nationalists continued to emphasize the primacy of intellectual leadership in cooperation with the nascent Korean bourgeoisie.

The cultural nationalists' elitism and gradualist approach shaped their conception of nationalism as a political movement. In terms of national identity, they emphasized their role as definitive examples of the modern Korean citizen. By implication, the masses needed to be tutored in the ways of the modern world to become full-fledged members of the nation. Therefore, rather than view the masses as an immediate source of power to be mobilized for political action, the cultural nationalists linked identity to a longer process of education, proper political orientation, and eventual national unity. The tactical implications of this attitude were obvious. Rather than direct nationalist passion outward toward immediate political goals, moderate nationalists seemed to be prescribing a long period of national soul searching and introspection. The emphasis on long-term education as a prerequisite for strong national unity also betrayed cultural nationalist distrust and contempt for the Korean masses. Apparently the masses in their present state were unprepared for national independence.

The emphasis on education and further economic development shaped their legal gradualist tactics. Behind this idea lurked the fear of class violence. They perceived growing class splits in Korean society as a threat to national unity; this led people like Yi Kwangsu to stress the apoliticism of *kaejo* as a way to pull Koreans away from their narrow class interests. In doing so, cultural nationalism diluted the power of nationalist sentiment and highlighted the ambiguity of its leadership's stance with regard to the Japanese colonial rulers. It was one thing to mention Gandhi as an inspiration for nonviolence, but shrinking from confrontation with the colonial authorities belied their commitment to Gandhian nationalism and tactics.

• The commitment to gradualism and legal means emphasized cultural nationalist acceptance of the colonial status quo. Yi Kwangsu tacitly accepted colonial rule for the foreseeable future, with his explicit apolitical stance in the *Kaejoron*. The failure of nationalist groups to either maintain or, after 1910, to regain independence was the strongest argument to men like Yi Kwangsu that a dramatic shift of tactics was necessary. The endless factional bickering and conflict among the exile movement simply reinforced this view for moderate nationalists within the colony. Although it is easy to label this passive view defeatist in retrospect, at the time that Yi published the *Kaejoron* there was considerable hope for significant nationalist gains in the colony. Had not the nonviolent mass demonstrations of 1919 united the Korean people and caused a significant shift in colonial policy? And the re-emergence of the press and the organizational renaissance after the Saitō reforms augured a brighter future for Korea.

In spite of the conservative drift of cultural nationalism, the Japanese were very concerned at the outpouring of nationalist activity after 1920. What most worried the authorities was the tendency, obvious by 1922, of amalgamation among legal nationalist organizations. The new head of the colonial police, Maruyama Tsurukichi, commented on the dangers lurking within the cultural nationalist movement in a major policy speech in April 1922. According to Maruyama, the cultural movement had a dual purpose, its legal

self-strengthening programs masked its long-range program to under- •
mine the foundations of Japanese rule; and its education program
attacked Japanese policy, subverted Japanese language use, and
strengthened national consciousness.[96] For this reason, Maruyama
warned that while in the short run the cultural movement was not
dangerous, its long-term effects could be disastrous for future Japanese rule. The cultural nationalists shared Maruyama's assessment; •
between 1922 and 1924, they mounted several movements they hoped
would realize these fears.

CHAPTER 3

Within Limits:
Moderate Nationalist Movements

The Cultural Nationalist Movement

Between 1920 and 1925, three movements emerged to address specific concerns delineated in the debate over national reconstruction. Responding to inequities and inadequacies of the colonial education system, the Society for the Creation of a National University (Minnip taehak kisŏng chunbihoe), established in November 1922, organized a centralized movement to raise funds for a Korean university. The movement addressed issues of discriminatory curriculum, opportunity for advanced training, and teacher training, all closely tied to nationalist concerns about cultural identity and the creation of a future generation of national leaders. A related movement focused on the Korean language. The amalgamation of separate Korean language research societies into the Korean Language Research Society (Chosŏn'ŏ yŏn'guhoe) in 1921 consolidated the effort to systematize and propagate the use of the Korean vernacular in the colony. This successful movement addressed directly the issue of Korean language education in schools as well as the problem of illiteracy in the colony. In addition, they linked directly the issue of language development to strengthening and maintaining national identity.

The largest movement mounted by moderates at this time was the Korean production movement led by the Society for the Promotion of Native Production (Chosŏn mulsan changnyŏhoe) formed in January 1923. The Korean production movement sought to stimulate the consumption of Korean-produced goods, both as a demonstration of national unity and as a method of stimulating the development of native industry in competition with Japanese capitalism. Although the movement was implicitly a boycott of Japanese and imported goods, nationalist intellectuals and Korean businessmen leading the movement hoped to avoid repression by emphasizing the positive aspects of "production." Moreover, the dominant intellectual leadership conceived the movement primarily in terms of its nationalistic goals of stimulating national unity and the ultimate expansion of Korean economic power.

These three movements put into operation the ideology of national reconstruction. Behind these organizations was the implicit goal of building on the gains made in the aftermath of the March First demonstrations. These movements were conceived by moderates who • wished to continue a program of national development within the confines of the colonial system. Some of its leaders drew inspiration from the contemporary Indian nationalist movement. British concessions to the Indian Congress party and promises for self-governing institutions provided precedents for the cultural nationalists in their drive for national reconstruction. Although, as we shall see, Korean nationalists misinterpreted the ideology of Gandhi's Swaraj movement, the symbolism of his native goods movement and emphasis on cultural identity as a weapon against British rule did inspire Korean intellectuals committed to reconstruction.

The campaigns of the early 1920s were part of a tremendous • efflorescence of cultural and intellectual activity of the decade. The leaders of the university, language, and Korean production movements were also involved individually in a wide range of cultural pursuits. As self-appointed creators of modern Korean culture, they viewed the gradualist national reconstruction campaign as totally compatible with their life missions as intellectuals. The ground was to ⨯ be prepared for the creation of a modern Korean nation and, having been denied a political outlet for their energies, they turned to cultural projects that would insure the autonomous development of the idea of a Korean nation.

Leading this cultural boom was the rapid growth of Korean • vernacular literature. Reaching a widening urban audience in the 1920s, Korean writers continued to expand the creative use of the vernacular and literary styles and schools proliferated, paralleling the growing ideological diversity in the 1920s. Journals devoted exclusively to literature appeared. Kim Tong'in's *Creation* (*Ch'angjo,* 1919) marked the advent of a "romantic" school of Korean literature.[1] Kim's magazine was complimented by *Ruins* (*P'yehŏ,* 1920) and *Tides* (*Paekcho,* 1922), both identified with a "pure literature" school of writing.[2] Politically oriented literary circles rose in reaction and, for a brief period, a proletarian literary movement flourished, first appearing in the pages of *Kaebyŏk.*

By 1925 Korean literature was fast establishing its own voice, a voice that expressed both universal emotions and Korean's unique sense of being. Kim Sowŏl's "Azaleas" (*Chindallaekkot*) and Han Yong'un's "The Silence of Love" (*Nim ŭi ch'immuk*) published in the mid-1920s marked the full flowering of Korean poetry and demonstrated the flexibility of the vernacular for a broad range of literary expression.[3] Not surprisingly, the new literature became a vehicle for expressing the deepening Korean political and cultural consciousness within educated circles.

Scholarly research into Korean history and folklore also expanded during the 1920s. The GGK had charged various committees with the task of "investigating old customs, manners, and systems in Chōsen [Korea]" in search of evidence to support the official line of "homogeneity of the Japanese and Korean peoples and intercourse between the two in olden times."[4] This official effort to interpret the Korean experience to fit long-range assimilationist goals was a major stimulus to nationalist studies on Korean history, folklore, customs, and religion. And many scholars were active in the broader cultural nationalist political campaigns.

Modern Korean historical studies, as we have seen, began as a nationalist reaction to the Confucianized official historiography of the Koryŏ and Yi dynasties. Chang Chiyŏn, Pak Ŭnsik, and Sin Ch'aeho had all begun the work of exhuming a national history from among the *sadae* line of official records. By the mid-1920s, historians such as Ch'oe Namsŏn, also a publicist and nationalist organizer, were counterbalancing the official Japanese line of "homogeneity" with a nationalistic theory of unique origins and political autonomy through the study of ancient history and mythology.[5] Ch'oe's interpretation placed Korea in the mainstream, if not in the forefront, of East Asian history, and he emphasized political autonomy and the power of ancient Korean states. He also stressed the antiquity and importance of the Tan'gun myth, and began the serious study of Korean shamanism, both aspects of Korean culture that served to separate Korea from Japan.

Yi Nŭnghwa's (1868–1945) work on Korean shamanism and religion, begun in the 1920s, popularized the study of native Korean religion and folklore as a key to understanding Korean society itself. Using classical Korean and Chinese texts, Yi traced the development of shamanism and its ritual use by ancient Korean royalty. And by tracing the East Asian distribution of "Korean-type shamanism," he concluded that ancient Korea had encompassed a vast territorial domain including large portions of present-day Manchuria.[6]

Ironically, the traditional Korean elite had often downgraded folklore and shamanism as unworthy of serious study. With the rise of nationalism and the critique of Korea's sinified elite tradition after the 1890s, however, the indigenous popular culture became a repository of national symbols and identity. Ch'oe and Yi's work legitimated scholarly studies of Korean culture while providing a counterargument to official Japanese scholarship that often supported the cultural argument for assimilation.[7]

Often working individually or in small study societies, the intellectuals of the 1920s laid the basis of a modern Korean culture. They expanded the intellectual movement that had begun before annexation and had continued after 1910 often with little recognition. The reforms of the cultural policy after 1920 stimulated national linkages of writers, scholars, and researchers, and their work gained a wider audience in the colonial press. The new national linkages and growing body of knowledge provided a base for participation of increased numbers of educated Koreans and, perhaps, more significantly, it heightened Korean intellectuals' own feelings about their mission to foster the growth of a truly national culture. Denied political outlets, intellectuals created organizations that would increase the impact of their cultural works. Although the growing national literature and expanding body of Korean studies scholarship united nationalist intellectuals and provided the cultural content for expressing national identity, its production and ultimate significance was circumscribed by the colonial context. Japanese domination of education, language policy, publication, organization, and economic life in the colony isolated cultural development to the intellectual stratum of the colony.

It is no surprise, therefore, that the cultural nationalist movement that burgeoned in the aftermath of the Saitō reforms sought to address issues of cultural autonomy and national identity. The university movement, language movement, and Korean production movement all addressed specific Japanese policies that affected moderate intellectuals and their vision of a future independent Korea. These organized movements attempted to expand on announced reforms in order to carve out a broader sphere of cultural autonomy as well as to address the primary economic plight of the Korean masses. In line with the ideology of national reconstruction, the potential core of the nation could be strengthened within the political context of the colony. It also assumed the primacy of intellectual leadership and the willingness of the Korean masses to respond to their appeal to national unity, just as they had responded to the call for independence in 1919.

University and Language Movements

The colonial education system had always been a target of nationalist criticism. Despite the creation after 1910 of an extensive mass education system and rapid expansion of enrollments at all levels, Korean nationalists were disturbed by the long-range implications of colonial educational policy.[8] The maintenance of a dual system, one for Japanese residents and another for Koreans, begged charges of discrimination in quality of instruction and facilities. Perhaps more insidious, official Japanese policy decreed that upper level education for Koreans, middle and secondary schooling, should focus on vocational subjects. Provisions for college and university level education were very limited, Koreans being judged unsuitable for advanced training. Curriculum at the common school level stressed Japanese language instruction, morals, citizen education, and other subjects deemed useful for the creation of "loyal subjects of the Japanese Empire."[9] Indeed, the Japanese self-consciously used the powerful tool of education in the colony to advance cultural assimilation (not social equality) and insure social control.

Educational reforms after the 1919 riots attempted to liberalize the educational system and diffuse some of the basic complaints. In 1920, Saitō convened a special investigative committee to recommend various changes. Concurrently, a textbook committee studied changes in materials and basic texts, many of which were criticized by Koreans as demeaning to Korean culture.[10] The result of these deliberations was the new Educational Ordinance promulgated in March 1921, followed by new regulations for normal schools announced a month later. The new regulations sought to bring education "into conformity" with education in Japan proper.[11] In addition, the GGK made a commitment to increase the numbers of common schools for Koreans, create new normal schools to train the required number of Korean teachers, and establish college preparatory schools in anticipation of the opening of an imperial university in Seoul. Finally, Korean language instruction, still only two hours per week, was made compulsory.

The GGK also took measures to reduce restrictions on Korean students bound for study at Japanese universities. Because of the limited opportunity for college-level training in law, economics, business, and humanities in the colony, many upper-class students sought university education in Japan. These students were joined by a smaller number of students on GGK stipends earned through meritorious performance in the colonial schools. Between 1910 and 1920, Koreans studying in Japan had been closely monitored by formal application to the GGK, requirements for a personal guarantor, and the necessity of reporting to the GGK education office in Tokyo. In 1920, Saitō simplified the procedures for study in Japan, and the number of colonial students in the metropole increased accordingly.[12]

Private schools in the colony continued to operate under strict regulations. Although they were permitted to offer more upper level courses and professional degrees, it was still difficult to compete with prestigious Japanese schools or the lure of study in the metropole. Another outlet for the increasing demand for education were missionary schools but, again, space was limited and not all qualified Korean students could be admitted. In the end, the private and mission schools continued to act principally as preparatory schools, and their graduates continued to seek admission to Japanese universities for higher level training.

Nationalists were not overjoyed by the GGK educational reforms. They argued that the pace of expansion of common schools was too slow, and, in addition, GGK requirements that new schools be financed locally placed an unfair burden on poor rural areas most in need of educational facilities. Too rapid an expansion of schools also lowered instructional quality as less qualified teachers were hired to staff the new schools. Fundamental to all attacks on colonial education was the fear that Japanese colonial education was having the long-range effect of denationalizing Korean youth. Clearly, no system dominated by the Japanese was tolerable, and the new educational ordinance of 1921, although providing limited concessions to Korean sensibilities, only stimulated further nationalist appetite for change, and a growing conviction that Koreans had to take more responsibility for providing alternatives to the colonial system.

Education had been a central issue from the inception of the nationalist movement. Before annexation nationalists intent on reform touted the spread of science and Western thought in the service of national development and survival and the new schools were centers of the movement. After 1910, educational issues became more complex as nationalist intellectuals worried that colonial schools would serve to spread literacy and modern skills but denationalize students. To counter the effects of the colonial system, private schools continued after 1910, but their numbers were reduced and their operations constrained by the restrictive private school regulations promulgated in 1909 in anticipation of annexation. An editorial in the *Korea Daily*

News lamented that there were only about ten good private schools (offering middle- and high-school courses) and some of these were dominated by foreigners and missionaries.[13]

The distress over the scarcity of Korean-managed schools was intensified by concern over the use of the Japanese language and lack of attention to formal Korean language instruction. Japanese became the "national language" (*kokugo*) after 1910, and the GGK proudly published statistics to show the rapid expansion of Japanese use in the colony.[14] Even after the educational reforms of the early 1920s, formal Korean language instruction remained limited. In its first months of publication the *Tonga ilbo* joined the fight over language use in favor of abolishing forced use of Japanese in the schools.[15] For nationalists, language was a key to identity, and expanding Korean private schools was one antidote to this problem.

Even as the colonial authorities were studying educational reforms, nationalists banded together to form the Korean Education Association (Chosŏn kyoyuk hyŏphoe) in June of 1920. Led by the venerable Yi Sangjae (1850–1927), ex-Yi dynasty official, Independence Club supporter, and veteran of the March First movement, the association centralized lobbying efforts for reform in colonial education. Assisted by Namgung Ŏk (1863–1939) and Chang Tŏksu, Yi's organization rallied nationalist forces in the fight to create changes in the educational system. Their goals were reform of the existing system, spread of educational philosophy, expansion of educational facilities, creation of libraries and publications, and recognition of meritorious teachers.[16] By the end of the year, Yi's organization had attracted 220 members, and it rallied opposition to the GGK studies on educational reform.

Educational issues were a natural rallying point for moderate nationalists. Teaching and journalism had become the main occupations of the colonial intellectual elite. And newspapers, journals, and schools became natural organizational foci for the spread of new ideas and efforts to mobilize Korean students. The cultural policy relaxation of regulations regarding assembly and organization paved the way for a mushrooming of youth groups. Organized originally for educational and recreational purposes, youth groups had always served as an outlet for nationalistic sentiment for idealistic Korean youth. After 1919, the movement became progressively more politicized as nationalist leaders, recognizing the potential power of these groups, competed for organizational control.

In June 1920, O Sanggŭn and Chang Tŏksu made the first serious attempt to create a national linkage of youth groups by convening a meeting to prepare for an all-Korea youth league.[17] The purpose of the league was to foster enlightenment, social reform, and encourage economic development through united efforts.[18] Clearly, its organizers wished to unify and direct the youth movement toward moderate nationalist reform goals. By the end of the year the Korean Youth League (Chosŏn ch'ŏngnyŏn yŏnhaphoe) was established, representing 116 different groups.[19] By the end of 1920, moderates had thus succeeded in organizing what they hoped would be a powerful force for cultural development in the colony.

In January 1922, the GGK announced a second set of reforms designed to reorganize higher education that included plans to open college preparatory schools (1924) and, eventually, an imperial university (1926).[20] This announcement galvanized cultural nationalists into action, and a movement was launched to establish a Korean-financed and -managed national university in November 1922. The desire for a national university was not new. In 1910, an attempt had been made to start a university, using money collected by the Repay the National Debt Movement (Kukch'ae posang undong), then defunct because of annexation. With much publicity in the nationalist press between 1907 and 1910, the Repay the National Debt Movement solicited contributions from all Koreans through churches and a variety of nationalist organizations. Often receiving jewelry and other "in kind" contributions, the movement raised upwards of six million yen by 1910. The movement foundered after annexation. Eventually, a group of well-respected nationalist leaders, led by Yun Ch'iho, was formed to dispose of the money, and they recommended the establishment of a national university (*minnip taehakkyo*).[21] Refused a permit by the GGK, the project lapsed and the money was diverted to other uses. The idea, however, remained alive, and in February 1919 the Tokyo Student Declaration linked inferior education in Korea to Japanese ascendancy in Korea, once again calling for the creation of a national university.[22] With announcements of educational reform, many believed the time ripe for a nationwide movement to create an institution of higher learning in Korea.

By the end of 1922, moderate nationalists rallied to mount a movement to raise funds for a national university. As one editorial remarked: "In thirty years of modernization Koreans had not created a truly modern university—in spite of our long cultural heritage and important contributions to Asian history we still have no university—it is a national disgrace."[23] It continued by asking the embarrassing question: "If we can't organize a university how can we criticize the Japanese—how did the great private universities in Japan (Keio, Waseda) get started?"[24] Yi Sangjae and Song Chinu (1889–1945), then editor in chief of the *Tonga ilbo,* were already preparing the ground for a centralized campaign. In November 1922 the Society for the Establishment of a National University (Minnip taehak kisŏng chunbihoe) was formed, with 1,170 supporters in attendance.[25]

The university movement drew to it a large group of moderates representing leaders from all important nationalist organizations. Educators, youth leaders, literary figures, journalists, and ministers joined in the cause, carrying the message back to their respective organizations or seizing pens to publicize the cause in the nationalist press. Broad coverage on the movement in the *Tonga ilbo* and *Chosŏn ilbo* throughout 1923 facilitated the spread of provincial committees and drummed up enthusiasm for the campaign. And the Association to Establish a National University sent representatives to Korean communities in Manchuria and North America to further solicit donations.

The underlying philosophy and declared principles of the association found wide acceptance among nationalist intellectuals. Indeed, its prospectus distilled what had been a central tenet of Korean nationalism from its inception, namely, the primacy of modern education to the process of enlightenment and national development. Even radical critics of the cultural movement agreed that education was a key to Korean survival. The prospectus of the association provided a concrete exposition of cultural nationalist goals in the 1920s, declaring that educational matters were a "fundamental precondition" to politics, foreign affairs, and industry.[26] It went on to declare that although mass education was necessary for overall development, a society was judged, in the end, by the quality of its upper level educational system, which, in turn, produced national leaders. Comparing Korea again to the Western model, the prospectus linked the power of the West to the early development (twelfth and thirteenth centuries) of great universities.[27] Attributing a central role for the European university in cultural development, the reformation, as well as the bourgeois and industrial revolutions, and the creation of modern law, medicine, and technology, the organizers rested their case as to the importance of establishing a great Korean center of learning.[28]

By March 1923, the plan for the organization and financial requirements of the national university were announced.[29] The plan divided the project into three phases. The goal of the first phase, betraying the organizers' own cultural and political biases, was to establish colleges of law, economics, literature, and philosophy. Technical colleges of engineering, medicine, and agriculture filled out the subsequent phases of the plan. Thus, the first phase addressed the issue of scarce opportunity for contemporaneously popular courses of study for Koreans in the colony. These courses were perceived to be the avenue toward upward mobility; already, many Korean students were going to Japan to pursue such study. The plan projected clearly cultural nationalist sentiments that linked elite education, national development, and their own pretensions to national leadership. The national university would serve as a focus for the recruitment and ideological indoctrination of the future leadership, taught by those who saw themselves in the primary role of creators and protectors of the national interest.

The projected endowment was set at ten million yen, four million for the first phase, and six million for the subsequent completion of the university.[30] The plan to raise this enormous amount of money was simple. They would appeal to the national pride of all Koreans, calling on them to invest in the national future. Notwithstanding the poverty of the vast majority of the population, Yi Sangjae announced that membership subscriptions would be set at one yen per person; the general hope was that if half the population (twenty million) sub-scribed, the goal could easily be reached.[31] As the campaign gained momentum in 1923, youth organizations and churches exhorted the population to donate. Temperance and antismoking campaigns urged citizens to contribute to the campaign money saved through absti-nence. And overseas Korean communities also sent donations.

In the beginning, the university movement generated tremendous enthusiasm among nationalist organizations. Branches were soon established in all major provincial cities, and successful circuit lectures and rallies were staged to maintain the momentum. In numbers of participants and organizational reach, the movement became the largest nationalist effort since the March First movement. Yet the movement stalled in its first year of operation. By the end of the first year, barely one million yen had been pledged, causing one contem-porary observer to quip: "Koreans are not very greedy, but we certainly are an excessively stingy people; having fallen, perhaps, into this vice because of our poverty, our desire for knowledge to the point we are willing to make financial sacrifices is yet insufficient."[32] Pledges made in the afterglow of patriotic meetings failed to materialize, provoking the coining of the contemporary slang term "independence on credit" to describe the troubled movement.[33]

Organizational problems and a failure of trust between provincial collection points and the central association plagued the movement. Local groups refused to remit collections to the center, arguing that expenses of the campaign were being mismanaged. Perhaps the most troubling obstacle encountered was the unremitting criticism of the left wing of the nationalist movement. Often joined by more moderate elements, leftist critics questioned the efficacy of establishing a university that would serve such a small segment of the population, and, as we shall discuss in detail in chapter 4, the patriotic motives of the movement itself were challenged decisively. In addition, the movement was jolted by the early withdrawal of support from the Korean Youth League, itself undergoing internal struggles as leftist leaders assumed control of the organization.[34]

By 1925, the movement once begun with so much promise had become moribund. Moreover, a major drought in 1925–26 diverted excess funds to relief efforts, further reducing contributions to the university campaign. Efforts in 1926 to revive the campaign failed. And it came to a formal end fully ten years after its hopeful beginning. In 1932, Kim Sŏngsu mounted a national endowment drive to establish a central library on the campus of the Posŏng School, one of the oldest and most prominent of the modern Korean schools. Funds raised for the defunct national university project were funneled to the library campaign that concluded with the opening of a central library to commemorate the thirty-year anniversary of the Posŏng School.[35]

The failure of the highly publicized patriotic movement to endow a national university was a direct contrast to the smaller, but highly effective and long-lived, language movement. Linguists and educators concerned with the standardization and spread of the Korean vernacular banded together in 1921 under the banner of the Korean Language Research Society (Chosŏn'ŏ yŏn'guhoe).[36] In the following twenty years, the society in cooperation with the nationalist press and private education system systematized language usage, orthography, the transliteration of foreign loan-words, and laid the basis for the compilation of a comprehensive Korean language dictionary.[37] These activities seemed superficially to be the exclusive province of linguists and intellectuals, with little connection to the political drama of colonial life, but they were, perhaps, one of the most important, if not most permanent, contributions of the cultural movement to the future of Korean national life.

The language movement had always been an important aspect of •
Korean nationalism, and its origins can be traced back to the heated
debate in the 1890s over the use of the Korean vernacular in official
government documents. Up to that time, classical Chinese was still the
official written language of the Yi bureaucracy. After the 1895 Kabo
Reforms, mixed script (Chinese ideographic word units, and Korean
alphabet combined in Korean syntactic usage), began to gain currency
in official use. The Independence Club propelled the language issue to
the center of the nationalist movement by equating vernacular use
with national identity; and they chose to use pure *han'gŭl* for their
organ newspaper.[38]

Perhaps no individual was more responsible for linking the scientific
study and popular use of vernacular Korea with nationalist politics
and culture than Chu Sigyŏng (1876–1914). Chu pioneered scientific
linguistic study of Korean and, in addition, never missed an opportunity to comment on the importance of language to the life of the
nation. He stressed the sophistication of the Korean phonetic alphabet, devised by King Sejong in 1443 and touted by Chu as Korea's
most important contribution to world civilization. Chu also stressed
its simplicity and flexibility, declaring it superior to both the "back-
ward ideographic Chinese script" and the "convoluted Japanese
writing system."[39] Chu believed firmly that language was the most
fundamental expression of national identity and character and without its continued development and systematization, a nation could not
maintain its sense of common experience. Furthermore, the simplicity •
of *han'gŭl* would ease the transition to mass literacy and aid Korea in
its drive to modernize. Chu classified Korean as one of seventy major
world languages, and as such, stressed Korea's undeniable contribution to world culture.[40]

Chu's disciples continued his work with the Korean language and
created the organized movement of the 1920s and 1930s for its spread
and development. Cultural nationalists were quick to use the language
issue politically because they instinctively grasped its potential for
unifying cultural development. The language movement faced none of
the obstacles of the contemporary Chinese Paihua movement. Korean
society was unified by a single spoken language and had inherited an
indigenously devised, easily learned phonetic alphabet. This endowment aided language activists in their effort to promote vernacular use
and presented Korean nationalists with an evocative unifying device in
language. Nationalist historians were also quick to build on Chu's
theories in their own effort to differentiate Korean culture from early

Chinese influence. They accomplished this by linking studies of the origins of the Korean language with contemporary research on the Tan'gun myth. In the end, language remained a prime component of
ꓮ the cultural nationalist agenda; it was the primary vehicle of socialization, a tool for modernization, and a key to national identity. It was not surprising, therefore, that after annexation nationalists equated the development and spread of the vernacular with national survival.

The language movement had faced an uphill struggle since the 1890s. Official Yi dynasty policy notwithstanding, the traditional elite had always denigrated *han'gŭl* as a low-class language, unsuitable for refined expression. Although the nationalist movement popularized its use, Japanese control after 1910 threatened all gains made by the movement. Official Japanese policy limited instruction of Korean and stressed literacy skills in the "national" language, Japanese. And between 1910 and 1920, restrictions on Korean vernacular publications limited seriously the continued refinement of the language. Moreover, the increasing importance of Japanese as the official language of the colony, and the rapid expansion of Japanese use among educated citizens threatened the solidification of Korean identity and the creation of modern Korean culture. Although censored for inflammatory content, an editorial in the *Chosŏn ilbo* in 1920 indicated the depth of concern in nationalist circles over the language issue. Pointing to the rapid spread of Japanese language use, even in the home setting, this editorial charged that such use of Japanese could lead to the acceptance of more basic customs and attitudes; ultimately, it might cause the acceptance of another peoples' consciousness.[41] Such concerns fueled the drive for language policy reform, the establishment of private schools, and the continued spread of vernacular use.

• The formation of the Korean Language Research Society in December 1921 laid the base for a unified movement to promote the use of the Korean vernacular.[42] The main research projects of the society were to publish standards for grammatical usage and to unify orthography and, having completed these tasks, begin the compilation of a comprehensive Korean dictionary.[43] In addition to their scholarly work, the society worked closely with Korean publishers and newspapers to implement unified usage. Another primary activity of the language researchers was to urge Japanese education officials to accept changes in Korean-language texts and to upgrade Korean language instruction in private and colonial schools. Although frustrated by Japanese official resistance to texts and curriculum, the society staged a series of training institutes for Korean-language instructors to elevate their teaching techniques. They also provided language instruction materials to the growing student population of Christian sunday schools.[44] Expanding the original focus on research and teacher training, the society began a successful series of circuit lectures in which members traveled to the provinces to report on research results and to promote the literacy movement.[45]

The efforts of the language movement, privately financed and dependent often on the individual efforts of poorly paid linguists, produced prodigious results. A decade of work on standard usage resulted in the publication of the *Unified Orthography* (*Matchumbŏp t'ongil'an*) in 1933. This was followed by agreements on standardized spelling and transliteration rules in the next few years.[46] By the mid 1930s, the society had also begun work on *The Big Dictionary* (*K'ŭn sajŏn*), a task that would continue through World War II and into the postliberation period.

The language movement survived and prospered throughout the 1920s and 1930s because of the consensus among nationalists, both moderates and radicals, as to its importance. As specialists and intellectuals, leaders of the language movement worked easily with publishers, journalists, and educators, and the goals of the society fit comfortably into the cultural nationalist program. Yet the members of the language society found considerable unity with more radical nationalist intellectuals. In spite of their opposition to the general cultural nationalist program, radicals supported the language movement because they were interested in the link between mass literacy and the creation of a truly mass culture in Korea. Society materials and contacts were instrumental in the success of the summer literacy campaigns staged by Korean university students with the cooperation of the major nationalist papers beginning in 1926.[47] This populist movement (*pŭnarŏdŭ*, Russ.: *v narod* [to the people]) was an attempt to involve directly the masses in nationalist consciousness raising and mass education, issues central to the growing Socialist movement among young nationalist intellectuals in the 1920s. These young leftists found fast, if unlikely, allies among the linguists of the language movement.

The language movement's successes were achieved without official government support, and often in spite of Japanese repression. Ch'oe Hyŏnbae (1894–1970), linguist, one-time president of the language society, and postliberation ROK education official, recalled the extraordinary unanimity the language issue brought to cooperative ventures among nationalists during the colonial period. Although individual members of the society could hardly agree on personal and political matters, the significance of language and spiritual bond it encouraged united nationalists in their work.[48] By the end of the colonial period, work in the language movement became a progressively dangerous act of political defiance. After the Japanese invasion of China in 1937, the GGK began a program of forced assimilation and forced mobilization to support their war effort. In line with this policy the Japanese eliminated the use of Korean in the bureaucracy (1937), schools (1938), and the press (1939). In spite of this pressure, the language society continued to work on the dictionary project only to suffer the arrest of fourteen members in 1942 for violation of the security law. The final report of the subsequent trial provided a fitting tribute to language society efforts by denouncing the society's efforts to "ensure the future independence of Korea by reviving the national spirit and fostering national strength through a cultural movement."[49]

The Korean Production Movement

As we have seen, cultural nationalists did stress the importance of economic growth to national development; however, it had always been subordinated to cultural development and education. It was somewhat ironic, therefore, that the largest cultural nationalist movement of the early 1920s formed around the issue of national economic growth and self-sufficiency. A combination of worsening economic conditions, GGK economic reforms, and renewed discussion of the issue of Korea's economic dependence created an atmosphere for the emergence of a nationalist economic growth campaign. The result was the moderate nationalist Korean production movement of 1923–24.

The genesis of the basic conditions of economic dependence lay in basic changes in the Korean economy since 1876. The opening of Korea to foreign trade in 1876 had an immediate impact. The arrival of foreign, machine-made consumer goods and commercialization of Korean agriculture forever altered its traditional economy. By the 1890s, Korea's trade with the outside world was severely unbalanced, with considerable wealth leaving the country to finance imports. Given the low level of technology of the Korean handicraft industry, competing with foreign manufacturers, increasingly Japanese companies, was exceedingly difficult. For example, foreign cotton textiles soon dominated the traditional Korean cloth markets. Japanese textiles competed initially with British cotton, but as Japanese political fortunes rose on the peninsula and more Japanese companies began to aggressively market their products, Japan's share of textile imports rose accordingly. By 1905, 53 percent of the popular unbleached cotton sheeting imported to Korea was Japanese, and by 1919 they controlled 97 percent of the import market.[50] This Japanese dominance was not accomplished with tariff relief after annexation because the Japanese had agreed to maintain the pre-1920 tariff structure in discussions with the major powers. Nevertheless, political domination of the peninsula paved the way for economic ascendancy. Moreover, World War I provided the Japanese with an opportunity to expand into markets throughout Asia previously dominated by European goods.

The commercialization of agriculture and efforts of the GGK to rationalize landownership rights after 1910 affected the lives of all Koreans. With growing commercialization of the economy after 1876, more and more rice was marketed for the cash to buy consumer items. As peasants became more dependent on the market, they also became more vulnerable to its vagaries. One of the first projects of the GGK was a comprehensive cadastral survey (1910–18). Land remained the most important avenue of investment and as the 1920s progressed, landholding became increasingly concentrated as peasant indebtedness and foreclosures rose.[51]

By the late 1910s, landlords began to look for investment in nontraditional areas. The GGK Company Law, however, required permits for Korean-owned businesses and restricted severely Korean entrepreneurship. Therefore, by 1920, Korea was increasingly dependent on imported manufactures and faced growing rural poverty and rising tenancy rates. Although Korean landlords prospered, opportunities for investment in the modern sector, already dominated by Japanese companies, remained scarce.

The cultural policy announced a series of reforms to address concerns over the economic situation in colony. Between 1910 and 1920 the Company Law had also restricted direct Japanese investment in Korea. After the war, domestic pressures from businessmen in Japan to liberalize the investment climate persuaded the GGK to liberalize the old Company Law.[52] In addition, the post-World War I recession had created a situation where Japanese firms were dumping products on the Korean market at prices no company in the colony could match. Concurrently, the tariff structure was about to be changed, creating a free economy between Japan and Korea, a situation calculated to overwhelm fledgling colonial industries, both

Korean and Japanese, that were competing with Japan-based enter-prises. To solve this problem, Saitō granted subsidies to some Japanese companies to sustain them as tariffs were removed.[53]

Saitō also had to worry about the political impact of the planned reforms in the colony. Therefore, he portrayed the economic reforms to Koreans as being in the spirit of cooperative development, part of the overall program of "harmony between Japan and Korea [*nissen yūwa*]." Cooperative development was in keeping with his earlier statement about creating a "bridge between Korean and Japanese capitalists," another part of the general cultural policy to build avenues of trust and cooperation among GGK officials, Korean intellectuals, and businessmen.[54] To publicize this new commitment, Saitō convened an Industrial and Economic Investigation Committee for Korea (Chōsen sangyō keizai chōsakai) in September 1921, a high level meeting of colonial bureaucrats and Japanese industrialists, to which important Korean businessmen were invited. Korean business-men took the opportunity to lobby hard for increased freedom of action. And encouraged by the talk of change, they also demanded subsidies for Korean firms, well aware that they faced an uphill battle against large Japanese companies, when and if the way was paved for unrestricted investment in the colony.[55]

As Korean capitalists lobbied for subsidies and freedom to partici-pate on an equal footing with Japanese business, cultural nationalists approached the economic crisis on a different tack. Their plan was to mobilize national sentiment in support of Korean industry and handicrafts to encourage self-sufficiency. They were supported imme-diately by Korean businessmen, who perceived the advantage of such political support in their struggle to compete with Japanese capitalism. The resulting joint effort heightened the political drama surrounding the GGK economic policy adjustments.

The Korean production movement repeated earlier efforts to stim-ulate Korean economic development in competition with foreign capitalism. The first Korean joint stock company, the P'yongyang Porcelain Company (P'yŏngyang chagi hoesa, 1908), had been estab-lished in conjunction with An Ch'angho's integrated plan for national development laid forth in the program of the New People's Associa-tion (Sinminhoe).[56] Company founder and Sinminhoe activist, Yi Sǔnghun (1864–1930), was a prototype for later Korean entrepre-neurs. He combined his business interests with a political commitment to national development, and he linked his economic activities directly to the cause of Korean nationalism; years later, he emerged as a leader in the Korean production movement. The Sinminhoe also organized their publishing house, the T'aeguk sŏgwan, as a joint stock company to encourage group investment and encourage participation in non-traditional money making ventures. Contemporaneously, the Repay the National Debt movement (Kukch'e posang undong) had also appealed to patriotic sentiments in the solution of national economic problems. In this case, the debt movement urged citizens to make personal sacrifices in consumption of "luxury" items (tobacco, liquor) to repay the national debt.[57] Antismoking and drinking movements continued after annexation, spurred on by social reformers and the Christian church. With the emergence of the later Korean production movement, these groups were invited to help in the dual effort to reduce economic waste and encourage savings for investment in Korean companies. Thus, nationalists had already linked economic growth with national development in the waning years of the Yi dynasty, stressing different programs for modernizing industry as well as frugality and savings in the national cause.

In 1920, separate organizations emerged with the shared purpose of addressing economic problems. The perception that Korean businesses were slowly being overwhelmed by outside economic forces galvanized nationalists into action. In July 1920, Cho Mansik (1882– ?) formed the Society for the Promotion of Native Production (Chosŏn mulsan changnyŏhoe).[58] Cho's organization was headquartered in P'yŏngyang, home of the old Sinminhoe, and maintained strong ties to the large Christian community in North Korea. Cho had become a Christian as a youth and was a graduate of Waseda University (1913). While in Japan, Cho came in contact with the ideas of Indian nationalist leader Gandhi's program of nonviolence and economic self-sufficiency for independence from British rule. Indeed, Cho's own self-deprecating style and personal commitment to these ideals earned him the label "Gandhi of Korea."[59] Later, Cho built on these ideas in creating the Korean production movement. Consumption of native goods would help economic development and encourage Korean solidarity as well.[60]

The Indian nationalist movement also inspired the formation of groups similar to Cho's in other cities. In Seoul, Yŏm T'aejin and Yi Kwangsu had already organized a group called the Self Production Association (Chajakhoe) in December of 1922. The organization's purpose was to raise national consciousness by rejecting the use of imported goods in favor of products made "by and for Koreans." To that end, the Chajakhoe opened a consumer cooperative that they hoped would become a model for similar cooperatives throughout the colony.[61]

In December of 1922, leaders of separate groups committed to the encouragement of native industries met to discuss plans for consolidating their efforts. And a month later the national native production movement was born, led by a new organization under the name of the original P'yŏngyang group (Chosŏn mulsan changnyŏhoe).[62] Over twenty separate groups merged into the national effort, and the new organization's moderate leadership strived to broaden the usual coalition of intellectuals, journalists, teachers, and students by including Korean businessmen. The participation of businessmen and shopkeepers was a unique development. Kim Tongwŏn, president of the Kyŏnggi Spinning Company, and Kim Sŏngsu, president of the *Tonga ilbo* and the Kyŏngsŏng Spinning Company, both played important roles in the genesis of the movement.[63] In another unusual move, a women's auxiliary organization (T'osan aeyong puinhoe) was created to involve wives, perhaps the most important Korean consumers, in the program and to coordinate efforts with women's organizations throughout Korea.[64]

The program of the Korean production movement was simple and direct. Korea faced an impending economic crisis from the growing dependence on foreign manufactures for all daily necessities. According to the organization's platform, the fact that Koreans "were selling themselves" to obtain even the most mundane items proved that Koreans were on the verge of economic annihilation.[65] Buying non-Korean-made goods simply enriched foreigners; the time had come for all Koreans, rich and poor, to support only Korean producers. Therefore, the movement urged all Koreans to patronize, whenever possible, Korean stores and to use Korean-produced clothing, foodstuffs (excluding sugar, salt, and fruits), and other daily necessities. Exceptions were made for medicine and other necessities not of Korean manufacture.[66]

• The Korean production movement stressed the positive value of production because they wished to avoid confrontation with Japanese authorities that a boycott might bring. More significant, they wanted to stress production for its spiritual effect on national unity. Clearly, leaders of the movement had the precedent of the contemporary Indian nationalist movement in mind when they created their program of action. In early 1923, articles appeared in the nationalist press describing the goals and ideology of Gandhi's Swaraj movement, comparing it with the Korean production movement. And Gandhi's ideas inspired both Cho Mansik and Yi Kwangsu's Buy Korean groups. Indeed, Gandhi's insistence on nonviolence, self-sufficiency, and national unity across class lines appealed greatly to cultural nationalists, intent as they were on gradualist national development within the colonial political framework.[67]

The Korean production movement generated tremendous enthusiasm in its first year. The movement planned rallies and parades for the lunar new year (February 14, 1923) that would be led by members in traditional Korean dress. The colonial police, worried that the rallies might get out of hand, forbade parades in Seoul and interrupted several rallies. In provincial cities, however, thousands of citizens joined in parades in a celebration of national unity.[68] Building on this initial outburst of support, the movement spread rapidly, establishing branch organizations in all provinces.

In its first year, the Korean production movement strove to build on this patriotic upsurge. It published a monthly magazine, *Industrial World (San'ŏpkye)*, as a clearing house for ideas and to advertise the movement. The magazine promoted regional specialty items, published results of economic surveys, encouraged the formation of consumer cooperatives, and sustained the patriotic line of self-sufficiency.[69] The movement's economic and survey sections conducted research on the Korean economy to uncover new areas for investment and sources of venture capital, and they conducted detailed surveys of regional economic conditions and consumption patterns.

At its height in the summer of 1923, the movement became the most successful mass mobilization of Koreans since the March First demonstrations. Consumption of Korean-produced goods increased to the extent that certain items became virtually unobtainable. Understandably, prices of Korean-made goods rose, demanding, ironically, further financial sacrifice for the patriotically inclined.[70] Clearly, the movement heightened mass awareness of economic issues, and it altered, at least temporarily, Korean consumption habits. Unfortunately, economic and political realities blocked its sustained growth, and by 1924 the movement was in steady decline.

The Korean production movement presented the GGK with a unique problem. Here was a movement that advocated economic development through legal means at precisely the time that the Japanese were contemplating reforms to ameliorate economic problems and win the support of Korean businessmen in the colony. Certainly, the implicit long-range goal of political autonomy threatened Japanese interests, but since the movement was not a formal boycott of Japanese goods, the GGK had to proceed with care to obstruct the movement without resorting to direct repression.[71] The most direct Japanese response was to limit the movement's publicity. The nationwide rallies and parades scheduled for February 14, 1923, had all the potential of a March First repeat. Accordingly, the police blocked the largest rallies in Seoul, but they permitted smaller, more isolated parades in the provinces.[72] They also censored advertisements in newspapers that directly implied that the movement was linked to Korean nationalist political goals and they warned movement leaders against taking an overt political line in program announcements.

Although Japanese obstruction hurt the movement, economic realities conspired with recent GGK policy changes to undermine its support more decisively. The Korean production movement assumed that nationalistic sentiment would be sufficient to overcome price differentials between cheaper, and often higher quality, imports and more expensive Korean-made goods. Initially, they were correct; however, over time, consumers slipped back to the more inexpensive foreign items.[73] Moreover, tariff revision in 1923 effectively reduced further the price of Japanese imports and increased the price of patriotism. Ultimately, the decision to proceed with tariff revision was one of the most effective GGK responses to the threat posed by the Korean production movement.

Having already modified the Company Law providing for more freedom for Korean entrepreneurs, Saitō continued discussions with Korean businessmen on the issue of subsidies. In 1923, the GGK responded to the private entreaties for subsidies backed by public pressure in the press and the rise of the Buy Korean movement by granting the first such subsidy to Kim Sŏngsu's Kyŏngsŏng Spinning Company.[74] The issue of subsidies was important because they were central to the profitability of Korean companies competing with Japanese textiles. With a subsidy, Kim's company could compete even without the support of the Korean production movement. Granting concessions to Korean businessmen gave the GGK leverage in their behind-the-scenes campaign to undermine the resolve of the Korean production movement leadership. Alternating intimidation and conciliation succeeded ultimately in driving a wedge between businessmen and nationalist organizers of the movement.[75]

By the end of the movement's first year in February 1924, additional leadership problems plagued the cause. Korean merchant cooperation was vital to the movement's success, but many merchants felt threatened by consumer cooperatives, fearing competition for customers.

Importers worried that the movement would drive them out of business. Soon there were reports of merchants profiteering from the increased demand for Korean-made goods, directly challenging the sincerity of the entire project.[76] In March 1924, one report cited the specific example of a merchant who imported cheaper Japanese cotton sheeting from Osaka and, switching to Korean labels, sold the sheeting at a higher price because it was "Korean-made."[77] Such activity presented the movement with serious problems. Noncooperation, indeed active exploitation by shopkeepers and importers, undermined seriously the movement's patriotic appeal.

Such problems opened the movement to growing criticism from within the ranks of the nationalist movement. Leftists charged that such an economic movement could never succeed in a colonial situation and that only Korean capitalists would profit in their own struggle against Japanese monopoly capitalism.[78] Even more to the point, critics declared that the very leadership that exhorted the masses to demonstrate their solidarity by using native manufacturers were, themselves, the most Westernized group in Korea, in dress, style, and education. Why, then, should the masses sacrifice to enrich a small group of Korean capitalists at the behest of foreign-educated intellectuals?[79] Such criticism challenged the ultimate sincerity of the entire cultural nationalist approach and, as we shall see, was the beginning of a significant division within nationalist ranks that ultimately discredited the moderate nationalist wing of the movement.

The Korean production movement responded to the reports of profiteering and the charges of its leftist critics by reaffirming their commitment to national economic development. Admitting that certain unscrupulous shopkeepers had abused the program, and that there was theoretical truth in the inherent ambivalent interests of Korean capitalists, the movement fought back by asserting that these problems were temporary and that the enormity of the problem facing Korea required a sustained effort, "if Korea was to avoid becoming the playground for foreigners."[80] Some members responded by justifying the Korean production movement with sophisticated arguments that turned Marxist bullets back on the Left.[81] In effect, these arguments insisted that since all Korean classes faced extinction in the present situation, it was futile to charge the production movement with exclusively supporting bourgeois interests. The Korean bourgeoisie was already becoming proletarian. Since political action was impossible under present conditions, like it or not, Koreans had to unite behind economic movements.[82]

Nevertheless the movement declined steadily in its second year. By the end of 1924, it even had problems meeting the rent for its central office in Seoul.[83] Although the movement continued to organize New Years' parades and enjoyed a brief revival during the depression years, its mass appeal and significance waned after its first year. The Korean production movement maintained, however, an official presence and continued publishing *San'ŏpkye* until the abolition in 1937 of all nationalist organizations, following Japan's invasion of China.

The Demise of the Cultural Nationalist Movement

By 1925, the major cultural nationalist movements, begun with so much promise and heraldry in the nationalist press, were in steady decline. The university movement united temporarily nationalist intellectuals, bridged organizational splits, and amassed significant contributions, but it failed to create a sufficiently strong mass base to sustain its program. From its inception, the Korean production movement aimed its program at the masses, and it achieved, in the short run, a significant response. Yet within its first year, the movement encountered serious difficulties that ultimately weakened its mass appeal and left it moribund. The cultural movement continued throughout the 1920s and early 1930s. It failed, however, to sustain its own promise as a solution to the long-term problems of Korean independence.

The cultural nationalist movement provoked a serious challenge from the expanding ranks of radical nationalists within the colony. Heavily influenced by their study of Marx and other Socialist writers, radicals attacked the fundamental precepts of the cultural nationalist program. They questioned the utility of national reform within the colonial system, arguing that without political independence talk of national development was meaningless. Furthermore, they questioned the basic motives of the cultural nationalist leadership's advocacy of cultural and economic development. Under Japanese colonial rule, did not such movements serve only the interests of the middle and upper class Korean elite? Such criticism diluted the mass appeal of cultural nationalism and, furthermore, split nationalist leaders over issues of class versus national interests as well as tactics for independence.

The Japanese also blunted the thrust of the cultural nationalist movement by skillfully evolving a cooptative policy of control. The rise of the university and Korean production movements did alarm the Saitō administration. Although committed to the softer cultural policy after 1919, the Japanese were careful not to let their "safety valve" blow too hot or too long. They did fear that they had gone too far in relaxing journalistic and organizational controls as they watched the mushrooming of political activity after 1920.[84] Moreover, as moderates began to link nationalist organizations together to further specific projects, most notably the university and Korean production movements, the Japanese worried about the potential of these projects for widespread disturbance. Additionally, the Japanese watched closely the proliferation of contacts between domestic and overseas nationalist organizations, well aware of the danger that more radical overseas groups might gain a foothold in the colony.[85] The national reform ideology of the cultural nationalists, while technically eschewing violence and illegal activity, threatened to sustain the nationalist fervor of the March First demonstrations. Furthermore, talk of Gandhian tactics threatened long-term Japanese interests in coopting the Korean elite and stabilizing Japanese control in the colony.

The Japanese handled the cultural movement with a two-pronged • policy of obstruction and conciliation. They used their power over the press and assembly to obstruct cultural nationalist rallies and promotional literature. They censored vigilantly more provocative publicity in the print media; articles explaining the goals of the university and Korean production movements were acceptable so long as they avoided inflammatory rhetoric linking these "legal" organizations with political independence.[86] And they worked hard to control both organizations in Seoul and inhibit their contacts in the provinces. On the other side of the coin, they allowed smaller rallies and meetings in the provinces while banning similar meetings in Seoul. The idea was to prevent where possible the forging of a strongly centralized movement.[87]

The Japanese authorities also pressured the cultural nationalist • leadership through continuous personal contact. From his first days in Seoul, Saitō established a habit of consulting directly with prominent Korean leaders. He was most interested in moderate intellectuals and wealthy conservatives because it was from these groups he hoped to obtain cooperation with long-term Japanese interests. Intellectuals were plied with concessions in the cultural sphere in the form of permits for publications and seats on advisory boards. The price for expanded freedoms embodied in the cultural policy was cooperation with the colonial regime. Indeed, the cultural nationalist movement • emerged at a time of continuous negotiation between Korean nationalists and the colonial administration, and, as we have shown above, this contact did affect the nature of the cultural nationalist strategy.

Japanese policy toward the cultural nationalist movement evolved gradually between 1920 and 1924. Saitō was in constant contact with major cultural nationalist leaders in 1922 and 1923, the most active period of the movement.[88] The Japanese chose to work hardest on returning exiled nationalists such as Yi Kwangsu and March First leaders emerging from prison after 1920. They hoped to further Yi's conversion to gradualism and his break with radicals abroad. Indeed, the conservatism of Yi's approach had already been noted by Saitō's political advisers. In November 1921, Abe Mitsuka had pointed out to Saitō that Yi's plans for a gradualist enlightenment program might, in the long run, serve to deaden the interest of youth in independence. He continued by advising a go-slow approach to fostering explicitly pro-Japanese organizations in favor of allowing some latitude for moderate cultural movements.[89] And after the publication of the "Minjok kaejoron," Japanese officials were convinced that their advantage lay in encouraging this conservative approach to nationalist issues.

The treatment of Ch'oe Namsŏn provided another example of the tacit encouragement of moderate nationalists. Ch'oe Namsŏn emerged from prison in 1921 and received, almost immediately, a current affairs permit for a weekly magazine (*Tongmyŏng*); Japanese officials agreed later to allow Ch'oe to convert his magazine to a daily newspaper (*Sidae ilbo*).[90] In another example of GGK largess, Kim Sŏngsu received a subsidy for his spinning company in 1923, at the height of the Korean production movement. In effect, Saitō expanded the use of rewards for cooperation, rewards first used in the form of stipends and peerages to gain the compliance of the Yi royal family and selected Yi dynasty aristocrats in 1910, to selected moderate nationalists after 1920.[91]

* The Japanese also worked hard to undermine the cultural nationalist program by speeding educational and economic reforms. Although the new educational ordinance of 1922 was responsible initially for the national drive to establish a Korean university, the * success of the reforms insured the ultimate failure of the project. By accelerating the schedule for the creation of an imperial university, the Japanese addressed successfully the criticism that access to higher education was limited in the colony. This left the university movement with only the issue of "national pride" in their arsenal. And given the fate of the university movement, it was clear that "national pride" was insufficient inducement for contributions from rich and poor alike.

Overall economic reform under the Saitō regime severely affected the course of the Korean production movement. Changing the Company Law to allow increased Japanese investment as well as the formation of more Korean companies undermined the critically needed support of Korean capitalists for the movement. In addition, the prospect of subsidies and closer cooperation between the GGK and Korean business helped to mollify longstanding grievances among the Korean economic elite. Finally, by moving ahead with tariff revision, the GGK effectively increased the competitive advantage of Japanese imports, thus furthering the burden on the Korean production movement. Tariff reform and revision of the Company Law had been planned long before the emergence of the Korean production movement. Thus, the conscious policy of conciliation toward Korean capitalists eroded their interest in the Korean production movement, providing further difficulties for a movement already in serious trouble.

Finally, as the cultural movement flowered in 1922–23, the Japanese moved to support and create numerous pro-Japanese reform organizations. The national reform ideology of the cultural nationalist camp was emulated by groups whose purpose was not to create an independent Korea, but to solidify Japanese political control while advancing their own interests in the colony. In 1923–24, political organizations dedicated to self rule within the Japanese Empire and representation in the Japanese Diet were active. Also landlord-tenant associations, alternative youth groups, and groups supporting cooperative relations between Korea and Japan emerged. In March 1923, eleven pro-Japanese groups amalgamated to form the All Parties Local Notables Association (Kakp'a yuji yŏnmaeng) as a response to the growing popularity of leftist ideas and organizations.[92] The emergence of these pro-Japanese organizations advocating political and social reform diluted the impact of the cultural nationalist program by blurring significantly the line between a gradualist movement for national cultural autonomy dedicated to future political independence and other groups devoted to "cooperation" or, worse yet, collaboration with the Japanese overlords.

The failure of the cultural nationalist movement to gain mass support exposed its program as increasingly irrelevant to the conditions of colonial Korea in the 1920s. In the first decade of the twentieth century, nationalist reform thought offered a radical alternative vision for Korean society. Twenty years later it proved unable to serve as the basis for mobilizing nationalist sentiment in the cause of independence. In the 1910s, the majority of the Korean nationalist leaders legitimated their own political and social prestige by advocating education, national consciousness raising, and economic development along the lines of the West as the way to the rebirth of the Korean nation. In the early 1920s, however, these ideas seemed to many passé, if not reactionary.

Ten years of Japanese rule had wrested the mantle of reform from the hands of nationalist intellectuals. Although they denied Koreans political power and served their own economic and strategic interests, the Japanese had begun the process of developing Korea in line with their own image of modernity. This development had served the economic and political interests of some Koreans, even as it held the bulk of the population in a cruel yoke of economic and political dependency. Korean landlords had profited from stable, rationalized landownership and tax system. The sons of landed families benefited from increased educational opportunities and study abroad. Education, however, did not automatically lead to upward mobility in the colonial system. By 1919, there was a large group of educated colonial intellectuals who, denied access to political influence, joined with the precolonial nationalist elite to work for political independence. The tremendous outpouring of discontent embodied in the March 1919 riots seemed to hold the promise of a successful nationalist movement and the possibilities for future political independence.

The Saitō reforms of 1920, however, significantly adjusted the climate for nationalist intellectuals in the colony. The cultural policy provided more outlets for creative energies, leadership positions in legal organizations, increased exposure in the colonial press, and, for those willing to actively cooperate, advisory positions in the colonial government. The dilemma for nationalists in the colony after 1920 was how to remain faithful to legitimate nationalist goals within the limits of the cultural policy without crossing the line to outright collaboration.

With increased options for cultural and quasi-political activity, the range of positions taken by influential Koreans broadened. Conservatives cooperated actively with the Japanese. Moderate cultural nationalists attempted to continue their work toward independence in the distant future by working within the system. Exiled nationalists returned to Korea, attracted by the possibilities for organization, and radicals continued their work underground and in exile to oppose Japanese rule. The major nationalist movements within Korea in this period, however, were dominated by the cultural nationalists. Adhering to the precolonial nationalist assumption that continued cultural and economic development was a prerequisite of political independence, the cultural nationalists attempted to mobilize patriotic sentiment toward the accomplishment of nationalist goals that fell far short of political independence. In doing so, they put themselves in an increasingly untenable position with regard to their own pretensions to national leadership.

As we have seen, cultural nationalists likened their program to the independence movement in India, especially true of the Korean production movement, leaders of which pointed to the obvious similarities between Gandhi's ideas on native production and their own project. Yet the Korean production movement leaders were attempting to strengthen Korean capitalism to compete, ultimately, on an equal footing with Japan and the West. Although many leaders were personally committed and sincere in their belief that economic development would benefit all Koreans, they ignored or never understood the symbolic importance to Gandhi of native production—his idea was not to become as modern as the West, but to disengage from competition based on the standards of Western civilization. Self-sufficiency in Gandhi's view was a means toward emphasizing a truly nationalist attitude; India did not have to be "elevated" to Western standards, she deserved independence as she was.[93] On the whole, the production movement was unable to capture the spiritual basis of noncooperation that was in Gandhi's Swaraj movement. While cultural nationalists searched for ways to operate within the limits of the cultural policy, Gandhi was urging Indian nationalists to ignore British law, constitutional reform, and the lure of appointments in the bureaucracy of the British Raj. To Gandhi, British schooling was not preparation for work in the nationalist future, it was a denial of one's own identity.[94] The Korean university movement was presented to the Korean people as an alternative avenue of modern education by and for Koreans, yet its failure demonstrated that the Korean elite were more interested in gaining validation from Japanese universities as a means of improving their chances for advancement in colonial society.

In the end, the cultural nationalist movement failed to gain mass support because it did not address the interests of the majority of Koreans. Ideas that served to create a class of nationalist intellectuals in the first two decades of the twentieth century were not attractive to the common Korean peasant or worker in 1922. While the masses demonstrated their emotional support for the idea of independence in 1919, this did not mean they were available to support the interests of the moderate intellectual elite in subsequent years. The idea of an independent Korea was, perhaps, firmly entrenched in the minds of the masses by the early 1920s, but how this conviction was to be translated into political action was still an open question. Clearly, a cultural movement might serve to strengthen the idea of Korean cultural identity and autonomy, and it bolstered the prestige of nationalist intellectuals who wished to assuage their alienation by gaining positions of leadership in the nationalist cause while avoiding Japanese jails. The fact remained, however, that the movement had utterly failed to change the political reality on the peninsula.

As the cultural nationalists presented their program to the Korean people after 1920, they discovered that although they might presume to speak as the inheritors of the precolonial nationalist mantle, this presumption did not silence the increasingly vocal critics within the overall nationalist movement, who challenged the core assumptions of cultural nationalism, and bitterly opposed the tactics of gradualism. In the end, the debate over the efficacy of cultural nationalism highlighted the growing ideological schism between Korean nationalists and marked a decisive change in the political climate in the colony. It is to the critics of cultural nationalism we must now turn.

CHAPTER 4

The Radical Critique
of Cultural Nationalism

The post-World War I era was a time of tremendous intellectual ferment in East Asia. The Versailles conference elevated expectations among Korean and Chinese nationalists alike by propagating the broad tenet of self-determination as a solution to conflicting demands for national autonomy and independence around the world. Although it was clear by 1920 that self-determination was aimed primarily at Europe, many East Asians continued to pin their hopes for a better world on the outcome of the series of international conferences on disarmament and world peace in the years after 1919. Other developments, however, augured well for radical change in intellectual and political circles in East Asia. The Russian revolution and the emergence of the Soviet Union as a champion of oppressed peoples throughout the world generated tremendous excitement. In contrast to the heavy sense of disillusionment with Western liberalism, the success of the Bolshevik revolution underscored the dynamism of its social revolutionary ideology. The subsequent rise of the Soviet Union and formation of the Comintern in the wake of the Third Communist Internationale convinced many intellectuals in East Asia that a new era had dawned.

The rise in the popularity of socialism among Koreans at home and in exile was rapid, and it affected deeply the intellectual development of Korea. The horrors of World War I raised questions as to the future of the West and the wisdom of emulating its political model. And although internationalism, panhumanism, and global cooperation became the slogans for those interested in establishing a new world order led by the victorious Allied Powers, the practical failure of these high-minded principles to alter the political and social reality in East Asia caused many to look toward the social revolutionary model of the Soviet Union. Socialism offered an alternate world view and a profoundly different mode of analysis for those concerned with the problems of socioeconomic reform and national liberation. Those caught up in the enthusiasm for social revolution were apt to view the Allied triumph in World War I not as a victory for liberal democratic thought, but as the last gasp of the capitalist system.

The disillusionment with Western liberalism was strong among certain groups of young Korean intellectuals. The failure of the March First movement to obtain any real political concessions, let alone independence, from the Japanese left many disheartened with the pacifism and nonviolent tactics of the movement. Subsequent Allied affirmation of Japan's suzerainty in Korea left many with a sense of betrayal. The continued failure of diplomatic appeals for independence and outside intervention at the Washington Conference (1921–22) heightened the sense of betrayal. The Russian revolution, therefore, and the evolution of the Leninist doctrine of national liberation movements in undeveloped areas of the world offered an attractive alternative to Western liberalism, and the failure of Western policies toward Asia only increased its appeal.

Although Korean intellectuals had undoubtedly encountered Socialist writings in translation before 1917, it was during the Russian revolution that socialism began to attract an increasing number of adherents among the nationalist intelligentsia. Given the nature of Japanese control in the colony after 1910, it was not surprising to see the spread of socialism, first among Korean exiles in the Russian Far East, Siberia, China, and then among Korean students in Japan. Korean nationalists abroad, free to read and discuss radical ideas and join groups professing principles of Marxism-Leninism, were attracted to a new vision of social and political development, a vision that offered insight into the causes of colonial subjugation of Korea as well as solutions to the problem of national liberation. In the early 1920s, national liberation remained a priority amongst a majority of intellectuals experimenting with Socialist ideas, and it was within the nascent Socialist movement in exile and the radical study groups in Japan and Korea that nationalists, with new ideological weapons, began to broaden their outlook on national liberation. It is impossible to separate nationalists from social revolutionary internationalists in the 1920s because Koreans who were studying radical ideas were doing so as patriots, intensely concerned with the issue of nationalist liberation. Their devotion to revolutionary means toward independence brought controversy to the nationalist movement and, as well shall see later, a concerted attack by the Left on the cultural nationalist movement.

The Rise of Socialist Thought after 1919

The first formal Socialist Korean organizations emerged in Russia and Manchuria. Bolshevik forces attracted Korean nationalists in Eastern Siberia to the common cause of fighting the remnants of Czarist forces and their Western and Japanese allies. In 1918, Yi Tonghwi formed• the first Korean Socialist party (Han'in sahoedang) in Khabarovsk; in the same year Nam Manch'un organized a Korean section of the Communist party in Irkutsk.[1] Both of these groups were competing for Soviet financial support by 1919.

Yi Tonghwi joined the Shanghai Provisional Government (SPG) in 1920, bringing with him many supporters from his organization in Khabarovsk. Yi joined the SPG to continue the fight against Japanese imperialism, but he was soon disenchanted with the SPG's moderate line. His group was instrumental in spreading the concept of armed struggle and social revolution among nationalists in Shanghai. In 1921, at the height of the power struggles within the SPG over tactics and ideology, he formed the first Korean Communist party (Koryŏ• kongsandang).[2] Yi had considerable success attracting followers, but his efforts to increase the influence of his radical line within the SPG was hampered by the continued controversy among members of the Korean Socialist movement. The split between the Shanghai and the Irkutsk group continued to broaden, and it escalated from disputes over ideology and the disposition of funds obtained from the Comintern to armed combat during the Alexeyevsk incident in March 1921.[3] Nevertheless, the idea of social revolution had gained considerable support and had spawned smaller fringe groups that dabbled in anarchism and other radical ideologies. In spite of fractional differences and disputes with Comintern advisers, the Communist movement continued to grow within the Korean exile community.

The second major spawning ground of socialism among Korean intellectuals was Japan. Always the primary destination for Koreans studying abroad, Japan lured increasing numbers of Korean students after World War I. Between 1919 and 1922 their number increased from 448 to 1,192.[4] Once in Japan, students encountered an intellectual atmosphere that was in stark contrast to the colony. In the relatively free climate of political dialogue supported by a rich number of publications in Japanese and Japanese translations of Western works, Koreans began to study socialism in earnest. In 1914, the GGK had already noted the radical drift among Korean students and their penchant for "obtaining mistaken ideas"; this warning was issued in 1914, five years before Saitō was to remove restrictions on Koreans studying abroad.[5]

In Japan, Korean students encountered a society that was beginning to feel the effects of a generation of rapid economic and social change. The post-World War I recession brought significant economic hardship to both industrial laborers and farmers, and labor and tenant strife increased. Yet, amidst the turmoil there was excitement among Japanese intellectuals: the advent of party government and the passing of the Meiji oligarchs seemed to presage a new era of leadership. In the 1910s, college students and young intellectuals began to address Japan's social and economic problems with an idealistic belief in the power of new ideas to transform society in general. Young intellectuals began to shift their personal ambitions toward social reform and mass enlightenment, and because of this new interest the works of Russian populists and later Socialists became popular. The exhortation of the Russian populists to "go to the people" struck a responsive chord among contemporary Japanese college students.[6] Journals such as *Kaizō* (*Reconstruction*) and *Kaihō* (*Liberation*) (their names indicative of the hope and idealism of the times), proliferated. These journals contained a sampling of the entire spectrum of political thought, with Socialist writers gaining increasing popularity after 1917. It was a time of doctrines; discussions of democracy, bolshevism, social democracy, syndicalism, guild socialism, anarchism, Fabianism, and National Socialism whirled about in an atmosphere of intellectual experiment and search for new directions.[7]

The increase of Koreans studying in Japan after 1918 coincided with the maturation of the Japanese university student movement. Beginning with small debating societies and study clubs, the Japanese student movement eventually expanded into national federations with links to youth and labor organizations as the 1920s progressed.[8] Although the exception, some Korean students found their way into Japanese organizations as Japanese leftists cultivated contacts with
• Chinese and Korean students to demonstratate their growing internationalist spirit. Kim Chunyŏn, later connected to both major nationalist newspapers and party secretary in the third Korean Communist party in the colony (1926), joined the Shinjinkai (New Man Society) at Tokyo Imperial University after the March First uprising.[9]

Korean students had always been organized in Japan. Early organizations such as the Korean Society for the Advancement of Learning (Taehan hŭnghakhoe), the Tokyo Korean Students' Friends of Learn-

ing Society (Choe Tonggyŏng Chosŏnin yuhaksaeng hag'uhoe), Korean Women's Society for the Advancement of Learning (Chosŏn yŏja
hŭnghakhoe), and the Korean Study society (Chosŏn hakhoe) provided
support for students far away from home.[10] The "self-help" aspects of
these organizations, however, receded as political activities increasingly
dominated student life. As we have seen, Korean students were greatly
excited by the events of 1919. However, with the failure of the March
first movement and the increasingly obvious impotence of the SPG,
student politics began to shift to the Left. In 1920, students created the
Korean Self-Supporting Students and Friends Association (Chosŏn
kohaksaeng tong'uhoe). Begun as a mutual aid group, this association
soon established itself as the first avowedly Socialist organization
among Korean students in Japan. By 1922, they declared their intention
to merge with the labor movement and involve themselves "directly
with the cause of class struggle": "Our fraternal organization in concert
with important Japanese ideological and labor groups will merge with
the labor movement by creating a university for workers and publishing
a magazine, *Comrade (Tong'u)*. Forsaking our former emphasis on
student and worker relief, we declare our intention to involve ourselves
directly with the cause of class struggle."[11]
    The 1922 declaration of the Chosŏn kohaksaeng tong'uhoe only
confirmed the trend already obvious to Japanese police as well as to
moderate nationalists in the colony.[12] The intellectual agenda was
becoming more complex, and the radicalization of Korean students in
Japan, whose nationalism had been inflamed by the events of 1919,
was beginning to affect significantly the colony's political life.
    Between 1920 and 1925, the Korean Communist movement in exile
tried unsuccessfully to organize a base in the colony. The Comintern
had urged the Koreans to establish their base in the homeland, but
factional disputes for Comintern recognition and Japanese police
vigilance hindered the attempted move. It was not until April 1925 •
that the first official Korean Communist party in Korea was formed.[13]
In spite of the organizational ineptness of the KCP, radical ideology
flourished in the fertile soil of the colony after 1920. In the end,
socialism came as the mental baggage of returning students and a
fewer number of exile patriots who began to work within nationalist
youth, labor, and intellectual organizations.
    The youth movement in Korea was a prime target for infiltration by
the Communist movement in exile. Returning students from Japan
soon gained positions of responsibility in the All Korea Youth League
led by O Sanggŭn and Chang Tŏksu. Yi Tonghwi also sent members

of the Shanghai Communist group to work within the youth league.[14] The yearly conference of the Youth League became an ideological battleground as various factions vied for control of its administrative board and fought bitter debates on public issues. In January 1921, a radical faction of the Youth League in Seoul broke away and established a parallel movement under the banner of the Seoul Youth Association (Seoul ch'ŏngnyŏnhoe). There was continued conflict between competing groups within the youth movement, and the leftward drift of the movement culminated at the 1923 conference of youth groups. The "Preamble" of the conference illustrated the ideological orientation and confusion felt at the time by the leadership:

> In these circumstances and considering the state of Korean society, let us examine the conditions of youth groups in Korea today. Their will is strong and their mission is a great one. However, if youth groups remain scattered and isolated they will not be able to unite in a common cause. We are weak in isolation. Furthermore, it is difficult to clearly delineate our mission. This is not the only problem. The intellectual climate has been shaken at its very foundation by the disorder and confusion of ideas. It becomes daily more oppressive. In this situation, we lose sight of our direction. There is definitely a feeling of urgency and expectation on the part of the Korean masses. Therefore, movements that are estranged from the masses have no clear way of continuing. Thus, the Youth Movement pledges itself to leading and helping the Korean masses and ameliorating their plight.[15]

This statement showed a significant shift from the more moderate enlightenment goals of the the original organization. As we shall see below, radicals in the youth movement leadership used their positions of influence to shift support of the league away from the moderate cultural nationalist programs just then gaining headway.

Returning radicals also joined and influenced the growing number of labor and peasant organizations. In 1920, Ch'a Kŭmbong organized the the Fraternal Worker and Peasant Association (Nonong kongjehoe). Founded as a mutual aid organization along Christian Socialist lines, the organization promoted education, savings, hygiene, and other relief projects aimed at laborers.[16] Almost immediately, the organization's leadership split along ideological lines: a radical faction worked to divert the relief emphasis toward a more activist approach by instilling class consciousness among its members and diverting the association's program toward political action. The association splintered between 1922 and 1924 into an array of different laborer and peasant organizations. Only in April 1924 was the movement brought together again into some semblance of unity with the creation of the Korean Labor-Farmer Federation (Chosŏn nonong ch'ong tongmaeng). Controlled by radicals, the organization claimed a membership of 110,100, divided into 79 labor, 78 peasant, and 37 mixed groups.[17]

Representatives of the Shanghai and Irkutsk factions of the Korean Communist movement fought for Comintern recognition and participated in the first Congress of the Toilers of the Far East in January 1922. Indeed, the congress had been organized as a radical alternative to the Washington Conference and an opportunity to reaffirm the Leninist principle of supporting national liberation movements in the Far East. Simultaneously, independent efforts were already underway to establish Socialist study groups in the homeland. The lineage and ideological positions of these groups within the colony were constantly shifting, with groups forming, renaming themselves, splitting, and reemerging with great rapidity.[18] Amidst this confusion between 1920 and 1925, three major strains of radical groups can be isolated.

One group rallied around the Seoul ch'ŏngnyŏnhoe, which had split off from the mainstream Korean Youth movement in January 1921. The Seoul ch'ŏngnyŏnhoe gradually took on the role of an intellectual society as members pushed the organization toward the goal of spreading social revolutionary thought. It maintained contact with Yi Tonghwi's faction in Shanghai and, ultimately, gave birth to the Socialist Alliance (Sahoejuŭi tongmaeng) in December of 1924.

An additional strain of leftist groups emerged with direct ties to the Korean Self-Supporting Students and Friends Society in Tokyo. In March 1922, members returning to Korea created the Proletarian Alliance (Musanja tongmaenghoe) to spread orthodox Marxism among the Korean laboring classes. In subsequent years, leaders of the alliance established separate groups such as the Saturday Society (T'oyohoe, 1923) and the New Thought Study Association (Sin sasang yŏn'guhoe, 1923), later renamed the Tuesday Society (Hwayohoe, 1924). Another group, the North Star Society (Puksŏnghoe, 1923) was formed in Tokyo after the Kantō earthquake by members of the original Tokyo Students and Friends Association. This group objected to the then popular anarchist line in favor of a more serious study of socialism. After establishing a presence in Korea, the leaders proceeded to build contacts with similar groups; in the summer of 1923 they organized a lecture tour of the colony by two prominent Japanese Socialists.[19]

Doctrinal and tactical convictions caused considerable friction among the radical study clubs. This was a natural result of the rapid spread of diverse shades of radical ideology among Korean intellectuals at the time. Compounding the problem was the major split between organized Communist groups in exile. Both the Irkutsk and Shanghai factions sent representatives to the colony to support their claims to the Comintern that they were acting on official directives to establish a formal presence in the homeland. Yet the establishment of a Korean Communist party in Korea was not achieved until 1925. Thus, four years before the founding of the KCP, radical ideology had already established roots in Korea and had begun to evolve separately from the "orthodox" movement in exile. The significance of the radical study clubs and press in the colony lay, therefore, in their independent effect on the general tone of the nationalist movement between 1920 and 1925.

The majority of leftists had little connection with the Korean Communist movement in exile. They were, in fact, not orthodox Communists at all. They did not submit to party discipline, and, as the Comintern had already pointed out, "nationalism," that is, the liberation and independence of Korea, was their primary motivation.[20] As nationalists, revolutionary thought provided them with new perspectives on the problems of national liberation and the hope that this could be accomplished through revolutionary means. These study clubs were essentially elite debating societies, concerned with ideological nuances and less interested in actual organizing of mass participation. Nevertheless, there were opportunities to influence and control mass organizations already in existence. Their main preoccupation was to win over other nationalists to the radical banner. To accomplish this, radicals turned to the mainstream nationalist press and the creation of specialized radical journals.

Journalism was one of the main occupations open to Korean intellectuals after 1920. It was not surprising, therefore, to see the growing diversification of political viewpoints in the *Tonga ilbo* and *Chosŏn ilbo* as their staffs were expanded by returning students after 1920. Although the mainstream nationalist press was owned and operated by men of moderate political views, their editorial and reportorial staffs represented a cross-section of the intellectual community. Editors came and went, and as controversy over the cultural movement and general direction of the nationalist movement increased during 1923 and 1924, the papers attempted to balance their editorial line and provide features presenting alternative views on various issues. Articles criticizing the university movement or Korean ● production movement appeared on the same pages as the announcements of rallies and cultural movement propaganda.[21] Similarly, the editorial line of *Kaebyŏk* broadened from its initial interest in nationalism, panhumanism, and Ch'ŏndogyo philosophy to include important features by radical intellectuals. Ultimately, *Kaebyŏk* was shut down in 1926 because of its increasingly radical content.[22]

The Japanese censor, of course, was responsible ultimately for the content of publications. Interestingly enough, between 1920 and 1924 the censors were relatively tolerant. Authors would avoid certain catch phrases and direct reference to Marx, revolution, class warfare, and imperialism, but, as we shall see below, the overall message was clear. Such indirect writing diluted the effect of the radical message, but it clearly introduced new ideas and concepts into the intellectual docket of the period.

Radical intellectuals took advantage of the relaxed publication ● climate in the early 1920s. Between 1921 and 1923, four radical magazines obtained permits and created a sensation in the colony during their brief runs. *Proletariat* (*Musanja*, 1922), *New World* (*Sinch'ŏnji*, 1921–22), *Light of Korea* (*Chosŏn chigwang*, 1922), and *New Life* (Sinsaenghwal, 1922) all featured radical themes.[23] *Musanja* survived only three issues as the organ magazine of the Proletarian Alliance (*Musanja tongmaenghoe*), and *Sinch'ŏnji, Sinsaenghwal,* and *Chosŏn chigwang* were all closed within a year and a half of their first issues. Their effect on the colonial intellectual community, however, was enormous. For a brief period, the colonial press was opened to radical ideas, and a true dialogue among nationalists ensued. If anything, the early suppression of these magazines only increased the power of their message as students continued to pass among themselves copies of this "forbidden fruit" long after their suppression.[24]

Sinsaenghwal, the brain child of two leftist journalists, Kim Myŏng-sik and Sin Ilyong, was representative of early leftist journalism in Korea. Establishing an independent publishing house, the Sinsaengh-walsa, in January 1922, and inviting Pak Hŭido, a well-respected moderate nationalist, youth leader, and hero of the March First movement to act as ceremonial leader, Kim and Sin gained permission to publish an intellectual journal with little difficulty. From its first issue, however, they ran afoul of the censor. Eventually, they received a current affairs permit, broadening their permitted scope. But the

Japanese took exception to the radical content of almost every issue. The *Sinsaenghwal* writers ridiculed the cultural movement and hammered away at economic and social problems in the colony. Although the *Sinsaenghwal* group was nominally independent, the Japanese were well aware of its ties to radical intellectual societies and the Korean labor movement, and in November of 1922 the police repressed *Sinsaenghwal* and indicted six members of the staff for thought crimes.[25] The subsequent trial in January 1923 was the first trial of Socialists for thought crimes and signaled a growing repression of leftist thought in the colony.[26]

The Japanese were aware of the dangers increased leftist activity posed for political control, yet having inaugurated the cultural policy, they were reulctant to repress immediately the early radical magazines. Political analyst and consultant to the GGK, Aoyagi Nammei, had warned repeatedly that having allowed press freedoms it was imperative to be vigilant in controlling its content, pointing out the contradiction between allowing a press as a safety valve and the dangers inherent in the spread of radical ideology.[27] Abe Mitsuka, adviser to Governor General Saitō, had been monitoring the stiuation among Korean students in Tokyo and the nationalists in exile, and his warnings to Saitō in April 1921 were a prelude to the Japanese crackdown on leftist publications the following year.[28] Still, the Japanese remained cautious, not wanting to provoke further unrest in the colony. In June 1922, the head of colonial police, Maruyama Tsurukichi, issued a series of warnings to Korean publishers about social revolutionary content. He warned that criminal charges would be brought against writers as well as publishers if orders to follow voluntarily censorship guidelines were not heeded.[29]

As we have seen, the Japanese made good on their threat in November 1922 by revoking *Sinsaenghwal's* publication permit and prosecuting its major writers. In early 1923, *Sinch'ŏnji* suffered a similar fate.[30] In spite of the increasingly hostile stance toward the Left, the Japanese continued to tolerate a high level of radical participation in organizations and publishing. Until the passage of the strict Peace Preservation Law in 1925, the repression of radicals remained an ad hoc policy. The police continued to operate within the guidelines of the cultural policy, preferring to monitor closely a relatively open political arena and repressing selectively those whose intransigence forced their hand.

The brief flourishing of radical publications provides a vivid glimpse into the evolution of socialism among Korean intellectuals.

The selective repression meted out by the Japanese created a sensation among intellectuals in the colony and created the first martyrs on the Left. In so doing, the Japanese inadvertently gave leftists more publicity than they might have achieved through their own efforts. The closure of *Sinsaenghwal* stimulated a unified protest by Korean publishers and the first national organization of journalists.[31] But, more important, the Japanese repression validated the ideas contained in these publications in a curious way. The suppression of *Sinsaenghwal* came at the height of the university movement and the ecstatic early days of the Korean production movement. The Japanese highlighted the status quo orientation of these moderate nationalist projects by repressing its fiercest critics. Therefore, the growing repression of leftist writers further inflamed the passions of nationalist intellectuals already burning red-hot over the issue of cultural nationalism.

The Emerging Korean Socialist World View

The introduction of socialism to the Korean intellectual community had a profound effect on the debate over the future direction of the nationalist movement. Korean nationalists had heretofore assumed that the continued evolution of Korean society along the path followed by Western democracies would eventually prepare Korea for independence. Indeed, the primary focus of cultural nationalism was nation building, the preparation of the groundwork for an eventually successful demand for independence within this context. After 1920, the unanimity that characterized the intellectual climate at the time of the March First movement degenerated as leftists challenged this fundamental assumption. Up to 1920, an abiding faith in the power of democracy, science, liberalism, and reason combined with a desire to destroy obstacles to change had united Korean nationalists. This unity was shattered by leftists, who offered different solutions to the problem of nation building and independence as Marxist ideas gradually took hold among some intellectuals.

The situation in Korea paralleled the political furor in China during the May Fourth era.[32] Liberals in China, like cultural nationalists in Korea, envisaged a gradual program of educational reform and enlightenment. Critics in each country scoffed at such programs and demanded political and social revolution. Socialism in both China and Korea offered an alternate set of assumptions for analyzing the present conditions and a new vision of the future; as such, it changed the nature of the debate among nationalists over how to obtain independence and over what form the new nation could assume.

This trend is obvious in any survey of Korean periodicals in the period between 1922 and 1925. With the first editions of *Sinsaenghwal* in the spring of 1922 leading the way, the influence of socialism on intellectuals and journalists became increasingly apparent in *Kaebyŏk* and the daily newspapers. And although no coherent political line emerged among leftist writers, it is possible to obtain a sense of the changing intellectual tone within the domestic nationalist movement.

One core Socialist assumption that helped widen the intellectual controversy after 1920 was historical materialism. This concept as delineated by Marx and Engels held that the ultimate cause and great moving power of all important historic events could be found "in the economic development of society, in the changes in the mode of production and exchange, in the consequent division of society into distinct classes, and in the struggle of these classes against one another."[33] Acceptance of this view of history focused attention on objective conditions in society and in concert with Marx's projection of historical stages of development that predicted the ultimate fall of capitalism, this vision provided Korean leftists with a very different political focus.

Historical materialism diverted leftists from the popular emphasis on education and value transformation that was an important component of the cultural nationalist thesis. Early evidence of a shift in thinking about social development was contained in the "Prospectus" of *Sinsaenghwal*'s first edition in March 1922:

 Society is based on man. It should protect and preserve his life first of all. If we are to reconstruct [*kaejo*] society we must first reform man and if we are to reform man we must reform the basic conditions of his life. We must establish freedom and equality in the place of economic slavery and political-social repression. Through the management of a new life of freedom and equality— in accordance with world trends—Koreans must throw off the shackles of convention, economic slavery, and repressive political power and blaze the way for a new movement toward a new life.[34]

Although this statement reflects a continuation of the Confucian idea of reforming men as a precondition to social reconstruction, there is evidence of a new interest in basic objective conditions in society. Without much evidence of appreciation for the nature of capitalism, the author still managed to focus on "economic slavery" as an important root of contemporary social unrest.

Kim Myŏngsik, a founding member of *Sinsaenghwal,* youth leader, and early activist in the Korean Fraternal Labor Federation (Chosŏn nodong kongjehoe), illustrated his understanding of the importance of objective conditions in the April 1922 issue of the magazine.[35] In this issue, Kim asserted that failure to understand how social structure served as the context for change rendered the concept of cultural change meaningless: "We do not mean (speaking of cultural change) the substitution of new culture for the old but creation (of culture) on an entirely new plane, a qualitative leap. The flow of culture from feudal aristocratic to capitalist was all on the same plane, they were minority cultures. The new age is a labor culture or mass culture. The new culture will be derived from the spirit of the masses."[36]

Unlike the cultural nationalists, Kim used the terms *culture* and *spirit* in a qualitatively different manner. He clearly viewed historical development along materialist lines and by emphasizing the quality of culture that emanated from different historical stages, Kim turned the nationalist concern for transmitting new values on its head. Here, objective conditions led to the formation of distinctive levels of culture and, to Kim, continued cultural development in Korea without attention to its objective structural base would only replace one "elite" culture for another.[37]

Yi Sŏngt'ae, managing editor of *Sinsaenghwal* and frequent contributor to *Kaebyŏk* and the major nationalist papers, was more direct in his analysis of objective conditions of Korean society.[38] Asserting that a particular structure and culture characterized each historical epoch, Yi linked the uncertainty and misery in contemporary society to the economic changes attendant on modern civilization.[39] Just as the economic structure of capitalism had created misery and uncertainty in Korea, it had also spawned an attendant ideology that served only to buttress this system.[40] Therefore, Koreans should cling to ideas that would serve the future, and avoid the platitudes and compromise philosophy that supported the present system.[41]

These brief illustrations show how an emerging materialist view was beginning to alter the perception of contemporary politics for some Korean intellectuals. In the context of the discussion over future independence and contemporary social and political conditions, this view begged questions that were quite separate from the moderate nationalist focus on values, identity, and education. It was a short step from this emerging materialist view of history and development to a rejection of cultural development as a means toward independence or the amelioration of economic misery in Korean society. As we shall see in our discussion of the radical critique of cultural nationalism, it also led to the direct questioning of the moderate nationalist view of society, economics, and tactics for political liberation.

Inherent in a materialist view of history was the important concept of class struggle as the engine of change. Historical change was driven forward as the mode of production in society changed, producing class divisions and, ultimately, struggle between different classes. Therefore, analysis of class alignments and interests in this process was the key to understanding political reality. Like all Socialists in East Asia, Koreans had difficulty applying orthodox views of class struggle in a capitalist society to their situation because of Korea's lack of development. They accepted the importance of class struggle to political analysis, but they differed widely among themselves as to the implications of class theory for Korean society in its present state of development. Class analysis did, however, alter many intellectuals' perception of the national problem. By focusing on class relations a very different picture of the fundamental political and economic situation facing Korea, as well as the solution to these problems emerged.

One early example of emerging class analysis can be taken from an article in the first issue of *Sinsaenghwal* by Chŏng Paek. As others in the *Sinsaenghwal* group, Chŏng was well connected in leftist circles in the early 1920s. He was a member of the Proletarian Alliance (Musanja tongmaenghoe) and he helped organize the short-lived organ magazine *Proletariat (Musanja)* in 1922. After the closure of *Sinsaenghwal,* Chŏng continued his activities in the labor movement and in 1924 he participated in clandestine activities to form a Korean Communist party in the colony.[42] Within a discussion of the "spirit of the masses," Chŏng described major class divisions in the world as "two major streams, the capitalist and laboring class—set on a course of inevitable clash."[43] He restricted his argument to a general recitation of Marxist theory relative to the inevitable fall of capitalism. In discussing Korea, however, he despaired that the masses, here undifferentiated, had yet to gain any subjective awareness of their situation.[44] Chŏng ran square into the problem of applying Marxist theory to Korea's unique conditions. Korea, as an agrarian society with no significant proletariat class, would have to wait until such a time that "dominant world trends" in development would affect local conditions; however, in the end, the "great clash" was still inevitable.[45]

Yi Sŏngt'ae, in a broad discussion of the source and direction of culture, pursued Chŏng's analysis of the two great streams.[46] Yi asserted that culture embodied the "spirit" of society and was shaped by the special circumstances of each great historical epoch. Thus the "spirit" of modern times was shaped by the economic and social structure of capitalism; although the spirit of capitalism stressed "freedoms," these freedoms were limited to the propertied class. It was a freedom to exploit labor and use capital to their own advantage.[47] Therefore, Yi believed that Marx was correct in predicting the division of capitalist society into opposing classes; he believed this division had already begun to occur in Korea between the "haves and the have-nots": "Capitalist society eventually divides itself into two classes, the haves and the have-nots. Class culture is formed from the confrontation of these two classes. The capitalists use their advantage of money and leisure to exploit labor for their own profit. The culture of the capitalists is not a mass culture but the culture of one class imposed upon another."[48]

Yet Korean leftists soon encountered the problem of delineating the "haves and have-nots" in the context of Korean society. Marxist theory focused on the struggle between capitalists and a wage-earning, industrial proletariat; in Korea of the early 1920s, neither class had emerged in significant numbers. Of course, Japanese imperialism represented the long arm of monopoly capitalism, but there was only a small group of native capitalists then emerging in Korea.[49] Furthermore, there was only a small class of Koreans that could be objectively labeled as an urban proletariat. To solve this problem, Korean leftists continued to use the general categories of "propertied" (*yusanja*) and "propertyless" (*musanja*). This formula pitted the small minority of the rich, comprised of capitalists, landlords, and elements of an urban leisure class, against the overwhelming majority of poor Korean peasants and laborers. This view did not make for precise class analysis, but it satisfied the need of Korean socialists to delineate major class alignments.

Analyzing the power of the "haves" or propertied class in Korea society, Chŏng Paek disparaged both its oppression of the propertyless as well as the ideology created by the original bourgeois revolution to support this oppression. The bourgeois revolution was a revolt in the name of "property rights and freedom against the special privileges of the nobility and clergy," yet eventually the bourgeoisie forsook freedom for all classes to "protect their own special privileges."[50] Therefore, democratic theory, voting rights, and social welfare legislation, all aspects of Western capitalist societies, were not insitutions that guaranteed true freedom: they were ideas calculated to prevent revolution from below and maintain the system of power and privilege for a few.[51] In this way, Chŏng attacked the very body of political ideas that an entire generation of Korean nationalists had so admired. Indeed, it was precisely the gradual accumulation of these rights and the spread of democratic values that cultural nationalists advocated in their gradualist program.

Without a sizable Korean capitalist class to attack, and unable to attack directly Japanese imperialism because of censorship, leftists finessed the issue by hammering away at a composite Korean upper class made up of landlords, intellectuals, petit bourgeois elements, and the odd capitalist. This composite class was often described as a "parasitic, urban leisure class." A vivid description appeared in another anonymous article in *Kaebyŏk*:

> In the last ten years the so-called new culture and education boom has fed an explosive growth in the population of our cities. The cities are now crowded with students, entrepreneurs and merchants leading an unproductive life. Students, of course, are not producers, and even after graduation they remain idle. They stay on in the cities and sell land in order to support themselves, or they go to Tokyo for more education. Because they are the new educated elite and are "gentlemen," they reject Korean clothes in favor of Western garb, eat beef and drink Western liquor instead of native foods. The merchants, petty bureaucrats, and so-called independent businessmen also ape this life-style, selling their land to live a luxurious life.[52]

This illustration underscored the unproductive nature of the urban elite and their parasitic relationship to Korean producers. It also questioned their identity as Koreans. Not only were they class enemies of the Korean masses, their Western education and life style cast aspersion on their national loyalties. The essay amplified the parasitic nature of this class in the following passage:

> This leisure class lives on the sweat and blood of the farmers. Without feelings of gratitude they teach their own children in the schools and read their self-centered books, magazines and news-

papers made possible by the work of the peasants. In the end, they sell the peasants' land, leaving them without a means of sustenance. Finally, the parasitic leisure class approaches the point of killing off its host. But the leisure class is only committing suicide in its own wisdom, for if the peasantry is brought down, so too will the parasites perish.[53]

The few examples cited above give some idea as to the direction of early Korean Socialists' class analysis. The jumble of categories used appeared vividly in a 1924 article in *Kaebyŏk*:

> The first allegiance of the Socialists in Korea is to the problem of the confrontation between rich and poor, not a call for liberation of the nation. The small class of rich Koreans exploit the masses of workers and live an idle life based on the sweat and blood of the farmers. The propertyless classes must realize who the real enemy is. From this beginning, tenants must organize to oppose landlords. And in accord with the call "workers of the world unite" strive to oppose capitalists on all fronts be they Japanese or Korean.[54]

This passage reflected the difficulty Koreans encountered when applying orthodox Marxist categories of analysis to the Korean situation. The author called on workers of the world to unite, but "workers" here meant the propertyless masses composed mainly of peasants. And seeing no industrial, wage-earning class of any size in Korea, the author lumps them together with the peasantry. Furthermore, "rich Koreans" became a generic substitute for capitalists, and landlords were the only specific target mentioned against which to direct the pent-up frustrations of the propertyless classes. As we shall see, the job of organizing and leading the masses fell upon the shoulders of Socialist intellectuals who understood the real conditions in Korean society.

Korean radicals believed that their ultimate destiny was linked with the oppressed masses, however they were to be defined. They also believed that they occupied a unique position in Korean society as intellectuals. This belief was grounded, in part, in the importance of intellectuals and reverence for learning in traditional Korea. More important, it was also a product of their interpretation of the pivotal position of intellectuals in modern society. While the majority of intellectuals supported the dominant class in society, it was also possible for intellectuals to lead or align with progressive forces in society.

Chŏng Paek provided his interpretation of the role of intellectuals in the political process. He argued that many modern Korean intellectuals were deluded in their belief that they could maintain their neutrality in the coming struggle between oppressors and the oppressed. He continued, however, to assert the advantage of what he considered to be the "amphibious position" occupied by intellectuals in society; they could choose their side in the ultimate struggle: "We must have a union of intellectuals and the workers in order to build a new society. Intellectuals must shed their middle-class psychology and gain class consciousness. They must now choose their side."[55] Such a union of intellectuals and the masses would augment the power of the social revolution, just as vacillation and neutrality by middle-road intellectuals had hindered the cause of the October revolution in Russia.[56]

Choosing sides was only part of the problem. Which group, laborers or peasants, should be mobilized? With only a nascent labor movement, leftists continued to wrestle with the problem of defining the proletarian masses, which led them invariably back to the Korean peasantry. There was a decidedly populist flavor to many articles that stressed the purity of spirit inherent in the peasantry. Just as they criticized the parasitic urban leisure class, Korean leftists extolled the virtues of peasant life as untainted by "urban corruption." One anonymous author went so far as to advocate a Return to Agriculture Movement (Kwinong undong) on the model of the Russian *narodniks*.[57] This populist argument can be compared with similar antiurban, propeasant sentiments of Li Ta-chao and other early Chinese Marxists.[58] Appearing at the height of the publicity surrounding the Korean production movement, this plan argued that the unique agrarian nature of Korean society should determine the direction of future political movements. As a nation of farmers, it was foolhardy to ape European development in the interest of capitalist growth. Only by merging with the agrarian masses and devising programs to alleviate their misery could Korea regain its independence.[59] Sin Paeg'u, committed Socialist, activist within the radical Tuesday Society, and participant in the first Korean Communist party in the colony, offered his view of the necessity for merging with the peasant masses.[60] To Sin, the masses represented the true backbone of Korean society and indeed, he directly equated Korean peasantry with the nation. Peasants had a real stake in the future, "having suffered hardships, spilled their blood in the fields, and having endured suffocating poverty."[61] Sin's focus on the spirit of the peasantry was reminiscent of earlier nationalist writing on the importance of the folk to Korean national identity. Sin believed that an intangible "spirit" of the peasantry exemplified not only the nation, but their destiny as the class upon which the future society would be built as well.[62]

Another example of this populist view of the agrarian masses appeared in the January 1924 issue of *Kaebyŏk:*

> The master of Korea is not the leisure class of forty or fifty thousand people, nor is it the commercial or landowning class. The true masters of Korea are the fifteen million peasants living on three million farms. Whatever system or movement ignores this fact loses all meaning, moreover, is truly evil. The fall of Korea was not the result of political, cultural, or commercial failure; it was the result of the fall of the peasantry. The life of the nation is the life of the farmer, its civilization is an agrarian civilization. Korea's wealth is the wealth of the land. In this fact lies the uniqueness of Korea.[63]

This statement expresses clearly the centrality of the peasantry to all facets of national life. Although the importance of the peasantry in the future class struggle was implied, even more interesting was the populist flavor of the language. The author was groping, it seemed, for a sense of national uniqueness not only in identity but also in the unique nature of the coming revolution.

This brief sampling of leftist writings shows that the intellectual agenda in the early 1920s was growing more complex. Although the examples shown above offer divergent interpretations of Marx and certainly little unanimity as to how Marxism should be applied to the special conditions of colonial Korea, they do indicate the growing acceptance of certain fundamental Marxist assumptions about historical development and the nature of class conflict in society. Korean leftists had to determine how social revolution might be accomplished in an agrarian society. In doing so, they began to speculate about the political and economic significance of the peasant masses, equating them, eventually, with future revolutionary movements.

The introduction of socialism to the intellectual debates in the colony placed the assertions of the cultural nationalists in a completely new light. Ideologically, Korean leftists writing in *Sinsaenghwal* and *Kaebyŏk* raised important questions as to the future course of Korean politics. From the beginning, new concepts of how society evolved and what economic forces shaped future development raised serious questions about the efficacy of cultural and educational movements as a solution to the problem of national independence. Belief in the ultimate collapse of capitalism diverted attention away from a slavish attempt to follow the path of evolution blazed by the West. Furthermore, class analysis raised nasty questions about the class interests of those who believed in gradualist cultural development or the strengthening of Korean capitalism as a solution to the problem of independence.

The passionate attachment of early leftist writers to the Korean peasantry, both as the core of the future revolution and as the repository of the true Korean national spirit, indicated that although they sought to expound an ideology of world revolution, they approached the exposition of this internationalist philosophy as nationalists. Indeed, most Korean Socialists had come originally to the study of Marx as nationalists searching for a solution to the problem of independence. In addition, they often studied classical Marxism in its Leninist form.[64] Thus, they grappled with the problem of national liberation at the same time as they attempted to apply Marxist analysis to their own society.

In the period before the formation of an organized Communist party in Korea, the primary influence of socialism was ideological. As Koreans wrote didactically on the major lessons of Marxism, its central assumptions laid a basis for controversy over the tactics and future of political movements in the colony. And as leftists widened their campaign to spread their newfound ideology in the colony, they focused their attention on the mainstream of the nationalist movement. The result was a scathing attack on the moderate cultural nationalist program.

The Radical Critique of Cultural Nationalism

The search for new truths within the classics of socialism and a growing appreciation of Leninist political tactics laid the basis for growing criticism of the present course of the Korean nationalist movement in the colony. The specific target of radical criticism was the cultural movement. At issue was not the overriding goal of Korean cultural autonomy or eventual political independence but disagreement over the ultimate political utility of a cultural movement for class liberation and the overthrow of Japanese imperialism. Indeed, radicals

questioned the class interest of the cultural movement's major propo-
nents, charging that the ultimate result of cultural nationalism would
be the perpetuation of imperialist oppression. Radicals questioned
ultimately the very culture such a movement would produce. Provid- •
ing their own answer, critics concluded that the cultural movement
would only strengthen the position of moderate intellectual leadership
within the continued evolution of Japanese imperialist rule.[65]

The appearance of Yi Kwangsu's *Kaejoron* stimulated a fierce
reaction by the left wing of the nationalist movement. Yi's pessimism
and elitism offended leftists' patriotic sensibilities, and his gradualist
tactics provoked their political and theoretical objections. Yi was the
first to admit the defeatist tone of the piece, but based his thesis on the
belief that Koreans had yet to demonstrate a true capacity for unified
action or the political capability to maintain their independence.
Therefore, according to the *Kaejoron*, long-term cultural and educational development was a necessary precondition to regaining independence.

It was precisely this attitude that offended many patriots in Korea.
If Korean society was without merit, why bother to transform its
culture at all? Such an opinion was offered by Sin Sang'u writing in
Sinsaenghwal in June 1922, a month after the publication of the
Kaejoron. Most offensive to Sin was Yi's callous and arrogant
judgment on the level of Korean civilization.[66] Dismissing Yi's charge
that Korean civilization still "bordered on barbarism," Sin criticized
Yi for disparaging the great historical and spiritual heritage of the
Korean people. How could Yi believe that a cultural movement could
undo the cumulative effort of 5,000 years of historical development?
Furthermore, Sin asserted that Koreans had nothing to be ashamed of,
considering general patterns of development worldwide.[67]

Sin concluded his critique of Yi with a stirring recitation of past
Korean cultural and political achievements. According to Sin, Yi's
formula for cultural development, based as it was on a mistaken
judgment of Korean capabilities and strengths, was tantamount to a
denial of his own identity. It is clear by Sin's remarks that, to some at
least, Yi's *Kaejoron* bordered on a total rejection of past Korean
accomplishments. If past cultural development had not laid a base for
the future of an independent Korea, upon what did Yi propose to
build?

As we can see by this early attack on the *Kaejoron*, some intellectuals were openly offended by Yi's attitude toward Korean culture.
Implicit in this attack was a hint of the *sadae* issue and past cultural

subservience to China. Was Yi advocating a similar bias by supporting a cultural movement to spread Western ideas and values? Certainly the cultural nationalists were vulnerable to this charge, given their heavy emphasis on modern education and Western liberalism. Yet, by pointing out in great detail the failures of Korean culture and linking the causes of colonial subjugation to flaws in Korean society, the *Kaejoron* came close to a curious backhanded justification of Japanese rule. To Sin Sang'u, Yi's theory was "base and worthless," an "insult" to the nation.[68]

Sin Ilyong, writing in the next issue of *Sinsaenghwal,* shared his colleague's disgust with Yi's worship of things Western, but his rejoinder to the *Kaejoron* was primarily on theoretical grounds.[69] To Sin Ilyong, Yi's premise that Korea's problems were primarily spiritual in nature was a fallacy. He asserted that from a materialist point of view the concept of reconstruction (*kaejo*) could not be limited to spiritual matters—primary social and economic structural problems also had to be addressed. Even if spiritual reconstruction was successful, and the thinking of the entire intelligentsia was reformed, without fundamental structural change the same elite would remain in power and the original structural conditions responsible for colonial repression would remain unchanged. Sin lambasted Yi for exhibiting a callous intellectualism that he believed anesthetized the "forming consciousness of the people."[70]

Sin Ilyong also criticized Yi's political naïveté with regard to organizations and ideology. A central theme of the *Kaejoron* was that strong organizations would drive the future transformation based on the ideal of "reconstructionism" (*Kaejojuŭi*). Sin was dumfounded by Yi's assertion that his organization could "rise above politics." Since organization is politics and the fundamental means for the class in power to maintain control, Sin charged that Yi's organization would simply be a means of perpetuating the present class alignment in Korea to the betterment of intellectuals.[71]

Sin saved his most scathing criticism for the end. He was outraged at Yi's belief that the Korean national character somehow placed no value on freedom. At the root of Yi's idea of spiritual transformation was the idea that Koreans should imitate the English because of their spirit of freedom and justice. Sin charged that only someone totally blind to current affairs or completely befuddled by the concept of freedom could make such an assertion. First, Yi obviously knew nothing about England and its political system, which oppressed the majority in the service of capitalism. And in terms of individual versus national freedom, Sin asked if Yi truly understood the fundamental nature of colonialism. How did the English domination of Egypt, India, and Ireland fit the supposed "value of freedom" inherent in the Anglo-Saxon race? Was Yi suggesting that Koreans should have their own colonies as well?[72]

Sin believed that Yi's reconstructionism was a concept that supported capitalist oppression in Korea. In spite of his plea for national unity, Sin could not accept the idealism and naïveté implicit in an argument that ignored structural and political reality in favor of a program of spiritual regeneration that would only unify like-minded intellectuals within the present system. In addition to its theoretical flaws, Sin joined the chorus of nationalists that were offended by Yi's pessimistic analysis of Korea's political culture and his excessive veneration of Western values explicit in his rampant Anglophilia.

As we have already noted, Yi's *Kaejoron* was a distillation of a broader consensus among moderate intellectuals. By the time of its publication in May 1922, a serious effort was already under way to create broad public support for education and native production within the framework of Japanese rule. Two months before, the first edition of *Sinsaenghwal* had already attacked the cultural movement as a serious distraction from the urgent task of social revolution. In a word, the *Sinsaenghwal* writers denied that cultural movements could have any lasting effect on the political situation in Korea. And as the cultural movement gained momentum, others joined them in attacking its goals and tactics.

Sin Paeg'u could find little use for the cultural movement writ large. In March 1922, before the consolidation of many separate cultural organizations into the university and Korean production movements had begun, Sin made his views on the cultural movement brutally clear:

> There is this thing called by everyone the culture movement. The cultural movement is vague and obscure; it is any organization hanging out a sign-post, financially supported by the aristocracy [*kwijok*]. It is a movement that, like so many controlled political parties, accommodates friendship networks from work or school. The culture movement is a bourgeois movement of people who collect money from the masses to fawn upon the old aristocracy and then disband after six months or so. The culture movement is dreaming of independence in the morning, lecturing about self-rule [*chach'i*] in the evening, and advocating participation in government to protect advantages [*ch'amjŏnggwŏn hodŭk*] the

> next day. So broad and amorphous is the movement, understanding it is impossible. Is this a useful movement for the property-less?[73]

This criticism of cultural organizations was part of Sin's argument for the formation of an intellectual vanguard to lead the masses. Sin despaired, however, that too few intellectuals understood the need for working with the common people. The intellectual vanguard needed to stir the masses to action by stimulating a true consciousness of their position in society. But, according to Sin, the majority of intellectuals in Korea alienated themselves from the masses by "waving their college degrees from Japan, the Unites States, and Europe and establishing countless do-nothing organizations that pandered to their own vanity." He continued:

> One gets the feeling they are the new aristocracy. They dominate the masses directly and indirectly—temporizing for the moment with false words, they deceive the people and advocate self-serving causes. If one lands in jail for work in an organization for one or two years, they clamor about bravery and nobility. Yet their deceit, arrogance, and lack of sincerity is blatantly obvious to the masses. Look at the suffering of the masses, wandering and begging. Yet, they don't boast, and they don't expose the baseness of this elite psychology.[74]

This brutal attack focused on the very intellectuals who formed the mainstream of the nationalist movement in the colony. Clearly, Sin rejected the political value of intellectual organizations. The moderates focused on independence (*tongnip*), self-rule (*chach'i*), or culture (*munhwa*) movements, but "few were concerned with the social or labor movements."[75] Sin believed that only social and labor movements held any promise for changing the abysmal conditions of the majority of Koreans and he worried that the proliferation of useless cultural organizations only confused Korean youth as to the correct direction for political action.

Sin's attack was one reason for the almost immediate notoriety of *Sinsaenghwal*. Heretofore, nationalist intellectuals had seldom denounced each other using such explicit language. Moreover, questioning the organizational and personal motives of cultural movement leaders in terms of political results raised disturbing questions. Membership in education and cultural organizations per se was no longer automatically coincidental with nationalist leadership. As Chŏng Paek had already observed, it was an "intellectual delusion" to believe that ideas and values could affect concrete political changes.[76] In a more sinister vein, this discussion raised the question as to whether or not educational and cultural movements might even support the colonial status quo.

In the same month that the university movement leaders announced their goal of creating a national university, an unsigned article in *Kaebyŏk* questioned anew the utility of educational movements. This indictment charged the education movement with ignoring the rural masses:

> What relationship is there between the current education move-
> ment and the rural masses? Furthermore, of what significance are
> newspapers, magazines, speeches, and publications to the peas-
> antry? Since these activities constitute the so-called cultural
> movement, what meaning can it have to peasants? It is not a bad
> thing per se, but it is merely the monopoly of the forty of fifty
> thousand who constitute the leisure class—neither the leisure
> class, bourgeoisie, nor landlord class are the masters of Korea; the
> masters of Korea reside in three million peasant households. Any
> movement that ignores this fact is meaningless.[77]

Such statements highlighted the growing separation between nationalist intellectuals who advocated modern education as a cure-all for
Korea's troubles and the rural peasantry who had little hope of
participating in the new urban culture of the colony. Cultural movements might be an excellent way to raise national consciousness and
unify the stratum of society that could afford the new schools, but the
process of reaching the bulk of the population in this manner was
necessarily long and incremental. Meanwhile, how did nationalist
leaders intend to solve the pressing problems of poverty and ignorance
that were endemic to Korean peasant life?

The relevance of the university movement to the Korean peasantry
emerged as a hotly debated subject at the March 1923 Conference of
Korean Youth Groups (Chŏn Chosŏn ch'ŏngnyŏndan taehoe). Leaders from the Seoul Youth Association (Seoul ch'ŏngnyŏnhoe) dominated the proceedings; the final resolutions on education passed by the
conference reflected vividly their Socialist stance. They charged that
the educational system was just another means of the capitalist class to
maintain their control of society. Too often, students were treated as
commodities with no consideration for individual needs and desires.

Moreover, youth leaders were angered that upper schools were monopolized by the propertied classes while lower schools were becoming vocational institutions to supply the manpower requirements of the capitalist economy. The resolution summed up the conference position as follows:

> Schools should not be places built for the propertied class, they must be a place for the creation of men of the masses. Schools don't produce commodities, they shape people. The uneducated masses, heretofore treated as commodities, are people who wish to learn, to express ideals and live as men. Therefore we resolutely reject the basic direction of the present educational system and offer the following resolutions:
>
> a. We reject the preservation and establishment of educational organs that exist for the purpose of promoting technical skills based on the idea of exploiting the people.
>
> b. We will work to create and expand general nonrepressive and nonspecialized education.
>
> c. We will work to establish night schools and weekend schools dedicated to developing class consciousness of the workers in order to oppose capitalism.[78]

This resolution was a blow to the university movement because it compromised the movement's standing with the important youth group constituency. As the resolution made clear, some youth leaders felt that education must become a tool for instilling class consciousness in the people. By juxtaposing the role of colonial education in meeting manpower requirements with statements about the Korean elite's dominance of higher education, the youth leaders directly questioned the ultimate motives of the education movement. One might ask on reading these resolutions—who would benefit most by the creation of a national university? Moreover, the demand for mass literacy projects and expanded opportunities for educating the lower classes turned the education philosophy of cultural nationalism on its head. The current situation demanded mass education, not the upper-level indoctrination and training of future cultural nationalist cadres.

Although there is no direct link between the attack by the youth conference and the declining fortunes of the university movement, it is clear that the resolution scored a direct hit on the prestige of the movement. Ironically, the members of the youth groups attending the conference were almost uniformly beneficiaries of the new educational establishment in colonial Korea. That they would militantly reject a movement that promised them future benefit is evidence of the importance they were beginning to attach to alternate political views. It was also a direct challenge to the older moderate nationalist leadership, as well as a demonstration of the growing attraction of socialism among young Korean intellectuals.

The Korean production movement also ran afoul of radical critics in the colony. One early attack on the movement directly questioned its ability to unite the bulk of the population under its banner. The problem, once again, was the class base and narrow interests of the project. In spite of the hot air generated by university and production movement leaders, these movements remained tied to narrow interest groups and had little chance of producing the mass unity required for the successful transformation of Korean society.[79] Furthermore, projects like the Korean production movement did not address the core problem in the colony, the plight of the Korean masses. As another article asserted, promoting Korean goods required broad support; the movement, however, was perceived by many people as a mere product of the leadership class (*chido kyegŭp*).[80] Returning to the popular metaphor of society as a critically ill patient, this article suggested that a radical cure was the only solution to the pervasive economic and political malaise in colonial society, and the palliatives offered by the Korean production and university movements fell far short of offering a remedy.[81]

Like the university movement, the Korean production movement was singled out for detailed criticism in 1923. Yi Sŏngt'ae, writing in the *Tonga ilbo,* presented a distillation of the major leftist objections to the movement in an article entitled "The Self-Serving Movement of the Bourgeoisie." The following excerpt represents the core of Yi's argument:

> Just who is behind the idea of the Korean production movement? Is it not the intellectuals of the middle class, a class that is unable to throw off its consciousness of social position and class identity and are the true representatives of their own profit interests, who are behind the movement? Frankly speaking, it is unnecessary to speak to the workers about promoting Korean goods. They have always done so. The bourgeoisie wear Western clothes made of fine silks and drink whiskey and brandy. Not the common man. The common man wears cotton and hemp and drinks coarse native liquors, not out of patriotism, but because cheap and shoddy goods are the only things he can afford in daily life.

Taken at face value, developing Korean productivity and resurrecting the Korean market in order to establish economic independence is all well and good. We must ask, however, to whose benefit is this movement directed? Clearly, there is a peculiar political taint behind the nationalistic and patriotic slogans of the Korean production movement. Because of the economic power of imperialism—[censored]—the Korean bourgeoisie assumes the attitude of following along with nationalist movements with profit in their minds. Mindful of the power of foreign capitalism, a power that can dominate Korean capitalism, Korean capitalists turn to patriotism and nationalism to buttress their own weak position vis-à-vis foreign economic interests. Thus with their own advantage in mind, and mouthing sentimental platitudes of patriotism, they hungrily seek aid from the working class, a class that stands in natural opposition to them. However, the enlightened members of the working class are well aware that the Korean capitalists and the foreign capitalists are on the same side of the line in the battle of class struggle.[82]

Yi expressed both nationalist and Socialist sentiments in his forceful critique of the Korean production movement. As a nationalist, Yi was contemptuous of the movement's patriotic appeal to the masses to use Korean goods exclusively; given the tastes and life style of the urban bourgeoisie, this appeal was blatant hypocrisy. This passage illustrated clearly Yi's identification with the masses as the true core of the nation. And his theoretical objections to the movement reinforced his disgust with the Korean production movement leadership's cynical manipulation of nationalist slogans.[83]

Yi believed that the Korean production movement was a pathetic attempt by the weak Korean bourgeoisie to strengthen its position in competition with predatory Japanese capitalism. Therefore, the Korean production movement served only the class interests of its leadership. Although Yi admitted that the Korean bourgeoisie had an interest in national liberation, this interest was calculated in terms of its struggle with Japanese capitalism. It was clear to Yi that in the end class loyalties would predominate, and he became one of the first to publicly charge the moderate nationalist leadership with collaborating with Japanese imperialists. At this point he was unwilling to offer a Leninist solution of temporary alliance with the Korean bourgeoisie. As we shall see, these ideas did emerge in 1924 and 1925 as a solution to the growing ideological split within the nationalist movement.

Nevertheless, the damage done to the Korean production movement by such attacks was already evident. As we saw in chapter 3, the movement was plagued from the beginning by organizational and political problems. The attack on the core interests of its leadership as well as the short-term nature of its goals added fuel to a fire already well established. The Korean production movement depended on a solid front of nationalist organizations to be effective. The leftist critique only further exacerbated squabbles among nationalist leaders and ultimately weakened the movement.

The examples cited above reveal the nature of the radical critique of cultural nationalism. From the theoretical criticism offered, it was clear that solutions to the national problem were open to wide interpretation. Moreover, the unanimity among nationalist intellectuals that followed the March First demonstrations was fast disappearing as a growing number of intellectuals began to drift toward socialism and involvement in radical groups.

Critics of culture nationalism grounded their attack on Socialist theory. Although widely variable, the theoretical objections to cultural nationalism seemed to stem from a new appreciation for historical materialism and the theory of class conflict. Increasingly, cultural and educational solutions to the national problem were seen by the leftist minority as hopelessly naive and narrow-minded. Cultural movements might alter the outer forms of political behavior, but they could never affect the fundamental structure of society from which the core problem originally stemmed.

That the projects of the cultural movement only strengthened the upper class monopoly of power in colonial society was even more objectionable. Few peasants would benefit from the creation of a national university, yet the idea was attractive to propertied Koreans, whose sons faced limited opportunities for higher education in the colony. Similarly, the Korean production movement promised to strengthen Korean capitalism, but it offered little hope for ameliorating peasant poverty and political subordination.

The emergence of the specter of class interest in 1922 introduced a vexing problem for nationalist leaders, whose motives had never before been so decisively challenged. Suddenly, their prestige and sincerity as a nationalist elite was being questioned. Although presented in theoretical form, there was still a strongly nationalist flavor to the leftist critique, for it was not representing a unified party line, and the Marxist base to its arguments, while clearly visible, remained fragmented and ambiguous. The concern of the Left however, for the masses as the true representatives of the nation stands out. By criticizing urban, Westernized intellectuals who were alienated from their own culture, the Left showed its distrust of the merging Korean bourgeoisie's economic interests as well as their national loyalties. Moreover, the Left rejected the cultural nationalist claim that their projects would serve to strengthen Korean national identity. Critics of cultural nationalism saw themselves as champions of the new political truths of Marxism, but they also envisaged themselves as the true leaders of the nation. Not only were they offended by cultural nationalist elitism and narrow-mindedness, they saw no potential in this movement for solving the immediate problem of national liberation.

The acrimony and bitterness produced by the radical critique accelerated the fragmentation of the Korean nationalist leadership into antagonistic factional camps. Although the cultural nationalists had succeeded briefly in producing the largest unified nationalist movement since the March First demonstrations, by 1923 consensus disintegrated as the cultural movement faltered under the ideological attack from the Left. In the next few years, this serious ideological split deepened within in the domestic nationalist movement.

Charges of accommodation or, worse yet, outright collaboration with Japanese rule became increasingly frequent in 1924 and 1925. And as the university and Korean production movements became moribund, nationalists began to jockey for position in an acrimonious atmosphere of charge and countercharge. The ultimate charge of collaboration was based on earlier attacks on the class interests of the cultural nationalist movement. Thus, as the cultural movement staggered under the weight of the leftist assault as well as the indifference of the masses, there was a growing sense of crisis among nationalist intellectuals. It is to the perceptions of this intellectual crisis and proposals for its resolution that we now must turn.

CHAPTER 5

Intellectual Crisis in Colonial Korea

Clearly, the ambiguity of the cultural nationalist line with regard to Japanese rule was a major problem within the movement. If gradualist tactics necessitated a long period of national development, what, then, should be done about the issue of national independence? Certainly this should be the primary goal for all nationalists, and its resolution could not be postponed indefinitely. On this issue, as we have seen, the nationalist intellectuals had become split to the point that the moderates' nationalist credentials were being seriously questioned. In 1924, the controversy over cultural nationalism came to a head, and in the following years both radicals and moderates cast about for a way to reunite the national liberation movement. The incident that precipitated the crisis within the nationalist movement was the publication of a controversial article in January 1924 by the principal architect of the cultural nationalist line, Yi Kwangsu. The ensuing controversy stimulated a new debate marked by charge and countercharge of accommodation and collaboration on the issue of Japanese rule and a search for a way to reunite national liberation forces in the colony.

The "Minjokchŏk Kyŏngnyun" and Accommodation

In the midst of the controversy over the ultimate intent and purpose of the cultural nationalist programs, Yi Kwangsu published a five-part editorial in the *Tonga ilbo* intended as a clarification and amplification of his by then controversial thesis on national reconstruction.[1] The series, entitled "National Statecraft" ("Minjokchŏk kyŏngnyun"), precipitated a short-lived boycott of the newspaper, Yi's resignation from its editorial board, and his ultimate "excommunication" from the nationalist movement. In addition to its grandiose title and tone resplendent with Yi's characteristic vague, social engineering formulae, "National Statecraft" (hereafter, *Kyŏngnyun*) startled intellectual circles by baldly advocating action within limits acceptable to the present colonial system. To the critics of cultural nationalism, this was proof positive of the movement's abnegation of national liberation for accommodation to colonial rule.

137

As we have seen, the ideology of cultural nationalism had always implied future independence. Yi's assertions in the *Kyŏngnyun,* however, made in the context of the already bitter denunciation of the two principal cultural nationalist programs, confirmed the suspicions of the movement's critics that such activity served only to consolidate and advance the interests of the bourgeois elite within the confines of colonial society. But after Yi's article appeared in January 1924, advocates of moderate cultural programs were placed increasingly on the defensive. Moreover, because of Yi's close association with the cultural nationalist thesis, the motives of the entire movement came under increased suspicion, and given the previous attacks on the movement, it was not long before the charge of accommodation escalated to an outright denunciation of collaboration. This brought the smoldering controversy over cultural nationalism to a head, and, ultimately, crystallized the deep split in the nationalist movement.

In his article, Yi called for the creation of a master plan for the future development of the nation.[2] This master plan had to be scientific and inclusive. Using the unfortunate analogy—given the increasing criticism of the Korean bourgeoisie—of a large company, Yi asserted that a people needed a comprehensive organization to accomplish any objective. Without a single mass organization, there would be no consensus and, therefore, continued factional strife. In addition, an organization was necessary to implement action on common projects. Yi thus offered again the cure-all of a single mass organization to solve the seemingly endemic factional divisions within the Korean nationalist movement.

Yi's "Great Association" (*tae kyŏlsa*) would divide itself between interdependent political, economic, and educational functions. In terms of the political aspects of his organization, Yi believed the first priority was to "gain national rights within the colonial system."[3] By "national rights" Yi meant that the principal political goal was to create and expand Korean organizations within the guidelines of present colonial policy and to achieve positive economic and educational results.[4] Ignoring the contradiction of "national rights" within a colonial system, Yi seemed to be saying that in spite of colonial government regulation of all organizational life, Koreans could maximize their efforts within the limits set by the Japanese by coordinating all existing organizations under the umbrella of one great association.

Yi was more explicit in the third installment. In discussing the economic problems facing Korean society, Yi concluded that "as a matter of life or death—Koreans had to create a program that worked within the limits of the present system."[5] Admitting that such a statement had heretofore been "unutterable," Yi asserted boldly that the economic crisis facing Korean enterprises demanded a realistic assessment of what could be done immediately. He argued that since infant Korean industries lacked protective tariffs and other benefits that might be forthcoming from a sovereign Korean government, it was necessary to pool resources and stimulate economic development from within. He reminded his readers of the already existing Korean production movement and the necessity of channeling the buying power of ordinary Koreans to stimulate native production.

Yi appended, however, a more forceful appeal to the familiar rhetoric on native production. He believed that Koreans needed to develop large companies to compete successfully with Japanese capitalism. To this end, he urged the pooling of capital to support larger, more successful enterprises. The economic arm of the Great Association was to be the mechanism to aggregate existing capital as well as a device to direct capital toward productive and profitable ventures. Therefore, without artifice or apology, Yi linked the fortunes of native capitalists with the future of the Korean nation. In addition, he anticipated his critics by asserting that whatever one thought of the national or class loyalties of Korean capitalists, they must be included in the overall plan.[6] Yi saw no contradiction here because he believed that economic leaders would be responsive to the political consensus of the overall organization.

The third and basic component of Yi's great plan was education, because without fundamental knowledge and an understanding of political rights, neither the political or economic goals of the movement could be achieved. Again, Yi intensified his stand on education already laid out in detail in the "Minjok kaejoron." In the fourth installment on "National Statecraft," Yi placed practical, utilitarian education ahead of national consciousness raising.[7] What made European nations superior was the spread of "scientific consciousness" (*kwahakchŏk ŭisik*) among all classes. Thus, Yi envisaged educational movements as a means to raise the level of practical skills among the peasantry by mobilizing and training a cadre of teachers to be sent among the masses. Yi believed that an educational revolution was necessary to elevate the common people by fostering habits of political association and economic skills.

Yi tied his argument together in the last installment by describing how the three arms of the great association were interrelated.[8] The political arm would channel the collective will toward accomplishing national development by encouraging and articulating consensus. To reflect the consensual goals of society, the political arm would have to develop a mass following that involved a broad spectrum of the population. Necessarily, the intellectual and economic elite would take the lead, and as peasants were drawn to educational and economic organizations they would, in turn, spread the goals of the organization downward. Educational groups would prepare the peasantry for political life by encouraging techniques for village self-rule (*nongch'on chach'i*); in this way, political and educational movements would be complementary.

Yi envisaged a huge economic movement managing all of Korean industry. He hoped this organization would be a focus for capital formation to develop a great industrial base. The base of this organization had to be peasants participating in village cooperatives. Such village-level economic organizations would bring peasants together for educational enlightenment programs as well as provide a new focus for political life. They would also be instrumental in teaching economic self-determination and spreading scientific knowledge. According to Yi, the economic movement would be the most difficult to nurture. Therefore, he proposed to begin with education, calling on underemployed intellectuals and students to form a vanguard willing to sacrifice in the cause of enlightenment.[9]

In summary, Yi proposed a very loose coordination among the three arms of his great association. A governing body would be necessary, but, given the political limits in colonial society, it was necessary to give the economic and educational organizations "functional independence"; if either assumed an overt political coloration the entire organization might be repressed by the colonial authorities.[10] Yi worried that direct confrontation with the Japanese would jeopardize the significant gains made since 1920; what was needed was a plan, a statecraft, that would focus the energies of all Korean organizations toward the singular goal of national development. He offered his plan as a blueprint for action.[11]

If he was hopeful for a positive response to his proposal, he was bitterly mistaken. Whereas his earlier proposals had helped spark action by moderate nationalists and, concurrently, intense debate, the *Kyŏngnyun* fell on deaf ears. Moreover, the overall tone of open accommodation provoked bitter denunciation of Yi by leftists and compromised his cultural nationalist defenders. Yi's thesis on national rights compromised the goal of independence by resonating with his earlier praise of the concept of commonwealth and cultural autonomy in British colonies.[12] To speak of national rights within the confines of Japanese sovereignty enraged independence advocates as much as it must have pleased the colonial authorities. Yi compounded this gaffe by asserting that peasants required basic training in political association, presumably an understanding of the political boundaries defined by the colonial system. Yi further betrayed his own moderate allies in the cultural movement by asserting that national consciousness raising should not be a primary goal of education. This assertion ran counter to the long-established nationalist goal of nurturing a strong national identity. It was fine to propose the strengthening of scientific consciousness in society, but by combining this with a basic tutorial on civics, Yi's plan began to sound like a movement to socialize the masses toward compliance with colonial rule.

Yi's economic ideas were also patently obnoxious to many nationalists, not to mention the more radical critics of the Korean production movement. The assumption that the nationalist movement would be better organized as a giant corporation added fuel to fires already destroying nationalist unity. Indeed, the insistence that businessmen would play a major role in his Great Association did not comfort those who already viewed Korean capitalists as collaborators. Yi anticipated his critics by maintaining that it was necessary to strengthen national capital to create an economic base for national life. Yet he was either unaware of or chose to ignore how this contradicted his political program, which directly acknowledged Japanese sovereignty. Finally, although Yi made soothing noises about the critical importance of involving the Korean peasantry in his grand scheme, they remained in his mind subordinated to the intellectual and economic elite. Clearly, Yi believed that peasant participation in what was supposed to be a movement to unify all Koreans would come only after a lengthy period of indoctrination.

Although Yi denied any premonition of the reaction his series would provoke, he left for Peking and meetings with gradualist exile leader An Ch'angho the week his series appeared, and he didn't return to Korea until April. Asked years later about the furor over the *Kyŏngnyun*, Yi recalled that his ultimate "excommunication" from nationalist circles stemmed from the controversy of January 1924.[13] Furthermore, Yi defended the newspaper itself saying "that the *Kyŏngnyun* was simply an attempt to concretize ideas previously expressed—and that it was not the expression of any group or organization."[14]

As Yi consulted with his mentor in Peking, his critics, at home and in exile, were expressing a different opinion. Whether or not Yi claimed sole authorship of the *Kyŏngnyun*, its appearance as a lead editorial in the *Tonga ilbo* provoked suspicion that the paper was swinging toward an accommodationist line. On February 20, representatives of ten student groups in Tokyo called for a formal boycott of the newspaper.[15] The boycott was provoked by intense discussion over the *Kyŏngnyun* and an additional editorial published on January 29 entitled "On Political Associations and Movements."[16] The Tokyo students listed their grievances and called for youth associations in Korea to join them in the boycott.

The reaction against the assumed shift of the *Tonga ilbo* toward accommodationism continued into the spring. The Korean Labor Farmer Federation (Chosŏn nonong ch'ong tongmaeng) condemned the *Tonga ilbo* in the strongest terms; resolutions passed by the league's Provisional Assembly on April 20 charged the paper with being "obstructionist," a "temple to reformism and the cultural movement."[17] The assembly intensified this attack by calling in the same resolution for the abolition of all pro-Japanese organizations, many of them recently federated in the All Parties Local Notables' Association (Kakp'a yuji yŏnmaeng). The debates held on the twentieth concluded with a broad attack on the class enemies of workers and peasants, and the assembly was halted abruptly by the Japanese police around six in the evening. Angry over police interference, the 600-odd delegates spearheaded riots in downtown Seoul far into the night.[18]

On April 23, the *Tonga ilbo* refuted the charges of reactionary ties. Their defense relied on a tedious explanation of the problems of publication under rigid censorship and the necessity of using euphemistic, vague, and overly theoretical language that facilitated misinterpretation and confusion.[19] They denied resolutely any softening of their position on independence or any links to organizations that advocated accommodation to Japanese rule.

Events in the second half of 1923, however, had conspired to weaken the *Tonga ilbo*'s defense. The rise of the coalition of explicitly pro-Japanese organizations as well as an increase in proposals of various schemes for self-rule (*chach'i*) had already compromised the moderate line of the newspaper. Moreover, in the fall of 1923, the paper's owner, Kim Sŏngsu, along with former editor Song Chinu and self-rule advocate Ch'oe Rin, had quietly organized the Political Study Club (Yŏnjŏnghoe) to study the feasibility of creating a broad nationalist coalition as a means to reverse the growing factionalism among nationalist organizations.[20] Given the explosive nature of the issue of accommodation, Kim and his associates were careful not to publicize their intentions, but since this group was involved heavily in reformist, cultural organizations and the Korean production movement, it was clear that their planned coalition would stress moderate goals and legal means. According to one account of the group's discussions, they accepted the idea that Japanese assimilation policy implied that Koreans would eventually be given rights of political participation; thus, it made sense to demand such rights now and hope for a sudden change in international politics that would favor a resumption of Korean independence.[21] Whatever their intent, the public outcry over the *Kyŏngnyun* caused them to abandon their plans to announce the formation of a nationalist coalition in early 1924.[22]

It is no mystery as to why the Yŏnjŏnghoe abandoned so quickly their grand plan. After all, both Kim Sŏngsu and Song Chinu were associated intimately with the *Tonga ilbo*. The outcry over accommodation and criticism of the newspaper placed them in an embarrassing position politically. Moreover, the well-known close relationship between Yi Kwangsu and Kim Sŏngsu caused their critics to speculate whether or not the *Kyŏngnyun* was a trial balloon launched by the Yŏnjŏnghoe to test the climate of public opinion for such a venture.[23] In addition, Kim Sŏngsu undoubtedly read with great sensitivity criticism of the economic ideas in the *Kyŏngnyun*. As a major industrialist then expanding his textile operations and using subsidies from the GGK, Kim was highly vulnerable to charges of economic collaboration. No doubt Kim was, therefore, anxious to avoid involvement in controversy over the ultimate goal of national capital formation or being accused of spearheading cooperation between Japanese and Korean capitalists.

Whether or not there was a link between Yi Kwangsu's *Kyŏngnyun* and the Yŏnjŏnghoe is immaterial. The public furor over accommodation clearly caused the Yŏnjŏnghoe to reconsider any organizational projects in 1924. As a result, a major initiative from moderate circles to create a grand coalition of nationalist organizations failed in the climate of suspicion and distrust inspired by the furor over accommodation. And, in the aftermath of the Yŏnjŏnghoe break-up, Kim Sŏngsu maintained an increasingly low profile in nationalist affairs. Moreover, it was several years before many of the Yŏnjŏnghoe group would be drawn back to the idea of a great nationalist coalition. Not until 1926 was another serious attempt made to heal the growing rift in the nationalist movement. This time the effort was initiated by the Korean Communists. Their proposal for a united front was manifested ultimately in the formation of the New Korea Society (Sin'ganhoe, 1927–31) of which we will speak below.[24]

In spite of leftist criticism, there were efforts in 1924 to create an accommodationist movement in the colony. Pro-Japanese organizations had been active since before 1910, and after the Saitō reforms the GGK had encouraged the formation of similar groups as well as the process of linking them in a national federation.[25] Even before the publication of Yi's *Kaejoron* in 1922, the Japanese had realized the implications of the cultural nationalist line on their attempts to foster support for Japanese rule. And while the cultural policy was still evolving in 1920, the Japanese had already made the decision to encourage the moderate cultural line. Hosoi Hajime, political adviser to Saitō, was convinced that moderate organizations were "soothing" and "represented ultimately the GGK cause."[26] Initially, the Japanese were tempted to openly support prominent cultural nationalists like Yi Kwangsu, but they soon realized that overt support would compromise the movement.[27] But after 1924, seeing that in spite of controversy many intellectuals continued to support accommodationist projects, the Japanese renewed their encouragement of moderate cultural and self-rule movements.

One nationalist who chose the overt accommodationist path was Ch'oe Rin. A signer of the March First Declaration, Ch'oe emerged from prison in the early 1920s to an active role in the Ch'ŏndogyo organization, and was subsequently prominent in moderate nationalist circles as a journalist and organizer. In 1924, after his involvement with the Yŏnjŏnghoe, Ch'oe became a leader in the Korean self-rule movement (*chach'i undong*). This little-studied movement sought to improve conditions by lobbying for a more active voice for Koreans in colonial government. The philosophy behind self-rule duplicated the cultural nationalist belief in national development within the colonial system but unlike the cultural movement, it was committed explicitly to political participation under Japanese sovereignty. Ch'oe's self-rule movement and other accommodationist organizations provided the perfect foil for leftists in their criticism of the entire cultural nationalist line. Indeed, by 1924 it was becoming progressively difficult to advocate the cultural nationalist line and not be associated with outright accommodationism represented in the self-rule movement.

Increasingly, political activists were asking who the real nationalists were. The debates over the limits of accommodation compromised intellectuals who called themselves nationalists but were committed to gradual strengthening of Korean economic and political power within the confines of colonial rule. And those committed to political liberation or social revolution began to assert that they alone had an unambiguous claim to the appellation "nationalists." In 1924, it remained for nationalists to solve the problem of division or reconstitute the forces that were still committed to overthrowing Japanese rule; a survey of political journals in 1924 and 1925 reveals that this topic consumed the energies of many political writers.

Redefining National Unity

The controversy over accommodationism stimulated speculation over the general conditions of political thought in the colony. There was a perception that, at least in terms of ideas, Korea had arrived at a turning point. In 1924–25, there was considerable discussion over changing trends in contemporary world politics and, naturally, Korean intellectuals began to speculate about Korea's position within this larger intellectual universe. Of consuming interest was the present disunity and the seemingly endless round of debilitating factional struggles among intellectuals. And as some intellectuals searched for a common ground as a solution to the discord among Korean nationalists, they began comparing the confusion in Korea to a general change in political thinking worldwide since World War I. Thus, the secret of national unity lay, for some, in realigning the intellectual base • of Korean nationalism with contemporary intellectual trends. One such attempt was made in a March 1924 *Kaebyŏk* article entitled "Conditions of Thought and the Direction of Movements."[28] The anonymous author, Min, posited that current disunity was the result of the general weakening of the intellectual coalition that had spawned the March First movement in 1919. "Liberal reformism" had reached its height in a burst of idealism that coincided with the Versailles conference and the publication of Wilson's Fourteen Points.[29] The high tide of idealism in Korea had led to the attempt to regain political independence by appealing to the world powers on the basis of principle, namely, self-determination. Likewise, other independence movements in India and the Philippines had been influenced by their belief in the ultimate altruism of the Western powers.[30]

Min believed that the idealism fostered by the Treaty of Versailles had caused otherwise well-intentioned nationalist leaders to "hibernate from reality."[31] Although the energy released in movements in Korea, India, and the Philippines was considerable, they had only stimulated reaction on the part of their colonial masters. In Korea, this reaction had taken the form of the insidious cultural policy, which had been calculated to play upon the reformist zeal of moderate nationalists while cloaking reality behind an ornamental facade. The cultural policy to Korea was the same as the concept of commonwealth to India: neither altered the fundamental reality of colonial control.[32]

Min's analysis continued with a discussion of how the economic conditions fostered by colonialism progressively separated idealist intellectuals from the masses. The entire idea of March First, to Min, was political, not economic liberation.[33] And although Min understood the well-intentioned motives of the March First leaders, he condemned their nearsightedness and lack of appreciation for the ultimate structural conditions that doomed cosmetic reform to failure and were progressively impoverishing the Korean masses. Furthermore, the economic conditions spawned by colonialism provided fertile soil for the growth of a new intellectual influence in Korea, namely socialism. Described by Min as "a huge whale" that had surfaced in Korea, socialism provided new standards that placed the idealism of the March First leaders in stark contrast with reality.[34] By focusing on the objective conditions of the masses, Socialists contradicted the glowing claims of progress contained in Japanese cultural policy rhetoric and, concurrently, criticized moderate Korean reformists for hibernating in misplaced idealism. Thus, to Min, the disunity among nationalist leaders was ultimately a product of the rise of socialism and the alienation of reformists from the Korean masses. This alienation was a direct cause of the moderate reformists' inability to see that the bulk of the Korean population could not profit from the cosmetic reforms of the cultural policy. Finally, Min linked his argument to the present controversy over accommodationism by attacking the Korean production movement as an effort to "expel foreign capital and enrich native capitalists" with the ultimate result of furthering the misery of the Korean masses.[35]

Although obviously sympathetic to a Socialist view, Min was careful not to reject the cause of nationalism. His concern was that nationalist intellectuals had failed to grasp a fundamental shift in world politics; where before World War I the liberal tradition might have seemed to be the wave of the future, in 1924 it was increasingly viewed as anachronistic. To Min, socialism was "cosmopolitanizing" the Korean intellectual community anew, and, unlike previous ideas, it provided "scientific methods and principles of social development" that would ultimately reunite Korean intellectuals, not only with each other, but with a wider community of intellectuals in colonies around the world.[36]

In January 1924, another lead article in *Kaebyŏk*, "1923 and 1924" ("Kyehae wa kapcha") (hereafter, *Kyehae*), had been even more explicit in seeking the roots of intellectual division in Korea.[37] This article, also anonymous, attempted to dissect objectively the causes of discord among Korean intellectuals; it considered the time ripe for rapprochement because of the temporary lull in the controversy in late 1923. Dividing Korea into two camps, nationalist and Socialist, the author traced the rise of social revolutionary ideas among intellectuals ● and showed how this had led to a growing number of radical journals, labor and tenant organizations, and parties. He believed that both sides sought to save the nation, but they focused on radically different ● methods. It was necessary to rediscover a common ground rather than ● to continue to struggle for one plan over another, and create a philosophy that could bridge the ideological gap between the two groups.[38]

He cited the Ŭiryŏldan (Righteous Fighter Corps), a Korean guerrilla group, as an example of how fervent nationalism and social revolutionary ideas could come together. The Ŭiryŏldan had surfaced in March 1923 with a series of attacks on Japanese police stations and officials.[39] The arrest and subsequent trials of Ŭiryŏldan members had been widely reported in the colonial press. According to *Kyehae*, the Ŭiryŏldan ideology combined a desire to expel the Japanese with a commitment to social revolution because its formulators had realized that the special conditions in Korea required a "special ideology and membership" for their movement.[40]

Both articles, particularly *Kyehae*, introduced the concept of a united front politics as a way to bridge the division among Korean groups. Neither mentioned Lenin by name nor was there any explicit reference to Comintern strategy for national liberation in colonial societies. Yet, both attempted to reappraise the importance of working with bourgeois forces in Korean society as a means toward unity. Min argued that although leftist criticism of the "compromise cultural nationalists" was justified, they had to retreat from their overly idealistic view of revolutionary potential in Korea.[41] Korean society had to undergo further development before the necessary forces for class warfare would emerge; thus, a tactical alliance with Korean capitalists was necessary. Min closed his argument with a reminder that, even in Russia, the main task was as yet economic. The Russian revolution had been political, not economic. And just as special

circumstances in Russia demanded special tactics, the unique charac-
teristics of Korean development demanded a flexible adaptation of
revolutionary ideas as well.[42] This adaptation required the joining of
forces, a tactical alliance between Korean capitalists and Socialists,
while creating bridges to the Korean peasantry.[43]

Kyehae approached the idea of united front politics differently.
Starting with an analysis of common goals, *Kyehae* built systematically a plan for unity. He believed Socialists had no quarrel with "true
nationalists" who advocated national liberation, autonomy, and
economic development. Furthermore, nationalist hatred focused, in
the main, on foreign capitalists.[44] Thus, Socialists and "true nationalists" had to focus on their common enemy, imperialism. Secondly,
Kyehae believed that in the future true nationalists, not cultural
nationalists, could eventually accept the economic ideas of Socialists.
Finally, the ultimate transformation of separate national liberation
movements into a "general struggle of subordinate nations against
rich, oppressor nations" would expand the parochial focus of Korean
nationalists toward a broader anti-imperialist stance.[45] This analysis
underlay a hope that if compatible groups recognized common short-
and long-term goals, the nationalist movement could be revived and
unified.

Kyehae divided intellectuals and political groups into four major
categories.[46] First, there were assimilationists and self-rule advocates
who openly supported Japanese rule and long-range amalgamation of
Koreans into Japanese society. These groups were outside the pale and
an obvious obstacle to unity. Second, there were the cultural nationalists. While they advocated eventual independence, they also diluted
the impulse for national liberation because of their gradualist orientation and ambiguous stance toward Japanese rule. Independence
fighters, mostly exiles who were struggling in a variety of ways to
overthrow Japanese rule by force, comprised the third category. And,
finally, there were the pure Socialists who advocated world class
struggle.

Kyehae posited that only the independence group and pure Socialists had any reasonable chance for union. The assimilationists were
collaborators, and the cultural nationalists were ultimately accommo-
dationists. The burden of forging a new union thus fell on the latter
two groups. More important, this union could succeed only if they
were able to appeal directly to the agrarian masses and build a broad
base of strength.[47] To do this, each would have to become more
realistic; Socialists would have to moderate their idealism and begin to

eschew theory for concrete work among the masses, and independence •
nationalists would have to adopt a more populist line, recognizing the
economic interests of the masses as well as their desire for liberation
from Japanese rule.

Clearly, the problem of a united front according to this analysis was
what to do with the cultural nationalists. National liberation had to be
the common goal for any coalition of nationalists and social revolu-
tionaries to succeed. The cultural nationalists' ambiguous stance with
regard to Japanese rule did not recommend them as "uncompro-
mising" nationalists yet these moderate reformists made up the
majority of nationalists active in the colony. The task for Korean
leftists was to find and unite with the core of "true" nationalists
within the colony and to create a program that could build and sustain
a mass movement in the face of Japanese repression.

These two articles represented an attempt to forge a link between
nationalism and socialism to lay the foundation for a united front
movement. Indeed, as *Kyehae*'s analysis demonstrated, the nationalist
leadership was divided in 1923 into at least three major constellations,
each supporting different plans for the ultimate liberation of Korea.
Of course Koreans had disagreed widely on tactics from the beginning
of the colony. What had changed, however, was the context of the
struggle. In 1910, few were concerned with the ultimate political and
social form an independent Korea would assume but, by 1924, tactics
for liberation were being closely linked with the future structure of the
nation. Thus, nationalists had assumed or been assigned labels such as
"compromise," "independence," or "radical." During the first decade
of colonial rule, to speak for the nation was automatically noble and
patriotic. In 1924, the act of wrapping oneself in the flag was no
assurance that ultimate political loyalties would not be questioned.

Toward a United Front

The issue of national liberation had been complicated by the rise of
Socialist thought in Korea after 1919. A materialist view of history
and the role of class struggle begged important questions for Korean
nationalists. By whom and for whom was the cause of national
liberation to be realized? How did the evolution of Korean society fit
into the course of world history? What role would intellectuals play in
the dual process of national liberation and social revolution? And how
did the class interests of nationalist leaders affect their programs for
independence? In addition to these fundamental theoretical questions,

Korean leftists were also influenced by Leninist theory with regard to the national liberation struggle in colonial situations and its importance in the overall scheme of world revolution. As we have seen from the attack on the cultural nationalists, they were concerned with broadening the national liberation struggle to Korean proletarian elements—here meaning peasants—and they were highly distrustful of the motives and goals of the bourgeois nationalists. Thus, by 1924, cultural nationalism was being tied increasingly to accommodation, if not outright collaboration. Such charges weakened the nationalist
• movement by questioning the utility of cultural nationalist participation in a united front.

Although ideological division within the movement was serious in 1924, there was evidence of willingness to reunite. The cultural nationalists had attempted, with disastrous results, to reconnect warring elements of the nationalist movement, and their failure demonstrated their increasing lack of credibility among nationalists in general. Yet for all the criticism Yi Kwangsu's *Kyŏngnyun* had received, it was floated at a time Korean nationalists were beginning to show concern for the problem of disunity. By 1924, radicals were offering their own plans for reuniting the nationalist movement to the service of their own aims. The discussion of a united front considered how the ideological differences between nationalist groups as well as Socialists might be reconciled. In joining the discussion, radicals indicated a new ideological sophistication, abandoning dogmatic application of Socialist principles to the Korean situation and making a more realistic assessment of how existing forces might be mobilized for action.

In 1924, groups from both the Right and Left within the nationalist movement were anxious that the movement enter a phase of concrete organizational activity. Each worried about the aimless drift of the movement, the Right stung by the failure of the Korean production and university movements, and the left concerned about factional infighting and increasing Japanese repression. As the memory of the March First movement faded, the Right realized the necessity of finding some way to mobilize the masses in the service of national development and education. But the criticism by the Left had already compromised the mass appeal of the cultural nationalist programs. For its part, the Left was also searching for a way to mobilize the masses, but as Japanese censorship became more stringent and arrests of tenant and labor organizers mounted, they found themselves increasingly isolated from the political mainstream of colonial society.

Therefore, after 1924, the most serious proposals for united front politics came from the forces of the Left within the nationalist movement.

Indeed, the debate over the role of the Korean agrarian masses in the nationalist movement was pivotal to both sides. The cultural nationalists wanted gradual enlightenment and future participation of the masses in the national development effort. Leftists wanted to harness the revolutionary potential of the masses against imperialism and, ultimately, for social revolutionary upheaval. The resulting debate over how to involve the masses marked a turning point in the nationalist movement in general. Each side realized that Korean nationalism had to be transformed from a predominantly intellectual movement to one of mass action. In this quest, the cultural nationalists were hampered by their own indecision as to how to mobilize mass action within the confines of colonial rule.

Practically from its inception, the Korean Communist party had been directed to establish a presence in the colony, eliminate its factional divisions, and participate in united front tactics.[48] Between 1920 and 1925, however, various factions competed for Comintern recognition and patronage and the party, such as it was, failed to establish an organized presence. Thus, in the early twenties the work of transmitting radical ideas and organizing the masses fell on the shoulders of individual leftists and radical nationalists in opposition to the moderate nationalist renaissance. Leftists were constrained by their own insistence that cultural nationalists were accommodationist and thus unacceptable partners in any coalition. Nevertheless, after 1925 there was a new push for creating a united front. Between 1925 and 1928, Korean Communists, in spite of extreme pressure from the Japanese police, finally established a party in the colony. Although repeatedly broken up—between 1925 and 1931 there were six separate roundups of Communists—the Korean Communist party labored to follow the Comintern line in united front tactics.[49] After 1924, therefore, there was an increased willingness by moderates and radicals to organize a united front, setting the stage for the creation of the New Korea Society (Sin'ganhoe) in 1927.

The early discussions of united front politics in 1924 coincided with a general Japanese crackdown on the Korean press. The high point of formal censorship actions (erasure, seizure, and publication bans) during the colonial period came between 1924 and 1927.[50] In 1925, the new Peace Preservation Law was applied to Korea by GGK order, providing even wider powers for the High Police. Radical publications had already been suppressed, and mainstream journals such as *Kaebyŏk* that still featured articles with radical political content suffered repeated seizures. Finally, in August 1926, the Japanese withdrew *Kaebyŏk*'s publication permit, ending the run of the most important intellectual journal of the period. These actions signaled a significant shift in Japanese policy toward tighter control of the press, organizations, and radical ideas. Socialists and radical nationalists were the first to feel the effects of the growing repression as their access to the media constricted and arrests mounted.

These developments had an enormous impact on the Korean intellectual community, and they signaled an end to the era of relatively open discussion of politics that had characterized the 1920–25 period. The nationalist leadership, fragmented as a result of five years of debate and controversy, faced the prospect of attempting to create a new nationalist coalition at a time of increased political repression. Moreover, the changing political climate skewed the opportunities for unity in a decisive manner. The repression was selective. It focused on containing the spread of radical thought and organizations while continuing to tolerate nationalist sentiment as long as it was presented in terms of accommodation. Accordingly, the cultural nationalist line was, within limits, acceptable, but any linkage of national sentiment to the overthrow of Japanese rule, class struggle, or anti-imperialism was not. The result of this selective policy on the media was clear by 1925.

One anonymous author despaired at the loss of political consciousness and spirit of struggle in the colonial press in a bitter indictment published in late 1925.[51] He believed that the Korean press was the most important weapon in the nationalist arsenal, having led in the struggle against Japanese rule. Recently, however, the press seemed "only concerned with selling goods and printing anything calculated to increase its readership; it considers itself the clarion of society, but, in reality, it only supports the class structure, money, and power."[52] Given this situation, the author wondered if political debate and continued nationalist struggle would even be possible.[53]

Subsequent developments provided the answer: commercial interests predominated. The criticism above reflected the view of only one author, yet history proved him right as well-financed, slickly produced publications replaced the small, politically oriented magazines of the early and mid-1920s.[54] This situation placed accommodationist forces in control of the media, and although the major newspapers continued to view themselves as the main representatives of Korean public opinion, the strident nationalism of the early 1920s gave way to a moderate, almost conciliatory tone in the press. Confrontation and possible censorship, after all, meant a large financial gamble in publishing, and seizure or suspension could involve tremendous losses.

By 1925, the Korean nationalist movement within the colony stood at a turning point. Divided by serious ideological differences, the consensus and optimism of the early post-March First era had faded. The controversy over accommodation had compromised a significant portion of the movement's intellectual leadership, and increasing Japanese repression was driving the radical wing of the movement underground. More insidiously, a major means for resolving internal factionalism, public debate in the media, was disappearing in the face of growing censorship and thought control. The situation produced a decisive intellectual crisis for the Korean nationalist movement. Some means for reunifying the movement needed to be found; either a new consensus had to emerge or some organizational mechanism devised to reconcile the division and maintain the movement's momentum.

The Sin'ganhoe, 1927–31, was the culmination of the search for a united front organization.[55] Founded in 1927 with top posts going to prominent moderate nationalists, the Sin'ganhoe provided a common base for cultural nationalists, radical nationalists, and Korean Communists. The moderate cultural nationalist leadership made Japanese approval possible; however, once formed, the leadership, especially at the branch level, fell to radicals and Communists. By 1930, the Sin'ganhoe claimed 386 branches and 76,939 members (Japanese reports cited lower figures).[56] It created a network that coordinated youth groups, labor and farmers groups, and intellectual societies, and it became a catalyst for coordinated nationalist activity and served, temporarily, the needs of both the Right and the Left in the Korean nationalist movement.

The struggling and faction-ridden Korean Communist party found respite in the Sin'ganhoe as well. Having failed repeatedly to establish their own organizational base, the Sin'ganhoe provided them with a mechanism for expanding their interests. Moreover, their participation brought them in line with Comintern directives. The success of Korean Communists and their radical nationalist allies within the Sin'ganhoe local branch organizations demonstrated that conditions were ripe for grass-roots organization. Nevertheless, their continued success in dominating the local branches of the united front engendered the resistance of the moderate leadership as well as repression by the Japanese.

The Japanese police carefully monitored the united front from the beginning. Its national conventions were prohibited, and periodic roundups of leftists within the leadership increased factionalism within its ranks. Ultimately, arrests of leading Communist members after the 1929 Kwangju incident precipitated the demise of the Sin'ganhoe. With a shift in the leadership to the Right, Communists began to advocate dissolution on the grounds that the organization was becoming an obstacle to class struggle.[57] Dissolution came in 1931 in a decisive leadership struggle, watched with relief, no doubt, by the Japanese authorities.

From its beginning, the united front had been the joining of two streams, each in search of a mass base.[58] For the Communists' part, the Sin'ganhoe represented a legal façade under which they might work to create and, ultimately, seize control of a mass national liberation movement. Unlike their Chinese counterparts, they were not joining an existing, strong nationalist organization, and this explains, perhaps, their initial success in gaining control of a portion of the movement. Indeed, the Communists' and radicals' success might have indicated that they were being seen as the true leaders of the national liberation movement. Furthermore, it was the Japanese, not bourgeois nationalists, that posed the greatest threat to the existence of a viable Korean Communist party. Therefore, even after the 1927 débâcle for the Chinese Communists, the Korean Communist party continued to pursue united front tactics. Indeed, given the difficulties of maintaining an independent party base, the united front represented one of the few opportunities available to the Communists at the time.

After 1930, the Comintern shifted its line toward an emphasis on "united front from below" and eschewed collaboration with the national reformists of all stripes.[59] And Korean Communists dissolved the Sin'ganhoe in 1931. One must question, however, the hold of the Comintern over the very weak and constantly shifting Korean Communist leadership. Indeed, given the enmity and distrust that had built up between moderate nationalists and radicals well before 1927, it was not surprising that Korean Communists could not work with the national reformists in the united front. The real problem was that the Japanese were not going to allow either group to create an anti-imperialist mass base. As long as moderates seemed in control of the Sin'ganhoe, the Japanese were content to harass and arrest the radicals within it, but allow the organization to exist. Directives to the Korean Communist party at this time indicated how little the Comintern knew about actual conditions in Korea. The well-known December Thesis

(December 1928) admonished the Korean party—even though the arrests in the Fourth Party incident left virtually no party to admonish—for failing to distinguish between a revolutionary and national reformist movement and for remaining isolated from proletarian elements due to the excessive number of intellectuals and students in the party.[60] Yet Korean Communists, as their radical forebears a few years before, were already aware of these problems.[61]

In the end, the weakness of the Sin'ganhoe stemmed from the original inability of the nationalist leadership to create a mass-based movement. As we have seen, the nationalist movement after 1920 was dominated by moderates who fought to create legal programs within the framework of colonial rule. The attempts of the moderates to create a mass base were first compromised by the radical attack in the early 1920s, and, later, by the rise of the overtly compromise-oriented self-rule movement. Although in some ways more effective, radical nationalists and Communists also failed to establish a mass base. And within the confines of the Sin'ganhoe, neither group was willing to yield to the other.

The debates within the Comintern about united front tactics revolved around the conditions under which a tactical alliance with bourgeois nationalist forces could help advance the larger cause of revolution. It assumed the presence of an anti-imperialist nationalist struggle in a colony. It also assumed that a Communist party would be able to maintain its integrity and discipline in a conditional alliance with hostile bourgeois nationalist forces and against the efforts of imperialist forces to repress it. In Korea, cultural nationalism scarcely constituted an anti-imperialist movement capable of garnering mass nationalist support, and efficient Japanese repression made it impossible to maintain a Communist party leadership in the colony, let alone effectively organize a mass base. It is no wonder, then, why united front tactics failed in Korea, not withstanding the fine tuning of Comintern directives to the constantly harassed Korean Communist leadership. Radicals and moderates alike came together to forge a mass nationalist organization in 1927, and they were still trying in 1931 when the Sin'ganhoe lapsed. In this sense, the issue of who torpedoed the organization was moot because, in essence, there was precious little there to scuttle.

Although nationalist resistance continued sporadically until the end of colonial rule—often in the form of spontaneous demonstrations and a great deal of sullen resistance—the demise of the Sin'ganhoe signaled, for all practical purposes, the end of a coordinated nationalist movement in the colony. The issues that divided the leadership and led to its failure were not new. Nor can its failure be blamed exclusively on Korean Communists' blind adherence to Comintern directives to first join and then dissolve the united front. The failure can be ultimately traced to the debate over nationalist tactics that preceded its organization. Was national liberation possible through a legal, gradualist program of national development, or did such a program play into the hands of Japanese colonial policy? Cultural nationalists believed in gradualism, but, as we have seen, their program lacked a sufficient mass following. Radicals refused to relinquish the tactics of struggle and confrontation and were subject to repression for their efforts. In the end, this decisive split provided the Japanese with the advantage of dealing with two movements. Conciliation and prevarication effectively controlled the cultural nationalists, and general repression decisively limited the efforts of the Left.

CHAPTER 6

Conclusion

While acknowledging the obvious fact that the Korean nationalist movement was unable to overthrow Japanese rule, it is often claimed that the by-product of the unsuccessful drive for independence was the creation of a strong national identity. This is correct if one assumes that hatred and loathing of Japanese rule was the main component of national identity. Certainly, the colonial experience produced such a feeling among the overwhelming majority of the Korean people. Yet it is also clear that although the force and depth of anti-Japanese sentiment was clearly evident after 1919 and was expressed sporadically in organized form, the nationalist leadership was unable to channel it into a sustained and purposeful program of action. Responsibility for this failure can be partially attributed to an efficient and often brutal Japanese repression, but it also must be shared by the Koreans themselves.

The formation of a national identity had proceeded since the late nineteenth century. The new Korean intelligentsia had nurtured the process of grafting symbols of the modern nation-state onto the existing ethnic and cultural identity in Korea and developed Korean nationalism as a political force. Moreover, the fall of the Yi dynasty and advent of Japanese colonial rule provided strong negative symbols that accelerated the growth of national consciousness as the movement transformed into a struggle for independence. Since 1905, Koreans had demonstrated time and again that they were willing to struggle against Japanese rule, and the March First demonstrations showed that nationalist passions among Koreans at all levels of society could be mobilized for political action. Yet the success of March First remains in history as the high-water mark of Korean nationalism during the colonial period. Japanese rule continued for another twenty-six years, but the nationalist movement was never again to experience such unanimity or strength of purpose.

The reasons for this are complex and, certainly, the Japanese response to March First was important. The cultural policy, the shift to cooptation that featured a softer stance on cultural autonomy and

157

identity while refining and strengthening the colonial control apparatus, served the Japanese well after 1920. Postwar histories have
adequately chronicled this development. Yet history is replete with
successful nationalist movements that have overcome equally adroit
repression. Why, then, did Korean nationalism falter when at first
glance it seemed, in the 1920s, to have acquired the requisites for
success in abundance? An explanation for this situation lies, at least in
part, at the feet of the Korean nationalist leadership and the enervating
ideological schism that developed after 1920 within the domestic
nationalist movement.

The cultural policy opened the way for a nationalist renaissance in
the colony after 1920. A significant portion of the nationalist leadership seized the opportunity to create a moderate program of national
development that would flourish within these political confines. To
work within these limits meant, at the least, that the most basic
nationalist demand, sovereignty, had to be deferred. This assumption,
accepted to varying degrees by most cultural nationalists, was not
considered an obstacle to national development because they believed
that Korea was not yet ready for independence. Thus, cultural
nationalists stressed a gradual program of reform, education, and
economic development to lay the base for future independence.
According to this line, the recent historical experience of Korea
supported such a view; the predatory ambitions of the Japanese and
other outside powers had been encouraged by Korea's internal
weaknesses and the unwillingness of the traditional political elite to
address this situation with significant reforms. Therefore, cultural
nationalists of the 1920s saw themselves as inheritors of the reform
program of the early nationalist movement. Although the political
context had changed—obdurate Confucian traditionalists leading a
corrupt regime had been replaced by Japanese colonialists as the main
obstruction, and the goal of transforming the traditional society to
maintain Korean political autonomy had given way to a struggle to
regain Korean independence—these moderate nationalists were focused still on the necessity of laying the basis for nationhood in Korea.

This assumption, that Korean society must be transformed along
the lines of other nation-states before it would possess the necessary
strength and solidarity to maintain its political independence, was
explicitly elitist. It was the conceit of a new elite, educated in modern
schools, assuming the mantle of nationalism and prescribing its
concept of national identity and model of the nation-state as the
cure-all to the colonial prostration of Korean society. As such an elite,

it fell upon cultural nationalists to articulate a program that encompassed their goals and provide a mechanism to carry them out. The elaboration of this ideology and program of cultural nationalism has been the major focus of this study. Yet as we have seen, the cultural nationalist vision was not shared by all. Although it evolved from the mainstream of Korean nationalist thought, it was challenged decisively in the 1920s by radicals whose view of what constituted the nation as well as what ought to be done about Korean independence was very different. The clash between these two views produced a deep division within the nationalist movement that revealed the core issues of identity and political programs were far from being sources of unity but were, rather, foci of dispute within the movement.

The cultural nationalist program contained an essentially elitist view of national identity. They accepted as given that modern intellectuals were the key component of the nation, and as leaders their task was to transmit core nationalist values to the masses. While early twentieth-century nationalist intellectuals had agonized over the content of national identity, cultural nationalists concentrated on programs that would encourage the transformation of Korean society toward the model of a Western nation-state. In doing so, they assumed the primacy of their leadership and their conception of what constituted the nation. The tutorial approach of the cultural nationalists resonated with the earlier nationalist stance toward the masses. As enlightened intellectuals they were seized by the conviction that national solidarity was a key to survival in the modern world and that their task was to create institutions and inculcate values that would support such unity.

In 1920, however, the nationalist leadership was faced with the reality of colonial rule. Where before the issue was reform of the traditional system, after 1910 Koreans faced the additional problem of regaining political independence. The inability to dislodge the Japanese, however, convinced some nationalists of the futility of direct opposition. Couching their program in pragmatic terms, the cultural nationalists seized the opportunity offered by the cultural policy reforms to embark on a gradual program of national development designed to lay the basis, once and for all, of national power. At the heart of their program was the assumption that they embodied the core of the future nation. Their concept of nation, their values, and their talents defined the future. The problem became how to widen the national core by increasing the circle of enlightenment. Korea would be ready for independence once a sufficiently large proportion of the population had acquired the rudiments of identity, the proper modern values, and the skills required for participation in the modern world.

There were decidedly traditional overtones to the style, if not the content, of the cultural nationalist ideology. At its core was the assumption that to reform social and political behavior it was necessary to readjust and affirm proper values. In Confucian thought, improper behavior stemmed from wrong thinking: rectify man's thinking and his behavior would be adjusted accordingly. Cultural nationalists placed a premium on transforming values. Although the content of the new value structure was very different from traditional Confucian concepts, the style continued to ring true. In terms of national identity, cultural nationalists asserted that they defined the new core values. Their identity was derived from their deep understanding of Korean history and culture and their struggle to rethink the idea of Korea and combine it with their understanding of the modern world. Therefore, they stood above the masses by virtue of their ability to distill the essence of nation and to articulate this identity within their program of value transformation. In early nationalist writing, the original spiritual source of identity was the people themselves, yet cultural nationalists assumed the posture of teaching the masses what it was to be Korean.

This posture was not inconsistent with other nationalist movements. It has been posited that the content of a specific nationalism is less important than the objective realization that it does, in fact, exist. Making people aware of group identity is very important; without consciousness of common identity there could be no political mobilization for group goals.[1] The problem with the cultural nationalist conception of identity was that it excluded the majority by identifying the core of the nation as a small group of enlightened individuals. Although the core would inevitably expand, the process was necessarily gradual because it required time to tutor the masses and elevate them to membership in the nation. The irony of cultural nationalism in terms of identity was that the leadership deliberately separated itself from the source of its original inspiration; and in so doing, it prolonged the process of independence and weakened the mass appeal of its program.

Another problem for cultural nationalism in terms of identity was the issue of *sadae*. Much of the early discussion of national identity had revolved around the foreign cultural domination in Korean history. As the idea of nationalism rose among Korean intellectuals at the turn of the century, the Confucian tradition came under attack as an obstacle to the creation of a strong national identity. Subservience to foreign ideas and cultural norms inhibited the development of a unique, self-conscious Korean identity. Nationalists, therefore, worked to exhume a Korean past as a repository of nationalist symbols smothering under a mantle of excessive veneration for Chinese culture. Even as early nationalists championed the new Korean consciousness, however, they fell under a spell of different foreign ideologies, this time from the West. Indeed, the idea of the nation-state and the philosophical tradition it implied was alien to the Korean tradition. And although the fight against *sadae* stimulated the creation of a unique and autonomous Korean identity, it provided an impossibly rigorous standard of morality for modern intellectuals. Taken in extreme, the fight against cultural subservience meant that all foreign ideas were suspect. Therefore, as the Korean nationalist movement developed, the issue of *sadae* remained closely linked with national identity. Although it was easier to ignore the contradictions posed by the standard of *sadae* in the early burst of enthusiasm for new ideas, by the 1920s when the cultural nationalists were offering specific programs for independence, they found themselves vulnerable to this issue because of their elitism and reverence for the Western model of development.

This dilemma highlighted another aspect of the traditional legacy and its effect on modern Korean nationalists. Intellectuals had always played important roles in traditional Korean political culture because of the heavy influence of Neo-Confucianism on Yi dynasty life, with its emphasis on the rule of men of cultivation. Although prestigious lineage and landed wealth were extremely important as a basis for political power in Yi dynasty Korea, it was also necessary to be successful on state examinations. The Yi elite maintained their intellectual credentials assiduously, and these credentials were expressed in terms of fluent knowledge of classical Chinese and familiarity with Confucian thought. One must wonder how this curious combination of attributes affected the political identity of the Yi elite. In a certain sense, their cosmopolitanism, that is, their connection with East Asian civilization writ large, was an important component of their legitimacy as leaders in Korean society. This leads one to wonder if a similar dynamic affected modern Korean nationalists. Modern Korean intellectuals, whether of the Right or Left politically, were also cosmopolitans; their position as the new elite was based on their special understanding of a new set of values derived from their study of the West. This alienated them from indigenous Korean culture at •

the same time that they were striving to build a new Korean cultural identity. Therefore, those who went to extremes in advocating the adoption of Western values and institutions were liable to the same attack earlier nationalists had leveled at the traditional Confucian elite.

Although not all Korean nationalists fell into this trap, cultural nationalists fit this pattern quite well. By placing themselves above the masses as an enlightened elite, their identification as cosmopolitans was clear. They referred frequently to their role as interpreters of the modern world. It was their leadership and example that would supply the synergy between native culture and modern ideas to create the new Korea. This strong identification as cosmopolitan intellectuals quite naturally distanced the cultural nationalists from the Korean masses. This gap was clearly manifest, particularly in the work of Yi Kwangsu, in his emphasis on modern education, the recruitment of a core elite, and the advocacy of colonial urban culture as the model for future Korean society. However attractive this vision might have been to urban intellectuals in colonial Korea, the fact remained that the overwhelming majority of the population was undereducated and lived in the countryside. The cosmopolitan orientation of the cultural nationalists, their degrees from foreign universities, their ability to read foreign languages, and their urban life style helped to legitimate their status as interpreters of the modern world, but, concurrently, it alienated them from the Korean masses for whom they purported to speak. The nationalist elite generally rose from among a modern intelligentsia that was alienated to a certain extent from its own culture.[2] Its response, however, was usually to build a new identity in opposition to colonial oppression that discriminates against them. In the case of the cultural nationalists, the resonance of this traditional cosmopolitan identification of the elite in Korea with the nationalists' conception of its leadership role conspired, perhaps, to weaken the nationalist side of its identification.

Radical nationalists shared with the moderates a strong sense of elitism. Indeed, Comintern directives to the fledgling Korean Communist party in the 1920s consistently criticized the elitist nature of the Communist leadership. Yet, as we have seen in the early writings of Korean radicals, there was a strong populist strain in the critique of cultural nationalism. In the 1920s, radical nationalists and Korean Communists found themselves separated from the masses and mired in their intellectual study clubs; however, their interest in either national liberation (not accommodation and gradualist reform) or revolutionary ideology predisposed them, at least in intellectual terms, to go to the masses, using the appeal of national liberation.

Indeed, at times it seemed that the ultimate nationalist goals of the cultural nationalist program had disappeared altogether. Certainly the underlying assumption was that education and economic development programs would strengthen Korean society for the ultimate attainment of nation-state status, but whose nation would it become? By downplaying confrontation with the Japanese and offering programs that paralleled Japanese projects that were either announced (as the establishment of an imperial university) or already under way, the cultural nationalists placed themselves in a position easily attacked by their enemies. In fact, one wonders if the ultimate goal of cultural nationalism was political independence at all? Certainly, the rise of the accommodationist self-rule movement after 1924 further highlighted the ambiguous stance of cultural nationalism with regard to national independence. In retrospect, cultural nationalism could be interpreted as an program that would allow Korean intellectuals to maintain their own status as a social and cultural elite by monopolizing a truncated version of nationalism that tolerated national cultural autonomy within the confines of Japanese sovereignty. Their class interest as members of the urban bourgeoisie was being served by the colonial system; although their political influence was marginal, they could attempt to retain their social status as cultural leaders.

As was clear from the debate during the 1920s, not all nationalists shared the cultural camp's sense of identity. The cultural nationalist elitism and, in particular, their attempt to lead the nationalist movement without confronting Japanese authority, offended their radical critics. Although critics of cultural nationalism exhibited a broad range of theoretical orientations, they were unified by a common view of what defined the nation. Time and again, they returned to the theme of the agrarian masses as the prime embodiment of the Korean nation. Clearly, their interest in class analysis encouraged this view, but their concern for the spirit embodied in the Korean peasantry was as much a part of the earlier nationalist search for the real Korea as it was a result of their search for proletarian revolutionary elements in colonial society. In fact, radical nationalists, in their quest to identify the objective bases of political and social transformation, were forced to come to grips with the significance of Korea as an overwhelmingly agrarian society. This led some radicals to underscore the importance of the Korean peasantry in the future struggle for national liberation as well as social revolution. And in early radical writings, in *Sin-*

saenghwal for instance, the emphasis on the peasantry as the embodiment of the spirit of the nation was as important as their analysis of the peasant role as a potential proletarian element in the future social revolution.

Indeed, as has been previously noted, radicals had come originally to their study of socialism as patriots. Consumed by their desire for national independence, they culled Marx and other Socialist sources for new ideas that might be relevant to Korea's political dilemma. They applied their early understanding of class and class conflict as well as Lenin's ideas of national liberation struggle in the colonial world to the Korean situation; as a result, they focused on the political problem of independence as well as the economic oppression of the peasantry. In doing so, they considered Korea's political dilemma and the problem of the Korean peasant as one and the same. Furthermore, their understanding of class conflict stimulated their disdain for the urban bourgeoisie and intellectuals who championed the cause of capitalism as not representative of the nation. The radicals' concern for the peasantry had a decisively populist ring. It expressed itself in unremitting hostility to the urban, Westernized intellectuals who championed cultural nationalism. The future Korea must be a product of a new mass culture built by and for the common Korean and embodying the true spirit of the nation.

The radicals' focus on the masses as the embodiment of the nation combined with social revolutionary theory to make, in their minds, national liberation synonymous with class liberation. Radicals were thus outraged at the accommodationist stance of cultural nationalism. To defer the drive for national sovereignty only meant to further strengthen the hold of Japanese capitalism. Such rhetoric confirmed, in the minds of radicals, the antinational dangers of cultural nationalism. Regardless of which hat, nationalist or social revolutionary, radicals were wearing while denouncing the accommodationist line, their attack exposed the moderate program at its most vulnerable point, making the case for gradualism increasingly difficult to justify on pragmatic grounds or otherwise. The only way for moderates to hold the middle ground and justify gradualism and legal activity was to hold to the future goal of independence. Yet, as the cultural nationalists elaborated their program, the issue of ultimate independence was downplayed in their concern to avoid Japanese reprisals. This made it increasingly difficult to separate themselves from accommodationist self-rule advocates, as well as those who were unabashedly pro-Japanese.

The isolated position on the issue of sovereignty held by cultural nationalists was a significant factor in the preliminary discussions of a united front in 1924–25. As we have seen, the moderate's call for national unity under the banner of cultural nationalism had fallen on deaf ears in 1924. Yet, similar proposals from the Left showed no promise of healing quickly the division in the movement. This was because leftists, in their search for a new anti-Japanese coalition, excluded the cultural nationalists from participation. Again, the issue was direct advocacy of independence, and the ambiguity of the cultural nationalists on this issue precluded, in the minds of leftists, their participation in any coalition of true nationalists and social revolutionary elements. Excluding cultural nationalists reduced the field of participants to independence fighters, mostly in exile, and radical nationalists, already being harassed and shackled by increasing Japanese repression. Although the eventual united front represented a compromise on this earlier hard line with regard to moderate nationalists, the controversy had already poisoned the atmosphere of compromise and seeded resentments and distrust between groups in the later Sin'ganhoe coalition.

The eventual Korean united front, represented by the Sin'ganhoe, failed because it could not bridge the gulf already opened between segments of the nationalist movement. The cultural nationalists did not represent a strong anti-imperialist movement, and they were highly suspicious of their radical allies, lest their participation and open advocacy of national liberation bring down the full wrath of the Japanese police. In the end, the moderate nationalists' ambiguous stance on independence diluted their nationalist appeal. Although radicals had a grasp on the potential power of direct appeal to mass nationalist sentiment, Japanese repression blocked their path. In this sense, the Sin'ganhoe represented a united front in potential only; its failure demonstrated the difficulty of mounting such an effort in a situation devoid of a military base and under the watch of a powerful colonial regime.

The development of ideological division within the Korean nationalist movement between 1920 and 1925 demonstrated that Korean nationalism was certainly no monolith.[3] The leadership of the domestic nationalist movement was divided by fundamentally different conceptions of nation. These views generated opposing strategies for independence and consequently diluted the impact of the entire movement's appeal to the people. The program of cultural nationalism became an appeal for patience, and in taking the long view they sought to work within the colonial system. In doing so, they became vulnerable to charges of aiding and abetting the creation of an exploitative class system that enslaved the majority. Indeed, if nationalism was to be the basis of any successful drive to overthrow Japanese rule, a way to focus the power of its appeal to the broadest segments of Korean society had to be found. Although cultural nationalists had gained the toleration of the colonial authorities, their program lacked broad appeal. On the other hand, radical nationalists and Socialists tried to link their politics to a mass base, but they were stymied by efficient Japanese repression and lack of cooperation by moderate nationalists. The nationalist movement, therefore, failed to create a mass base in the first half of the 1920s.

Such a conclusion forces a rethinking of the place of the March First movement in Korean history. Although it demonstrated the potential power of nationalist sentiment, in the years following 1919 this potential remained dormant. Certainly the Japanese worked hard to subvert any attempt to activate a repeat performance. The cultural policy marked a successful modification of their control, but the cultural policy could not have succeeded without the positive, in Japanese eyes, response of a significant segment of the domestic nationalist leadership. The response of the cultural nationalists, although initially worrisome, was viewed eventually by the Japanese as benign. This allowed the Japanese police to concentrate with great effectiveness on the radical camp in the nationalist movement. Therefore, the domestic movement was enervated by the split between a cluster of moderate leaders advocating a self-limiting program of national development and a more radical group calling for direct action by the masses but harassed, imprisoned, and otherwise cut off from organizing their appeal. Korean nationalism developed after 1910, nurturing within itself the seeds of internal division; by the mid-1920s, the seeds had sprouted, fertilized by the bitter realities of life under Japanese colonial rule. And throughout the balance of the colonial period, the differences among nationalists leaders that had appeared by the mid-1920s continued to plague the unity and purpose of the nationalist movement.

Notes

Introduction

1. Chong-sik Lee, *Politics of Korean Nationalism* (Berkeley and Los Angeles: University of California Press, 1964), pp. 114–18.

2. Dae-yeol Ku, *Korea Under Colonialism: The March First Movement and Anglo-Japanese Relations* (Seoul: Royal Asiatic Society, Korea Branch, 1985), pp. 37–45.

3. Frank Baldwin, Jr., "The March First Movement: Korean Challenge and Japanese Response" (Ph.D. diss., Columbia University, 1969), pp. 214–24.

4. Michael Robinson, "Colonial Publication Policy and the Korean Nationalist Movement," in R. H. Myers and Mark Paettie, eds., *The Japanese Colonial Empire, 1895–1945* (Princeton: Princeton University Press, 1984), pp. 312–45.

5. Lee, *Politics of Korean Nationalism*, pp. 129–55. Also Robert Scalapino and Chong-sik Lee, *Communism in Korea* (Berkeley and Los Angeles: University of California Press, 1972) 1: 10–24. For a standard work in Korean see Lee Hyunhi, *Taehan minguk imsi chŏngbusa* (Seoul: Chimmundang, 1982).

6. The terms *munhwa undong* (cultural movement) and *munhwap'a* (cultural faction) were in common use after 1920 in the colonial press. They were both general designations for moderate nationalists who favored long-term national development, both cultural and economic, as an ultimate solution to the problem of independence.

7. The literature on nationalism as a form of sentiment or, at its roots a psychological phenomenon, is voluminous. Two good examples of this approach are Carlton Hayes, *The Historical Evolution of Modern Nationalism* (New York: Richard Smith, 1931); and Hahns Kohn, *The Idea of Nationalism* (New York: Macmillan, 1967). This writing stresses the state of mind or consciousness that fuses patriotism and cultural identity with nationalism. For a quick review of nationalism theory see also Arthur N. Waldron, "Theories of Nationalism and Historical Explanation," *World Politics* 37, no. 3 (April 1985): 416–31.

8. One good example of nationalism linked to theory of development is Karl Deutsch, *Nationalism and Social Communication* (Cambridge, Mass.: M.I.T. Press, 1953). The literature on modernization and development in the

postcolonial world also links nationalism with broad categories of "modernization." See J. S. Coleman, *Nigeria, Background to Nationalism* (Berkeley and Los Angeles: University of California Press, 1958).

9. Anthony Smith, *Theories of Nationalism* (New York: Holmes and Meier Publishers, 1983), pp. 41–64.

10. Political movements that base their programs on nationalist sentiment can develop highly diverse ideologies to support their political claims. An analysis of the use of nationalist appeals and manipulation of nationalist symbols is contained in Paul R. Brass, *Language, Religion, and Politics in North India* (London: Cambridge University Press, 1975).

11. This definition is a modification of Smith, *Theories of Nationalism*, p. 171.

12. Ibid., pp. 86–150. See also Elie Kedourie, *Nationalism* (London: Hutchinson of London, 1960); Ernst Gellner, *Thought and Change* (Chicago: University of Chicago Press, 1964); Clifford Geertz, ed., *Old Societies and New States* (New York: Free Press, 1963).

13. Any cursory glance at the titles in Korean historiographical literature indicates the close link between the independence movement and modern Korean history. The major work in English on Korean nationalism is Lee, *Politics of Korean Nationalism*. Lee's book is a landmark work in the study of modern Korea. His history is a narrative of Korean history as first a reformist struggle against the Yi dynasty and from 1910 an anticolonial struggle.

14. The same point is made about Chinese nationalism by Lin Yü-sheng, *The Crisis of Chinese Consciousness: Radical Antitraditionalism in the May Fourth Era* (Madison: University of Wisconsin Press, 1979), p. 10. See also the classic studies of late Ch'ing intellectual history: Benjamin Schwartz, *In Search of Wealth and Power: Yen Fu and the West* (Cambridge: Harvard University Press, 1964), and Joseph Levenson, *Liang Ch'i-ch'ao and the Mind of Modern China* (Cambridge: Harvard University Press, 1959).

1. The Rise of Korean Nationalism

1. James B. Palais, *Politics and Policy in Traditional Korea* (Cambridge: Harvard University Press, 1975), p. 9.

2. For a general discussion of the Ming tributary system and Korea's position within the system, see M. Fredrick Nelson, *Korea and the Old Orders in Eastern Asia* (Baton Rouge: Louisiana State University Press, 1946); John K. Fairbank, ed., *The Chinese World Order* (Cambridge: Harvard University Press, 1968); Haejong Chung, "Sino-Korean Tributary Relations during the Ch'ing Period," in Fairbank, *Chinese World Order*, pp. 90–111. An excellent and detailed account of the creation of Korean-Chinese relations at the beginning of the Yi dynasty is contained in Donald Clark, "Autonomy, Legitimacy, and Tributary Politics: Sino-Korean Relations in the Fall of Koryŏ and the Founding of the Yi" (Ph.D. diss., Harvard University, 1978). Also

James B. Palais, "Han Yongu's Studies of Early Chosŏn Intellectual History," *Journal of Korean Studies* 2 (1980): 209–10.

3. Palais, *Politics and Policy*, p. 9.

4. The term *yangban* originally denoted the "two files" of officials, civilian and military, that lined up outside the royal audience hall of the king during the Koryŏ dynasty (918–1392). During the Yi dynasty, the term gradually took on a wider meaning, referring, in general, to the officialdom. By the nineteenth century, yangban came to connote aristocrat or high status person. The general requirements for the usage revolved around the maintenance of status through a combination of factors that included public officeholding, land, and wealth, or aristocratic lineage.

5. Palais, *Politics and Policy*, p. 5.

6. Ibid.

7. Ibid., p. 285.

8. Joungwon Kim, *Divided Korea: The Politics of Development* (Cambridge: East Asian Research Center, Harvard University, 1975), p. 8.

9. Recent research on Yi social history stresses the influence of Neo-Confucian orthodoxy on Korean society, tracing the gradual Confucianization of Korea after 1400. See Edward Wagner, "Two Early Genealogies and Women's Status in Early Yi Dynasty Korea," in Laurel Kendall and Mark Peterson, eds., *Korean Women: A View from the Inner Room* (New Haven, N. J.: East Rock Press, 1984), pp. 23–32; also Mark Peterson, "Women Without Sons: A Measure of Social Change in Yi Dynasty Korea," ibid., pp. 33–44.

10. Palais, *Politics and Policy*, p. 2.

11. Ibid., p. 285.

12. Martina Deuchler, *Confucian Gentlemen and Barbarian Envoys* (Seattle: University of Washington Press, 1977).

13. Ibid., p. 92.

14. Ibid., pp. 104–7.

15. Key-hiuk Kim, *The Last Phase of the East Asian World Order* (Berkeley and Los Angeles: University of California Press, 1980), pp. 1–38.

16. This group is referred to variously as the Independence party (T'ongnipdang), Enlightenment party (Kaehwadang), or the Progressive party (Chinbodang). The major leaders of this group were Kim Okkyun (1851–94), Pak Yŏnghyo (1861–1939), Hong Yongsik (1855–84), Sŏ Kwangbŏm (1859–?) and Sŏ Chaep'il (1864–1951). See Yong-ho Ch'oe, "The Kapsin Coup of 1884: A Reassessment," *Korean Studies* 6 (1982): 105–24.

17. In 1882 there was a fairly widespread acceptance of the necessity of using Western technology. The debate around selective adoption of technology, "enriching the well-being of the people by taking advantage of the useful" (*iyong husaeng*) was reminiscent of the *ti-yung* debates in China, also in the 1880s. See Deuchler, *Confucian Gentlemen*, p. 151.

18. Harold Cook, "Kim Okkyun and the Background of the 1884 Emeute" (Ph.D. diss., Harvard University, 1968), pp. 449–88.

19. Ch'oe, "Kapsin Coup," pp. 109–18.
20. Sources on the Tonghak Rebellion abound. A few standard works include: Kim Sanggi, *Tonghak kwa Tonghangnan* (Seoul: Han'guk ilbosa, 1975); Yi Sŏngŭn, "Tonghak undong kwa Han'guk ŭi kundaehwa kwajŏng" (The Tonghak movement and its meaning in modern Korean history), *Han'guk sasang* 4 (August 1962): 14–28; for English sources see Lee, *Politics of Korean Nationalism,* pp. 19–33; Young-ick Lew, "The Kabo Reform Movement: Korean and Japanese Reform Efforts in Korea, 1894" (Ph.D. diss., Harvard University), pp. 50–121; Benjamin Weems, *Reform, Rebellion, and the Heavenly Way* (Tucson: University of Arizona Press, 1964).
21. Lew, "Kabo Reform Movement," pp. 60–84.
22. Ibid., p. 105.
23. Ibid.
24. For a detailed analysis in English of the Kabo reforms see ibid; see also Lew's "An Analysis of Reform Documents of the Kabo Reform Movement," *Journal of Social Science and Humanities,* no. 40 (Dec. 1974).
25. C. I. Eugene Kim and Han-kyo Kim, *Korea and the Politics of Imperialism, 1876–1910* (Berkeley and Los Angeles: University of California Press, 1967), pp. 83–84.
26. Sin Yongha, *Tongnip hyŏphoe yŏn'gu* (Studies on the Independence Club) (Seoul: Ilchogak, 1976). Also, Vipan Chandra, "Nationalism and Popular Participation in Government in Late 19th-Century Korea: The Contribution of the Independence Club (1896–1898)" (Ph.D. diss., Harvard University, 1977).
27. Gari Ledyard, "The Korean Language Reform of 1446: The Origin, Background and Early History of the Korean Alphabet" (Ph.D. diss., University of California, Berkeley, 1966).
28. Chandra, "Nationalism and Popular Participation," pp. 184–220.
29. Ibid., p. 23.
30. Ibid., p. 154.
31. Sin Yongha, *Studies on the Independence Club,* pp. 666–67.
32. Yi Kwangnin, *Han'guk kaehwa sasang yŏn'gu* (Seoul: Ilchogak, 1979). Yi Kwangnin, *Kaehwadang yŏn'gu* (Studies on the Progressive party) (Seoul: Ilchogak, 1973).
33. Ch'oe Ch'un, *Han'guk sinmunsa* (Seoul: Ilchogak, 1968).
34. The Korean Enlightenment spawned numerous study societies and clubs devoted to examining Western thought and introducing new institutions to Korea. These groups were the source of many of the early Korean publications that contributed in this period to Koreans' understanding of the outside world. The following organizations were among the most prominent: the Korean Self-Strengthening Society (Taehan cha'ganghoe); Friends Society (Tong'uhoe); National Education Society (Kungmin kyoyukhoe); the Korea Club (Taehan kurakbu); the Great Eastern Study Society (Taedong hakhoe); North Korean Study Society (Hanbuk hakhoe); the Northwest Study Society (Sŏbuk hakhoe); the Kyŏnggi and Honam Study Society (Kiho hakhoe); and

the South Chŏlla Study Society (Honam hakhoe). For a discussion of these groups and their publications see Cho Yongman, "Ilcheha ŭi uri sinmunhwa undong" in Cho Yongnam, ed., *Ilcheha ŭi munhwa undongsa* (Seoul: Asea munje yŏn'guso, 1969), pp. 3–208.

35. Sin Yongha, "Pak Ŭnsik ŭi kyoyuk kugak sasang e taehayŏ," *Han'guk hakbo* 1, no. 1 (Fall 1975): 84.

36. Ibid.

37. Sin Ilch'ŏl, *Sin Ch'aeho ŭi yŏksa sasang yŏn'gu* (Seoul: Koryŏ tae-hakkyo Ch'ulp'anbu, 1981), pp. 65–70.

38. Lee Kwang-rin, "Korea's Responses to Social Darwinism," *Korea Journal* 18 (April–May, 1978): 45.

39. Sin Yongha, "Pak Ŭnsik ŭi kyoyuk kugak sasang e taehayŏ," p. 59.

40. Hao Chang, *Liang Ch'i-ch'ao and Intellectual Transition in China, 1890–1907* (Cambridge: Harvard University Press, 1971). See also Joseph Levenson, *Liang Ch'i-ch'ao and the Mind of Modern China*, and Lin Yü-sheng, *The Crisis of Chinese Consciousness*, for their discussions of intellectual transition and the reformulation of Confucianism.

41. Chang, *Liang Ch'i-ch'ao*, p. 306.

42. Michael Kalton, "The Neo-Confucian World View and Value System of Yi Dynasty Korea" (Ph.D. diss., Harvard University, 1977), pp. 33–35. Thomas Metzger discussed the concept of activism and struggle in the context of the Confucian concern for overcoming evil and realizing the good nature within oneself. Koreans of this period, however, were concerned that excessive formalism in Korean Confucian thought had stifled activism and hence the will to reform the political system. Thomas Metzger, *Escape from Predicament: Neo-Confucianism and China's Evolving Political Culture* (New York: Columbia University Press, 1977).

43. I draw here on Lin Yü-sheng's analysis of the universality of the Confucian tradition in China and the impetus for a totalistic approach to changing values. Lin Yü-sheng, "Radical Iconoclasm," p. 26.

44. Sin Ch'aeho, for one, repeatedly stressed this theme in his early writing as well as his later historical works. Sin Ilch'ŏl, *Sin Ch'aeho ŭi yŏksa sasang yŏn'gu*, pp. 4–16; 140–52.

45. Deuchler, *Confucian Gentlemen and Barbarian Envoys*, p. 105. In the 1880s dynasty officials had rallied against adopting outside ideas and technology under the slogan "protect orthodoxy, ban heterodoxy" (*wijŏng ch'ŏksa*).

46. Chu Sigyŏng, "Kungmunnon," *Tongnip sinmun*, April 27, 1897, p. 1.

47. Pak Ŭnsik, *Han'guk t'ongsa* (Seoul, 1910); Sin Ch'aeho, *Toksa sillon* (Seoul, 1908).

48. Michael Robinson, "National Identity and the Thought of Sin Ch'aeho: Sadaejuŭi and Chuch'e in History and Politics," *Journal of Korean Studies* 5 (1984): 121–42. For an example in Sin's writing on this line of thought see Sin Ch'aeho, "Ae'guksa wa ae'guksim ŭi kwangye" (The relationship between patriotism and history), *Tanje Sin Ch'aeho chŏnjip* 2 (Tanje Sin Ch'aeho sŏnsaeng ki'nyŏm saŏphoe, 1979), pp. 71–82.

172 *Notes*

49. Ch'oe Hyŏnbae, *Chosŏn kaengsaeng ŭi to* (Seoul: Chŏngŭmsa, 1962), pp. 32–33. First published in serial form in the *Tonga ilbo* in 1926.

50. A standard account of the Christian missions in Korea is presented in George L. Paik, *The History of Protestant Missions in Korea, 1832–1910* (Seoul: Yonsei University Press, 1971). See also Donald Clark, *Christianity in Modern Korea* (New York: University Press of America, 1986) and Kenneth Wells, "Civic Morality in the Nationalist Thought of Yun Ch'i-ho, 1881–1911," *Papers on Far Eastern History* (A.N.U.)28 (1983): 107–51.

51. Michael Robinson, "Nationalism and the Korean Tradition, 1896–1920: Iconoclasm, Reform, and National Identity," *Korean Studies,* vol. 10 (1987): 25–53.

52. Roger Janelli, "The Origins of Korean Folklore Scholarship," *Journal of American Folklore* 99 (1986): 24–49.

53. For a general account of the 1905–10 period see Kim and Kim, *Korea and Politics of Imperialism;* also Hilary Conroy, *The Japanese Seizure of Korea 1868–1910: A Study of Realism and Idealism in International Relations* (Philadelphia: University of Pennsylvania Press, 1960).

54. For a full text of the 1907 Newspaper Law (Shimbunshi hō), the 1908 Newspaper Regulations (Shimbunshi kisoku), and the 1909 Publication Law (Shūppan hō) see Chōsen Sōtokufu, *Chōsen hōrei shuran* (Keijō: Chōsen sōtokufu, 1915), pp. 15–23.

55. Kim and Kim, *Korea and Politics of Imperialism,* pp. 169–71.

56. Standard English-language sources on the 1910–45 period are Lee, *Politics of Korean Nationalism;* Scalapino and Lee, *Communism in Korea;* Andrew Grajdanzev, *Modern Korea* (New York: John Day and Co., 1944); Ku, *Korea Under Colonialism;* Bruce Cumings, *The Origins of the Korean War* (Princeton: Princeton University Press, 1983); Dae-sook Suh, *The Korean Communist Movement* (Princeton: Princeton University Press, 1967): Gregory Henderson, *Korea: The Politics of the Vortex* (Cambridge: Harvard University Press, 1968). Among numerous Ph.D. dissertations: Wonmo Dong, "Japanese Colonial Policy and Practice in Korea, 1905–1945: A Study in Assimilation" (Georgetown University, 1965); Baldwin, "The March First Movement: Korean Challenge and Japanese Response"; Edwin Gragert, "Landownership Change in Korea Under Japanese Colonial Rule: 1900–1935" (Columbia University 1982); Joung Yole Rew, "A Study of the Government-General of Korea, with an Emphasis on the Period Between 1919 and 1931" (American University, 1962); Michael Robinson, "The Origins and Development of Korean Nationalist Ideology, 1920–1926: Culture, Identity, National Development and Political Schism" (University of Washington, 1979); Karl Moskowitz, "Current Assets: The Employees of Japanese Banks in Colonial Korea" (Harvard, 1979); Arthur Gardner, "The Korean Nationalist Movement and An Ch'angho, Advocate of Gradualism" (University of Hawaii, 1979); Carter J. Eckert, "The Origins of Korean Capitalism: The Koch'ang Kims and the Kyŏngsŏng Spinning and Weaving Company, 1876–1945" (University of Washington, 1986).

57. Government General of Korea, *Results of Three Years of Administration of Chōsen Since Annexation* (Keijō: Government General of Korea, 1914), p. 242.
58. Ibid., p. 49.
59. Ibid., p. 54.
60. Chōsen sōtokufu, Keimukyoku, *Chōsen ni okeru shuppanbutsu gaiyō* (Keijō: Keimukyoku, 1930), pp. 51, 64, 138.
61. Gragert, "Landownership Change in Korea," p. 328.
62. Ibid., p. 329. For a separate discussion of land-tenure issues see Karl Moskowitz, "The Creation of the Oriental Development Company: Japanese Illusions Meet Korean Reality," *Occasional Papers on Korea*, no. 2 (March 1974), pp. 73–121.
63. Yi Son'gun, "Ilche ch'ongdokbu ŭi hŏnp'yŏng chŏnch'aek wa sasang t'anap," *Han'guk sasang* 8 (June 1966): 7–42.
64. Gardner, "The Korean Nationalist Movement and An Ch'angho," pp. 41–58.
65. Kim Kŭnsu, *Han'guk chapchi kaegwang mit hobyŏl mokch'ajip* (Seoul: Han'gukhak yŏn'guso, 1973).
66. Cumings, *Origins of the Korean War*, pp. 12–16.
67. See Baldwin, "The March First Movement"; also Ku, *Korea Under Colonialism.*
68. Lee, *Politics of Korean Nationalism*, p. 114.
69. Dong, "Japanese Colonial Policy in Korea," p. 266.
70. Baldwin, "The March First Movement," chap. 8.

2. The Rise of Cultural Nationalism

1. Lee, *Politics of Korean Nationalism*, chap. 8.
2. Suh, *Korean Communist Movement*, pp. 8–9.
3. Lee, *Politics of Korean Nationalism*, pp. 148–49.
4. Ibid., p. 137.
5. Ibid., p. 177.
6. Dong, "Japanese Colonial Policy in Korea," pp. 281–83. Figures quoted in Dong are from Archives of the Japanese Ministry of Foreign Affairs, *The State of Public Peace and Order in Korea*, 1922, sect. 1, pp. 171–72.
7. Chōsen sōtokufu, Keimukyoku, *Chōsen chian jōkyō* (Keijō: Chōsen sōtokufu, 1922), p. 76.
8. By custom, social and reform organizations invariably published their goals and philosophy upon their establishment. These were usually contained in a "Ch'wijisŏ" (Prospectus) published in an organ journal or publicized in the nationalist press.
9. *Saitō Makoto Kanken bunsho*, 724, "Chōsen tokuritsu undō ni tsuite taisaku" (Policies regarding the Korean independence movement, Aug. 27,

1920). Quoted in Kang Tongjin, *Ilche ǔi Han'guk ch'imnyak chǒngch'aeksa* (Seoul: Han'gilsa, 1980), p. 385.

10. Kang, *Ilche ǔi Han'guk ch'imnyak chǒngch'aeksa*, p. 384.

11. For a complete text of the censorship standard for Korea see: Chōsen sōtokufu, Keimukyoku, *Chōsen shuppan keisatsu gaiyō* (Keijō: Keimukyoku, Toshoka, 1940), pp. 68–73.

12. Keimukyoku, *Keimu ihō* 288 (April 1930): pp. 73–74 (Seoul, Chōsen sōtokufu).

13. Cho Yongman, "Ilcheha ǔi uri sinmunhwa undong," in Cho Yongman, ed. *Ilcheha ǔi munhwa undongsa* (Seoul: Asea munje yǒn'guso, 1969), p. 121.

14. Chōsen sōtokufu, *Chōsen ni okeru shuppanbutsu gaiyō 1930,* pp. 19–34.

15. Michael Robinson, "Publication Policy and the Korean Nationalist Movement," pp. 335–36.

16. For a compilation of publication seizures of colonial publications between 1920–1939, see ibid., p. 327. Quoted from Chǒng Chinsǒk, "Nōhon kenetsu," *Asea Kōron*, vol. 3, no. 10 (Oct. 1974).

17. Kim Sangman, *Tonga ilbo 50 nyǒnsa* (Seoul: Tonga ilbosa, 1975), p. 113.

18. Ibid., pp. 93–95.

19. "Chuji rǔl sǒnmyǒng hanora" (Declaration of principles), *Tonga ilbo*, April 1, 1920, p. 1.

20. Ibid., p. 1.

21. Paek Sunjae, "Chapchi rǔl t'onghae pon ilchesidae ǔi kǔndaehwa undong," *Sindonga* 18 (Jan. 1966): 393–95.

22. Ibid., p. 396.

23. Cho Yongman, "Ilcheha ǔi uri sinmunhwa undong," p. 57.

24. Ibid., p. 97.

25. Paek Sunjae, "Chapchi rǔl t'onghae pon ilchesidae ǔi kǔndaehwa undong," p. 365. There was an ambivalent attitude toward the term *chonghap chapchi*. Some felt that the mass-circulation magazines had lost their political consciousness and zeal, a quality that had characterized the earlier *tong'in chapchi*. For an example of such a critique see: XYZ Saeng "Hyǒnha sinmun chapchi e taehan pip'an," *Kaebyǒk*, vol. 6, no. 10 (Dec. 1925).

26. Cho Yongman, "Ilcheha ǔi uri sinmunhwa undong," p. 121.

27. *Kaebyǒk (Creation)* began publication in June 1920 and ceased publication in August 1928 after seventy-two issues. It resumed publication using several different names in the 1930s. For a complete listing of the table of contents of *Kaebyǒk* see Kim Kǔnsu, *Han'guk chapchi kaegwan mit hobyǒl mokch'ajip* (Seoul: Han'gukhak yǒn'guso, 1973), pp. 279–322.

28. Paek Sunjae, "Chapchi rǔl t'onghae pon ilchesidae ǔi kǔndaehwa undong," p. 335.

29. Other Ch'ǒndogyo publications during the 1920s and 1930s included *Children (Ǒrini)*, *Wives (Puin)*, and *Student (Haksaeng)*.

30. Ch'oe Tŏksin, "Kaebyŏk kyŏng'in ŭl naemyŏnsŏ," *Kaebyŏk kyŏng'-inbon* (Seoul, Kaebyŏksa, 1969), Frontpiece, p. 1.
31. Ibid., p. 3.
32. Chow Tse-tung, *The May Fourth Movement: Intellectual Revolution in Modern China* (Stanford, Calif.: Stanford University Press, 1960), p. 45.
33. Ibid., chap. 9.
34. Yi Kwangsu appears ubiquitously in general accounts of the colonial period. While his contributions to the early nationalist movement and the development of modern Korean literature are acknowledged, his withdrawal from politics and later collaboration with the Japanese in the 1930s as head of the All Korea Writers League are the subject of much controversy. Yi was tried and convicted as a collaborator in a show trial after 1945, and was kidnapped and presumed executed by North Korean forces in 1950. Sources on Yi are Yi Kwangsu, "Na ŭi kobaek," *Yi Kwangsu sŏnjip* (Seoul: O'mungak, 1979); *Han'guk inmyŏng taesajŏn* (Biographical dictionary of important Koreans) (Seoul: Sinbyŏng munhwasa, 1967); Song Uk, "Han'guk chisig'in kwa yŏksajŏk hyŏnsil," *Sansaggye*, (April 1965), pp. 206–27; Pak Kyŏngja, "20 segi ch'ogi ŭi Han'guk minjokjuŭi ilsaeng: Ch'unwŏn ŭi minjok kaejoron chungsim ŭro," *Sukdae saron* 7 (Dec. 1972): 169–85. For an account of Yi's trial after 1945 see Kil Chinhyŏn, *Yŏksa e tasi mut'nŭnda: panmin t'ŭkwi wa ch'in'ilp'a* (Seoul: Sam'minsa, 1984).
35. General descriptions of *Kaebyŏk* and its role in the political ferment of the 1920s abound. See Paek Sunjae, "Chapchi rŭl t'onghae pon ilchesidae ŭi kŭndaehwa undong"; Cho Yongman, *Ilcheha ŭi uri sinmunhwa undong;* Ch'oe Ch'un, "Han'guk ŭi ch'ulp'an yŏn'gu: 1910 ŭrobutŏ 1923 kkagi," *Souldae sinmun yŏn'gu hakbo,* vol. 1 (1964).
36. Segye rŭl alla," *Kaebyŏk* 1, no. 1 (June 1920): 3.
37. Ibid., p. 6.
38. "Segye sam taemunje ŭi p'agŭp kwa Chosŏn'in ŭi kag'o yŏha," *Kaebyŏk* 1, no. 2 (July 1920): 2–17.
39. Ibid., p. 6.
40. Ibid.
41. O T'aehwa, "Kŭppyŏn hayaganŭn singu sasang ŭi ch'ungdol," *Kaebyŏk* 1, no. 1 (June 1920): 80–84.
42. Pak Yŏnghyo, "*Kaebyŏk* ŭi ch'anggan ŭl munhago," *Kaebyŏk* 1, no. 1 (July 1920): 31.
43. Pak Sajik, "Chosŏn sahoe ŭi suyang munje," *Kaebyŏk* 1, no. 2 (July 1920): 45–49.
44. Ibid., p. 49.
45. Hyŏn Sangyun, "Kŏdŭm naja," *Kaebyŏk* 3, no. 1 (Jan. 1922): 20–30.
46. Ibid., p. 28.
47. Chang Tŏksu, "Saesidae ŭi saesaram," *Kaebyŏk* 3, no. 1 (Jan. 1922): 34.
48. Ibid., p. 34.

49. Yi Tonhwa, "Chosŏn sinmunhwa kŏnsŏl e taehan t'oan," *Kaebyŏk* 1, no. 4 (Oct. 1920): 12.

50. Ibid., p. 15.

51. Yi Tonhwa, "Saenghwal ŭi chokkŏn ŭl ponwirohan Chosŏn ŭi kaejo saŏp," *Kaebyŏk* 2, no. 11 (Oct. 1921): 19–20.

52. Yi Tonhwa, "Chosŏn sinmunhwa kŏnsŏl . . . ," p. 13.

53. Ibid., pp. 13–14.

54. Yi's early contributions to *Kaebyŏk* are included in a collection of Yi's works in *Ch'unwŏn ŭi myŏngjak nonmunjip: minjok kaejoron* (Seoul: Usinsa, 1981).

55. Yi Kwangsu, "Sonyŏn ege," *Kaebyŏk*, vol. 2, no. 11; vol. 3, no. 3 (Nov. 1921; March, 1922).

56. Yi Kwangsu, "Chungch'u kyegŭp wa sahoe," *Kaebyŏk* 2, no. 7 (July 1921): 24–31.

57. *Chungch'u* could be translated as "pivot" or "core." In this case, Yi implies "core" because of his plan for the spread of a "reconstructionist" consciousness outward in concentric circles, beginning with the "core" class of society.

58. Yi Kwangsu, "Chungch'u kyegŭp wa sahoe," p. 27.

59. Ibid., p. 29. Yi elaborated on "cultivation and education leagues" in his "Minjok kaejoron" a year later.

60. Ibid., pp. 30–31.

61. The contemporary press of the 1920s labeled the various cultural and educational projects sponsored by nationalist organizations as the "cultural movement" (*munhwa undong*). This should not imply that there was any strong coordination between projects. In only two cases, the Korean production movement (Chosŏn mulsan changnyŏhoe) and the Society for the Creation of a National University (Minnip taehak kisŏng chunbihoe), the first of which became one of the largest mass efforts of the nationalist movement in the colony, was there a significant centralized leadership. These movements will be treated in the following chapter. Those advocating such programs earned the title of "cultural faction" (*munhwap'a*), a term usually used derisively by leftist critics in the colonial press.

62. Yi Kwangsu, "Minjok kaejoron," *Kaebyŏk* 3, no. 5 (May 1922): 18–72. *Kaejo* is translated here as "reconstruction." Yi sometimes used the weaker term *hyŏksin* reform, but he generally followed the usage of others, who preferred *kaejo* to describe their plans for Korean society. Yi avoids *hyŏngmyŏng* (revolution), perhaps because of censorship, but more probably because of his own interest in avoiding identification with socialism and the class struggle then becoming popular in intellectual circles. When Yi did use *hyŏngmyŏng*, it was to describe the effects of *kaejo*.

63. Yi Kwangsu, *Na ŭi kobaek*, quoted from *Yi Kwangsu sŏnjip*, pp. 552–54.

64. Ibid., p. 553.

65. The Chinbohoe, organized by Tonghak leader Son Pyŏnghŭi, was a

political association built on Tonghak networks. The Chinbohoe had merged with the Ilchinhoe in 1904. After the split in 1905, Son Pyŏnghŭi formed a separate religious movement, the Ch'ŏndogyo, that continued the earlier Tonghak faith.

66. The chronology in *The Selected Works of Yi Kwangsu* dates the first publication of *Mujŏng* in 1910 in *Taehan hunghakbo;* it was republished in the *Maeil sinbo* (the only Korean vernacular newspaper of the 1910–19 period, run by the GGK), in 1917. Undoubtedly the second serialization reached a dramatically wider readership than the first.

67. Song Minbo, "Ilcheha ŭi han'guk chohang munhak," in Cho Yong-man, ed., *Ilcheha ŭi munhwa undongsa,* pp. 257–58.

68. Gardner, "The Korean Nationalist Movement and An Ch'angho, Advocate of Gradualism."

69. Lee, *Politics of Korean Nationalism,* pp. 104–6.

70. Ibid., chap. 8.

71. Yi Kwangsu, *Na ŭi kobaek,* pp. 247–48.

72. It seemed to be Yi's intent to use reconstructionism (*kaejojuŭi*) as a replacement for "nationalism" (*minjokchuŭi*). The whole idea of a large, coordinated cultural movement could thus be neatly summed up as the *kaejo undong,* read "nationalist movement."

73. Yi Kwangsu, "Minjok kaejoron," p. 18. The preface of the *Kaejoron* closes with the phrase "on the opening day of the Pacific Conference" (T'aepy'ŏngyang hoeŭi). This conference was convened to lobby the Western Powers and Japan at the Washington Conference then in session. See Kim Chunyŏp and Kim Ch'angsun, *Hanguk kongsanjuŭi undongsa* (Seoul: Asea munje yŏn'guso, 1962) 1: 155–56.

74. Ibid., p. 19.

75. Ibid., p. 26.

76. Ibid., p. 72.

77. Ibid., p. 32.

78. Ibid., pp. 33–34.

79. Ibid., pp. 37, 41.

80. Ibid., p. 35.

81. Ibid., p. 41.

82. Ibid.

83. Ibid., pp. 44–45.

84. Ibid., p. 45.

85. Ibid.

86. Ibid.

87. Ibid., pp. 40–41.

88. Ibid., p. 29.

89. Ibid., p. 49.

90. Ibid., p. 31.

91. Ibid., p. 41.

92. *Tonga ilbo,* July 29, 1921. Quoted in Daniel S. Juhn, "Nationalism and

Korean Business Under Japanese Colonial Rule," *Korea Journal* 17, no. 1 (Jan. 1977): 4–12.
93. Yi Kwangsu, "Minjok kaejoron," p. 31.
94. Ibid., p. 67.
95. Ibid., pp. 22–23.
96. Maruyama Tsurukichi, *Chōsen chian no genjō oyobi shōrai* (Keijō: Chōsen sōtokufu, Jimuka, 1922).

3. *Within Limits: Moderate Nationalist Movements*

1. Cho Yongman, "Ilcheha ŭi uri sinmunhwa undong," in Cho Yongman et al., eds., *Ilcheha ŭi munhwa undongsa* (Seoul: Asea munje yŏn'guso, Han'guk yŏn'gu ch'ongsŏ, III, Minjung sŏgwang, 1970), pp. 154–55.
2. Ibid., p. 155.
3. David McCann, "Arirang: The National Folksong of Korea," in David McCann, ed., *Studies on Korea in Transition* (Honolulu: Center for Korean Studies, University of Hawaii).
4. Government General of Chōsen, *Annual Report on Reforms and Progress in Chōsen, 1918–1921* (Keijō: Government General of Chōsen, 1921), p. 10.
5. Roger Janelli, "The Origins of Korean Folklore Scholarship," *Journal of American Folklore* 99 (1986): 30–33. Ch'oe Namson's work published in the mid and late 1920s: "Tan'gunnon" (A theory of Tan'gun), *Tonga ilbo*, March 3, 1926; "Untitled Introduction," *Kyemyŏng*, vol. 19 (1927); "Shaman'gyo ch'agi" (Survey of shamanism), *Kyemyŏng* 19, no. 2: 51; "Purham munhwa non" (A theory of Purham culture), *Chosŏn kŭp Chosŏn minjok* (Korea and the Korean people).
6. Janelli, "Korean Folklore," p. 16.
7. *Kyemyŏng (Enlightenment)* was published between 1921 and 1933 in twenty-four issues. The May 1927 issue (no. 19) published important papers by both Ch'oe Namsŏn and Yi Nŭnghwa on Korean shamanism and folklore.
8. For general discussions in English of the Japanese colonial education system see Dong, "Japanese Colonial Policy and Practice in Korea, 1905–1945: A Study in Assimilation"; Rew, "A Study of the Government General of Korea, with an Emphasis on the Period Between 1919 and 1931"; Grajdanzev, *Modern Korea;* Paul Anh, "Education as an Instrument of National Assimilation: A Study of Japan in Korea" (Ph.D. diss., Columbia University, 1931). Government General of Korea, *Annual Report on Reforms and Progress in Chōsen, 1914–1930* (Keijō: Government General of Korea) (hereafter *ARGGK*). Government General annual reports contain generally reliable statistics on enrollments and school numbers by type.
9. *ARGGK*, 1914, p. 54.
10. Rew, "Study of the Government General of Korea," p. 179.
11. *ARGGK*, 1922–1924, pp. 88–90.

12. Ibid., p. 90.

13. *Chosŏn ilbo,* "Chosŏn minnip taehak p'algi e ch'wihayŏ," Dec. 1, 1922.

14. *ARGGK,* 1923–24, p. 97. Figures cited for the "proportion of Koreans more or less conversant with Japanese" were: 1913, 7 per 1,000; 1921, 26 per 1,000; and 1923, 40 per 1,000.

15. "Chosŏn'in ŭi kyoyuk yong'ŏ rŭl ilbon'ŏro kangjeham ŭl p'yeji hara" (On abolishing the forced use of Japanese for Koreans in the schools), *Tonga ilbo,* April 11, 1920.

16. Kim and Kim, *Han'guk kongsanjuŭi undongsa* 2: 8–9; 10: 224.

17. Ibid., pp. 104–6.

18. "Chosŏn ch'ŏngnyŏn yŏnhaphoe ch'wijisŏ," *Tonga ilbo,* July 15, 1920.

19. Kim and Kim, *Han'guk kongsanjuŭi undongsa,* p. 107.

20. Rew. "Government General of Korea," pp. 181–82; *ARGGK* 1930– 32, p. 75.

21. *Tonga ilbosasa, 1920–1945* (Seoul: Tonga ilbosa, 1975), p. 214.

22. Ibid., pp. 214–16. For an extended discussion of the February 8 declaration See: Kim Sŏnsik, "Ilcheha Han'guk haksaeng undong" (Student movements under Japanese rule) in Ch'oe Yonghŭi et al., eds. *Ilcheha ŭi minjok undongsa* (Seoul: Asea munje yŏn'guso, 1971) 4: 137–53. Also: Chŏng Sehyŏn, *Hang'il haksaeng minjok undongsa yŏn'gu* (Seoul: Ilchisa, 1975), pp. 46–92.

23. "Chosŏn minnip taehak palgi e ch'wihayŏ," *Chosŏn ilbo,* December 1, 2, 1922. In *Chosŏn ilbo myŏng sasŏl obaeksŏn* (Seoul: Chosŏn ilbosa, 1972), pp. 21–25.

24. Ibid.

25. Kim and Kim, *Han'guk kongsanjuŭi undongsa* 2: 12. Prominent members of the society included Yi Sanjae, Hyŏn Sangyun, Han Yong'un, Yi Sŭnghun, Hŏ Hon, Song Chinu, Chang Tŏksu, Yi Sangch'im, Yi Kapsŏng, Pak Hŭido, Kang Int'aek, Namgung Ŏk, Hong Tŏg'yu, Chang Tobin. For a complete listing of early subscribers to the movement see *Tonga ilbo,* March 30, 1923.

26. "Chosŏn minnip taehak palgie ch'wihayŏ," *Chosŏn ilbo,* Dec. 1–2, 1922.

27. Ibid.

28. Ibid.

29. "Minnip taehak saŏp kyehoeksŏ" (A plan for a national university), March 29, 1923. Quoted in *Tonga ilbosa,* pp. 218–19.

30. Ibid.

31. "Yŏnnae ilch'ŏnmanwŏn kyehoek" (A plan for one million wŏn within the year), *Tonga ilbo,* April 4, 1923.

32. XYZ [pseud.], "Cheundong ŭi hoego kwa pi'pan," *Tonga ilbo,* Jan. 1, 1924.

33. Kim and Kim, *Han'guk kongsanjuŭi undongsa* 2: 14.

180 *Notes*

34. Ibid., p. 15.

35. Cho Yongman, "Ilcheha ŭi uri sinmunhwa undong," p. 126.

36. The Chosŏn'ŏ yŏn'guhoe was formed in December 1921 to bring together language scholars then working privately or affiliated with separate scholarly societies. The founders of the society included: Im Kyŏngjae, Ch'oe Tuson, Yi Sŭnggyu, Chang Chiyong, Kwŏn Tŏkkyu, Yi Pyŏnggu, Yi San-ch'un, Yi Kyubang, Sim Myŏnggyun, and Kim Yŏn'gyŏng. Han'gŭl hakhoe, *Han'gŭl hakhoe 50 nyŏnsa* (Seoul: Han'gŭl hakhoe, 1971), p. 5.

37. Ibid., pp. 3–18.

38. Chu Sigyŏng, "Kungmunnon," *Tongnip sinmun*, Apr. 24, 1897.

39. Sin Yongha, "Chu Sigyŏng ŭi aeguk kyemong sasang," *Han'guk sahoehak yŏn'gu cheilchip pyŏlswe* 1 (Jan. 1977): 30.

40. Ibid., p. 28.

41. "Kyoyukyong ilbon'ŏ e taehayŏ," *Chosŏn ilbo*, May 19, 1920.

42. The Korean Language Research Society (Chosŏn'yŏn'guhoe) became the Korean Language Study Society (Chŏsŏn'ŏ hakhoe) in 1931, and after 1945, it became the Han'gŭl Society (Han'gŭl hakhoe).

43. Han'gŭl hakhoe, *Han'gŭl hakhoe 50 nyŏnsa*, pp. 11–13.

44. By 1933, there were 402,300 students enrolled in Korean sunday schools (figures quoted in Cho Yongman, "Ilcheha ŭi uri sinmunhwa undong," p. 126).

45. Ibid., pp. 150–54.

46. Ibid., pp. 164–71.

47. Pak Pyŏngch'ae, "Ilcheha ŭi kug'ŏ undong yŏn'gu" (The language movement under Japanese rule), in Cho Yongman et al., eds., *Ilcheha ŭi munhwa undongsa* (Seoul: Asea munje yŏn'guso, 1973) 3: 469.

48. Ch'oe Hyŏnbae, *Han'gŭl ŭi parŭnkil* (Seoul: Chŏng'ŭmsa, 1945), p. 46.

49. Lee Hi-seung, "Recollections of the Korean Language Society Incident," in Marshall Pihl, ed., *Listening to Korea* (New York: Praeger, 1973), p. 41.

50. Eckert, "Origins of Korean Capitalism: The Koch'ang Kims and the Kyŏngsŏng Spinning and Weaving Company, 1876–1945," p. 160.

51. Hoon K. Lee, *Land Utilization and Rural Economy in Korea;* Cumings, *Origins of the Korean War;* Gragert, "Landownership Change in Korea Under Japanese Colonial Rule."

52. Eckert, "Origins of Korean Capitalism," p. 112.

53. Ibid., pp. 161–66.

54. Ibid., pp. 98–101.

55. Ibid., pp. 162–64.

56. Cho Yongman, "Ilcheha ŭi rui sinmunhwa undong," pp. 23–38. See also Cho Kijun, *Han'guk ŭi minjok kiŏp* (Seoul: Han'guk ilbosa, 1975), pp. 128–36.

57. "Tosan changnyŏ kŭm'il put'ŏ silhaeng" (Encouraging native production begins today), *Tonga ilbo*, Feb. 16, 1923.

58. Cho Kijun, *Chosŏn chabonjuŭi sŏngnip saron* (Seoul: Taewangsa, 1973), p. 559.

59. K. M. Wells, "The Rationale of Korean Economic Nationalism Under Japanese Rule, 1922–1932: The Case of Cho Man-sik's Products Promotion Society," *Modern Asian Studies* 19, no. 4 (1985): 829.

60. *Inmyŏng taesajŏn* (Biographical dictionary) (Seoul: Sinbyŏng munhwasa, 1967), p. 872.

61. Kim and Kim, *Han'guk kongsanjuŭi undongsa* 2:10. See also Yi Kwangsu, *Na ŭi kobaek*, pp. 252–53.

62. On Jan. 9, 1923, representatives of twenty organizations met and formed a preparatory committee to establish a national organization, the Chosŏn mulsan changnyŏhoe palgi chunbihoe. On January 20–25 formal meetings of the new national organization, Chosŏn mulsan changnyŏhoe, produced its formal charter and plan of action. Officers of the organization were Chŏn Songjun, director; Sŏl Ch'unhŭi, Chŏng Nosik, Kim Ch'ŏlsu, Kim Kansu, and Paek Kwansu, economic officers; Na Kyŏngsŏk, Kim Tonghyŏk, Ch'oe Sunt'ak, Pak Pongso, Kim Tŏkch'ong, survey officers; Yi Ch'angnin, Yi Kapsŏng, Pak Tongwŏn, Yi Tŏg'u, Han Inbong, Yi Siwan, Ch'oe Kyŏngho, Ko Yonghwan, propaganda officers.

63. Cho Kijun, *Han'guk chabonjuŭi sŏngnip saron*, p. 532.

64. The T'osan aeyong puinhoe (Wives association for use of native products) was formed as an auxiliary organization on Feb. 5, 1923.

65. For a full text of the charter of the Chosŏn mulsan changnyŏhoe see "Chosŏn mulsan changnyŏhoe ch'wijisŏ," *San'ŏpkye* 1, no. 1 (March 1923): 55–56.

66. Ibid., pp. 55–56.

67. Sankar Ghose, *Political Ideas and Movements in India* (Bombay: Allied Publishers, 1975); Francis G. Hutchins, *India's Revolution: Gandhi and the Quit India Movement* (Cambridge: Harvard University Press, 1973); Paul F. Power, *The Meanings of Gandhi* (Honolulu: University of Hawaii Press, 1971).

68. Cho Kijun, *Han'guk chabonjuŭi sŏngnip saron*, pp. 535–36.

69. Although the Buy Korean movement soon faltered, their publishing effort continued into the 1930s. *San'ŏpkye* (*Industrial World*) 1923–24 was followed by the *Chosŏn mulsan changnyŏ hoebo* (*Bulletin of the Native Production Encouragement Association*) between 1924–1931. In 1931, it was again retitled *Changsan* (*Encouraging Production*) and, later, *Silsaenghwal* (*Practical Living*), 1931–37.

70. One contemporary analyst estimated that prices almost doubled in 1923. See Chu Chonggŏn, "Musan kyegŭp kwa mulsan changnyŏ," *Tonga ilbo*, April 6–17, 1923.

71. Kim and Kim, *Han'guk kongsanjuŭi undongsa* 2: 17–18.

72. Cho Kijun, *Han'guk chabonjuŭi sŏngnip saron*, p. 535. Cho cites figures for parades in P'yŏngyang and other provincial cities with 10,000 or more participants.

73. Cho Kijun, "Chosŏn mulsan changnyŏ undong ŭi chŏn'gae kwajŏng kwa ku yŏksajŏk sŏnggyŏk," in An Pyŏngjik, ed., Han'guk kŭndae saron (Seoul: Chisik san'ŏpsa, 1977) 3: 62–91.

74. Eckert, "Origins of Korean Capitalism," p. 165.

75. Cho Kijun, Han'guk chabonjuŭi songnip saron, p. 546; see also Kang Tonjin, Ilche ŭi han'guk ch'imnyak chŏngch'aeksa, pp. 377–424, passim.

76. "Ilchu'nyŏn ki'nyŏm ŭl tanghayŏ," San'ŏpkye (March 1924), p. 1.

77. Ibid.

78. Yi Sŏngt'ae, "Chungsan kyegŭp ŭi igijŏk undong," Tonga ilbo, March 20, 1923.

79. Ibid.

80. "Ilchu'nyŏn ki'nyŏm ŭl tanghayŏ," p. 1.

81. Yun Yŏngnam, "Cha'myŏl inga, tosaeng inga?" (Shall we work or die?), Tonga ilbo, April 26, 1923; Na Kyŏngsŏk [Kongmin], "Sahoe munje wa mulsan changnyŏ" (Products promotion and social problems), Tonga ilbo, April 26–29, 1923.

82. Wells, "Rationale of Korean Economic Nationalism," pp. 844–47.

83. Cho Kijun, Han'guk chabonjuŭi sŏngnip saron, p. 543.

84. Saitō diary, quoted in Kang Tongjin, Ilche ŭi Han'guk ch'imnyak chŏngch'aeksa, p. 384.

85. Ibid., p. 380.

86. Robinson, "Colonial Publication Policy and the Korean Nationalist Movement," pp. 332–33.

87. Cho Kijun, Han'guk chabonjuŭi sŏngnip saron, pp. 536–39.

88. Governor General Saitō Makato's diary from 1919 to 1926 records the following numbers of his meetings with various important moderate nationalists: Kim Sŏngsu 14, Chang Tŏksu 12, Song Chinu 15, Yi Kwangsu 8. See Kang Tongjin, Ilche ŭi Han'guk ch'imnyak chongch'aeksa, p. 397.

89. Letter from Abe to Saitō, Nov. 11, 1921. Saitō Makoto kankei bunsho (Tokyo: Kokkai toshokan), quoted in Kang Tongjin, Han'guk chongch'aeksa, p. 397.

90. Ibid., p. 395.

91. Imamura Takeshi, "Hanseikizen no Chōsen" (Korea a half century ago), Chōsen kindai shiryō kenkyū shisei (Collected historical materials of modern Korea) 3: 167–208 (Tokyo: May 1960). In Henderson, Politics of the Vortex, p. 77. See also Grajdanzev, Modern Korea, pp. 45–46.

92. Kim Chunyŏp and Kim Ch'angsun provide a list of "bogus nationalist groups," Han'guk kongsanjuŭi undongsa 2: 22–24.

93. Hutchins, India's Revolution, pp. 123–30.

94. Ibid., pp. 44 and 112.

4. The Radical Critique of Cultural Nationalism

1. For a discussion in English of early Korean Socialists see: Scalapino and Lee, Communism in Korea 1: 3–66 (hereafter, Scalapino and Lee). See also

Suh, *Korean Communist Movement, 1918–1948,* and idem, *Documents of Korean Communism 1918–1948* (Princeton: Princeton University Press, 1970).

2. Scalapino and Lee 1: 22–23.

3. Ibid., pp. 32–37.

4. Chŏng Sehyŏn, *Hang'il haksaeng minjok undongsa yŏn'gu* (Seoul: Ilchisa, 1975), p. 85.

5. Government General of Korea, *Results of Three Years Administration of Chōsen,* p. 54.

6. Henry Smith II, *Japan's First Student Radicals* (Cambridge: Harvard University Press, 1972), pp. 29–30.

7. Ibid., p. 71.

8. Ibid., preface. For Kim Chunyŏn's subsequent role in the KCP, see Scalapino and Lee 1: 85, passim.

9. Ibid., p. 54.

10. Kim and Kim, *Han'guk kongsanjuŭi undongsa* 2: 30–31 (hereafter, Kim and Kim, vol. 2). See also Chŏng Sehyŏn, *Hang'il haksaeng minjok undongsa yŏn'gu,* passim.

11. Chōsen sōtokufu, Keimukyoku, *Chōsen chian jōkyō* (Keijō: 1922), p. 17. The original declaration was published in *Tonga ilbo,* Feb. 4, 1922. Quoted in Kim and Kim 2: 33.

12. "Nonsŏl" (Editorial), *Tonga ilbo,* Feb. 12, 1922.

13. Scalapino and Lee 1: 58–61.

14. Ibid., p. 60.

15. "Ch'ŏngnyŏndang taehoe kaech'oe" (The opening of the conference of Korean youth groups), *Tonga ilbo,* Jan 30, 1923.

16. "Chosŏn nodong kongjehoe ch'wijisŏ" (Prospectus of the Korean Fraternal Labor Association), *Tonga ilbo,* April 17, 1920.

17. Scalapino and Lee 1: 69.

18. Kim and Kim 2: 56.

19. Ibid., p. 38.

20. The Comintern was already disgusted with the lack of unity within the ranks of Korean Communists. They were also concerned about ideological purity. Comintern policy dictated coalition politics and united front tactics within the colony. It remained, however, a difficult problem to get Koreans to work together. For a general discussion of the left within the Korean colony, see Scalapino and Lee 1: 51–61.

21. See *Tonga ilbo* and *Chosŏn ilbo* for this period.

22. Chŏng Chinsŏk, *Han'guk ŏllon t'ujaengsa* (Seoul: Chŏng'ŭm mungo, 1975), pp. 84–85.

23. For a list of articles and features contained in these magazines see Kim Kŭnsu, *Han'guk chapchi kaegwan mit hobyŏl mokch'ajip* (Seoul: Han'gukhak yŏn'guso, 1973).

24. Koryoku, "Chōsen ni okeru shuppanbutsu no kosatsu," *Keimu ihō* 296 (December 1930): 39.

25. Chŏng Chinsŏk, *Han'guk ŏllon t'ujaengsa*, pp. 102–5.
26. Ibid., p. 105.
27. Aoyagi Nammei, *Chōsen tōchiron* (Keijō: Chōsen kenkyūsha, 1923), p. 296.
28. "Letter from Abe Mitsuka to Saitō, April 10, 1921," quoted in Kang Tongjin, *Ilche ŭi Han'guk chimnyak chŏngch'aeksa*, p. 381.
29. Chŏng Chinsŏk, *Han'guk ŏllon t'ujaengsa*, p. 43.
30. Ibid., p. 106.
31. Ibid., pp. 155–65.
32. Lucien Bianco, *Origins of the Chinese Revolution* (Stanford, Calif.: Stanford University Press, 1971), p. 45.
33. Tom Bottomore, ed., *A Dictionary of Marxist Thought* (Cambridge: Harvard University Press, 1983), p. 206.
34. "Chwijisŏ kŭp chojik" (Prospectus and organization), *Sinsaenghwal* 1 (March 1922): 68.
35. Kim Myŏngsik began his career in journalism on the editorial board of the *Tonga ilbo* in 1920. He was also a rival of Chang Tŏksu in the struggle to create a national youth federation in 1920. Kim's activities leaned increasingly toward radical organizations after 1920. He was a founding member of the Korean Fraternal Labor Association, editor of its organ magazine *Kongje*, and, in 1922, he helped to found *Sinsaenghwal*. He was sentenced in the *Sinsaenghwal* trial and served six months of his two-year sentence, being released early for health reasons.
36. Kim Myŏngsik, "Ku'munhwa wa sinmunhwa," *Sinsaenghwal* 2 (March 1922): 6.
37. Ibid., p. 6.
38. Yi Sŏngt'ae, "Sanghwal ŭi pullan," *Sinsaenghwal* 1 (March 1922): 24.
39. Ibid., p. 27.
40. Ibid., p. 28.
41. Ibid.
42. Chŏng Paek (Chŏng Chihyŏn) was active in radical circles in the 1920–25 period. He was part of the founding group of *Sinsaenghwal*, and a leader in the Socialist Alliance (Sahoejuŭi tongmaeng) that was formed in 1924. In the late 1920s, he joined the Chinese Communist party in the aftermath of the failure of the United Korean Independence party in 1927. After liberation, Chŏng was a member of the preparatory committee for the establishment of the Korean Communist party. See Suh, *Documents on Korean Communism*, pp. 145, 476, 524; Scalapino and Lee 1: 170. Also Kim and Kim, vol. 2, passim.
43. Chŏng Paek, "Minjung chŏngsin ŭi il koch'al," *Sinsaenghwal* 1, (March 1922): 32.
44. Ibid., p. 30.
45. Ibid., p. 32.
46. Yi Sŏngt'ae, "Hyŏndae munhwa ŭi panghyang," *Sinsaenghwal* 1, no. 9 (Nov. 1922): 2–8.
47. Ibid., p. 4.

48. Ibid., p. 7.
49. The standard secondary work on the development of Korean capitalism is Cho Kijun's *Han'guk chabonjuŭi sŏngnip saron*. The issue of when and in what manner Korean capitalism developed remains controversial in Korean historical literature because of the important link between early Korean industrial entrepreneurs and the Japanese colonial economy. English-language sources on the subject have also been affected by the debate over when and if modern economic growth began, in spite of or as a result of the colonial experience. See Sang-chul Suh, *Growth and Structural Change in the Korean Economy, 1910–1945* (Cambridge: Council on East Asian Studies, distributed by Harvard University Press, 1978). This important topic is only beginning to be explored in English-language studies. A recent Ph.D. dissertation (Eckert, "The Origins of Korean Capitalism: The Koch'ang Kims and the Kyŏngsŏng Spinning and Weaving Company, 1876–1945"), has recently provided ground-breaking material on the subject. Bruce Cumings also discusses the political impact of capitalist development on the colony and its effect on the political leadership of the postliberation era. See Cumings, *Origins of the Korean War*.
50. Chŏng Paek, "Minjung chŏngsin ŭi il koch'al," p. 32.
51. Ibid., p. 32.
52. "Chosŏn ŭi t'ŭki han ch'ŏji wa iedaehan t'ŭki han kujech'aek," *Kaebyŏk* 3, no. 1 (Jan. 1923): 25.
53. Ibid., p. 26.
54. Min, "Sasang ŭi ch'ase wa undong ŭi panghyang," *Kaebyŏk* 5, no. 3 (March 1924): 44–45.
55. Chŏng Paek, "Chisik kyegŭp ŭi mimang," *Sinsaenghwal* 1, no. 3 (May 1922): 18.
56. Ibid., p. 19.
57. "Chosŏn ŭi t'ŭki han ch'ŏji wa iedaehan t'ŭki han kujech'aek," p. 28.
58. Maurice Meisner, "Leninism and Maoism: Some Populist Perspectives in Marxist-Leninism in China," *China Quarterly* 45 (Jan.–Mar. 1971): 17–21.
59. "Chosŏn ŭi t'ŭki han ch'ŏji wa iedaehan t'ŭki han kujech'aek," pp. 23–24.
60. By the 1920s, Sin Paeg'u (1887–1959) had a long record of service in nationalist organizations. He had been a member of the Sinminhoe (1907) and had spent most of the 1910–20 decade in exile in Manchuria. He joined the Korean Fraternal Labor Association in 1920 and wrote for its organ magazine *Mutual Aid* (*Kongje*). In 1922, he helped found the Tuesday Society (Hwayohoe). He was also active in the Seoul Youth Association (Seoul Ch'ŏngnyŏnhoe) and the Proletarian Alliance (Musanja tongmaenghoe) (1923). In addition, he was a frequent contributor to *Sinsaenghwal*.
61. Sin Paeg'u, "Sahoe undong ŭi sŏn'guja ch'ullae rŭl ch'ok hanora" (A call for leaders of social movements to step forward), *Sinsaenghwal* 1, no. 2 (March 1922): 19.
62. Ibid.

63. "Chosŏn ŭi t'ŭki han ch'ŏji wa iedaehan t'ŭki han kujech'aek," pp. 24–25.

64. For a discussion of the Chinese intellectuals' attraction to Leninism, see Maurice Meisner, *Li Ta-chao and the Origins of Chinese Marxism* (New York: Atheneum, 1970).

65. Kim Myŏngsik, "Ku'munhwa wa sinmunhwa," pp. 2–6.

66. Sin Sang'u, "Ch'unwŏn ŭi minjok kaejoron ŭl tokhago," *Sinsaenghwal* 1, no. 6 (June 1922): 73.

67. Ibid., p. 74.

68. Ibid., p. 77.

69. Sin Ilyong, "Ch'unwŏn ŭi minjok kaejoron ŭl p'yŏng ham," *Sinsaenghwal* 1, no. 7 (June, 1922): 2–18.

70. Ibid., p. 6.

71. Ibid., p. 10.

72. Ibid., p. 15.

73. Sin Paeg'u, "Sahoe undong ŭi sŏn'guja ch'ullae rŭl ch'ok hanora" 1, nos. 2–3: 19–20.

74. Ibid., pp. 18–19.

75. Ibid., no. 2: 34.

76. Chŏng Paek, "Chisik kyegŭp ŭi mimang."

77. "Chosŏn ŭi t'ŭk'i han ch'ŏji wa iedaehan t'ŭk'i han kujech'aek," pp. 24–25.

78. Chŏn Chosŏn ch'ŏngnyŏn taehoe, March 1923, "Kyoyuk munje sŏn'ŏnsŏ" (Declaration on the problem of education), Kim and Kim 2: 118.

79. "Minjok ilch'i taedong tangyŏl ŭl unwi hanŭn i ege," *Kaebyŏk* 4, no. 3 (May 1923): 14–15.

80. Ibid., p. 15.

81. Ibid., p. 14.

82. Yi Sŏngt'ae, "Chungsan kyegŭp ŭi igijŏk undong," *Tonga ilbo,* March 20, 1923.

83. Yi Sŏngt'ae's biting criticism of self-serving middle-class movements provided an ironic footnote to personal relations between nationalists during this period. Just two years before, according to Yi Kwangsu's own memoirs, Yi Sŏngt'ae had tried to win the older Yi Kwangsu over to the leftist cause. According to Yi Kwangsu, the younger Yi lamented that Yi Kwangsu had chosen to return to Korea and had tried to convince him to stay in Shanghai to work on mediating the growing split within the Shanghai Provisional Government leadership. Yi Sŏngt'ae's blast at the cultural movement demonstrated that the ideological gap between the Left and Right had widened precipitously (Yi Kwangsu, "Na ŭi kobaek," pp. 251–52).

5. Intellectual Crisis in Colonial Korea

1. Yi Kwangsu, "Minjokchŏk kyŏngnyun," *Tonga ilbo,* Jan. 1–5 (1924).

2. Ibid., Jan. 1.

3. Ibid., Jan. 20.

4. Ibid.

5. Ibid., Jan. 4.

6. Ibid.

7. Ibid., Jan. 5.

8. Ibid., Jan. 6.

9. Ibid.

10. Ibid.

11. Ibid.

12. Yi Kwangsu, "Minjok kaejoron," *Kaebyŏk* 3, no. 5 (May 1922): 33–35.

13. Sŏl Hwasa, "Segŭn simnyŏn p'ilhwa," *Samch'ŏlli* 5, no. 14 (May 1931): 13–14. See also Yi Kwangsu, "Na ŭi kobaek," pp. 251–52.

14. Sŏl Hwasa, "Segŭn simnyŏn p'ilhwa," p. 14.

15. Kim Sangman, ed., *Tonga ilbosa*, p. 231.

16. "Chŏngch'ijŏk kyŏlsa wa undong e taehayŏ," *Tonga ilbo*, Jan. 29, 1924.

17. Nonong ch'ong tongmaeng imsi taehoe, "T'oŭi kyojŏng" (Debate resolutions), *Tonga ilbo*, April 21, 1924.

18. *Tonga ilbo*, April 22, 1924. Quoted in Kim and Kim 2: 97.

19. "Nonong imsi taehoe esŏ non'ŭi toen ponsa ŭi sasŏl munje wa myŏng'wŏlgwan sagŏn" (The Myŏng'wŏlgwan incident and editorial concerning the resolutions of the workers and peasants interim conference), *Tonga ilbo*, April 23, 1924.

20. Song Kŏnho, "Sin'ganhoe," in An Pyŏngjik, ed., *Han'guk kŭndae saron* (Seoul: Chiŭi sanŏpsa, 1977) 2: 440.

21. Yŏ Sang'il, "Habbŏp undong kwa pihabbŏp undong e kwanhan sa'gyŏn" (A personal view of legal and illegal movements), unpublished manuscript quoted in Kang Tongjin, *Ilche ŭi Han'guk ch'imnyak chŏngch'aeksa*, pp. 413–14.

22. Song Kŏnho, "Sin'ganhoe," p. 441.

23. Yi Kwangsu, "Na ŭi kobaek," pp. 252–53.

24. Korean Communists had been under pressure from the Comintern to form a united front with militant nationalists since 1920. However, internal factional strife among Korean Communists abroad and in Korea weakened any coherent organization. By 1925, however, a core movement among Korean Communists began to emerge. It was from this core, in alliance with leftists in the colony, that the impetus for organizing a united front finally emerged in 1925–26.

25. Kang Tongjin, *Ilche ŭi Han'guk ch'imnyak chŏngch'aeksa*, pp. 375–427.

26. Ibid., p. 408.

27. Ibid., p. 388.

28. Min, "Sasang ŭi ch'use wa undong ŭi panghyang," pp. 41–48.

29. Ibid., p. 42.

188 *Notes*

30. Ibid.
31. Ibid.
32. Ibid., p. 43.
33. Ibid., p. 44.
34. Ibid., p. 43.
35. Ibid., p. 45.
36. Ibid., p. 46.
37. "Kyehae wa kapcha" (1923 and 1924), *Kaebyŏk* 5, no. 1 (Jan. 1924): 2–12 (hereafter, Kyehae).
38. Ibid., p. 7.
39. Kim Ch'angsu, "Minjok undong ŭrosŏ ŭi Ŭiryŏldan hwaltong" (The activities of the Ŭiryŏldan as a nationalist movement), in An Pyongjik, ed., *Han'guk kŭndae saron II* (Historical papers on modern Korean history) (Seoul: Chisik sanŏpsa, 1977), pp. 382–400.
40. Kyehae, p. 7.
41. Min, "Sasang ŭi ch'use wa undong ŭi panghyang," pp. 47–48.
42. Ibid.
43. Ibid., p. 48.
44. Kyehae, p. 8.
45. Ibid., p. 10.
46. Ibid., p. 11.
47. Ibid.
48. Scalapino and Lee 1: 51–53. See also Suh, *Korean Communist Movement, 1918–1948*, pp. 85–114.
49. Scalapino and Lee, vol. 1, chap. 2.
50. Chŏng Chinsŏk, *Han'guk ŏllonsa yŏn'gu* (Seoul: Ilchogak, 1983), pp. 120–30.
51. XY Saeng, "Hyŏnha sinmun chapchi e taehan pihan," pp. 46–56.
52. Ibid., p. 50.
53. Ibid., p. 56.
54. Paek Sunjae, "Chapchi rŭl t'onghae pon ilchesidae ŭi kŭndaehwa undong," *Sindong'a* 22 (May 1966): 382–400.
55. For accounts on the Sin'ganhoe, see Scalapino and Lee 1: 94–103; Lee, *Politics of Korean Nationalism*, pp. 250–56; Suh, *Korean Communist Movement, 1918–1948*, pp. 85–116. For an account in Korean, see Song Koňho, "Sin'ganhoe."
56. Scalapino and Lee 1: 113–14.
57. Suh, *Korean Communist Movement*, p. 129.
58. Ibid., p. 88.
59. Franz Borkenau, *World Communism: A History of the Communist International* (Ann Arbor: University of Michigan Press, 1962), pp. 328–31. See also Lyman P. Van Slyke, *Enemies and Friends: The United Front in Chinese Communist History* (Stanford, Calif.: Stanford University Press, 1967), chap. 3.

60. Suh, *Documents of Korean Communism*, pp. 243–56.
61. Suh, *Korean Communist Movement*, pp. 112–14.

6. Conclusion

1. Brass, *Language, Religion and Politics in North India*, pp. 8–10.
2. Gellner, *Thought and Change*.
3. Korean historiography is curious with regard to nationalism because it ascribes a certain universality to national patriotism that does not jibe with the reality of the colonial period. This is due, I believe, to many studies of the twentieth-century Korean independence movement being influenced by the ideological warfare waged between the two post-World War II Korean states, each of which claims to be the true representative of the Korean nation. In terms of the intellectual history of the independence movement, there is a tendency to create a dichotomy of nationalist versus Communist, a division that neatly reproduces the ideological division between North and South Korea. Therefore, South Korean historiography tends to stress the importance of the domestic and exile independence movement during the colonial period. Accordingly, in some treatments of the colonial period, leftist elements, Socialists, and Korean Communists, in the colony and abroad, who espoused social revolutionary ideas for the solution of the national problem are written off as internationalists (i.e., nonnationalist). Similarly North Korean historiography of the period excoriates moderate nationalist elements as collaborationists—the only true nationalist movement was the national revolutionary movement to free Korea from the yoke of Japanese imperialist rule. Perhaps most insidious, colonial intellectuals whose ideas fell somewhere between these extremes are claimed by both historical traditions, yet the elements of their thought that do not fit the ideological framework of either side are frequently not considered. Such interpretations of the colonial nationalist movement informs us more about postcolonial Korean politics and the struggle of two Korean states to legitimate their rules as the only true inheritors and protectors of the nationalist mantle, but they confuse the issues that faced Korean nationalists at this time and ignore their complexity.

Guide to Romanization

Sin Paeg'u 申伯雨
Sŏ Chaep'il [Philip Jaisohn]
　　徐載弼
Sŏ Kwangbŏm 徐光範
Son Pyŏnghŭi 孫秉熙
Song Chinu 宋鎮禹
Terauchi Masatake 寺內正毅
Yen Fu 嚴復
Yi Ha'ŭng [Taewŏngun]
　　李昰應
Yi Kap 李甲
Yi Kapsŏng 李甲成
Yi Kwangsu 李光洙
Yi Nŭnghwa 李能和
Yi Sangch'im 李相沈
Yi Sangjae 李商在
Yi Sŏngt'ae 李星泰
Yi Sŭnghun 李昇薰
Yi Sŭngman [Syngman Rhee]
　　李承晚
Yi Tonhwa 李敦化
Yi Tonghwi 李東輝
Yŏm T'aejin 廉台鎭
Yun Ch'iho 尹致昊

Terms, Titles, and Associations
amhŭkki 暗黑期
Budan seiji 武斷政治
Bunka seiji 文化政治
chach'i 自治
Chach'i undong 自治運動
Chajakhoe 自作會
Ch'angjo 創造

chido kyegŭp 指導階級
Chinbodang 進步黨
Chinbohoe 進步會
chisikja 知識者
Choe Tonggyŏng Chosŏnin
　yuhaksaeng hag'uhoe
　在東京朝鮮人留學生
　學友會
chowa t'ong'il 調和統一
Chŏn Chosŏn ch'ŏngnyŏndan
　taehoe
　全朝鮮青年黨大會
Ch'ŏndogyo 天道敎
Ch'ŏndogyo ch'ŏngnyŏnhoe
　天道敎青年會
Ch'ŏngch'un 青春
Ch'ŏngnyŏn hag'uhoe
　青年學友會
Chōsen sangyō keizai chōsakai
　朝鮮產業經濟調查會
Chosŏn chigwang 朝鮮之光
Chosŏn ch'ŏngnyŏn yŏnhaphoe
　朝鮮青年聯合會
Chosŏn' ŏ hakhoe 朝鮮語學會
Chosŏn ilbo 朝鮮日報
Choson kohaksaeng tong'uhoe
　朝鮮苦學生同友會
Chosŏn mulsan changnyŏhoe
　朝鮮物產獎勵會
Chosŏn nodong kongjehoe
　朝鮮勞動共濟會
Chosŏn nonong ch'on tongmaeng
　朝鮮勞農總同盟

Chosŏn wangguk 朝鮮王國
Chosŏn yŏja hŭnghakhoe
朝鮮女子興學會
Chosŏn'ŏ yŏn'guhoe
朝鮮語研究會
chungch'u kyegŭp 中樞階級
Hanbuk hakhoe 韓北學會
Han'gŭl hakhoe 한글學會
Han'in sahoedang 韓人社會黨
Honam hakhoe 湖南學會
Honam hakhoe wŏlbo
湖南學會月報
Hsin ch'ing nien 新青年
Hŭngsadan 興士團
hwangje 皇帝
Hwangsŏng sinmun 皇城新聞
Hwayohoe 火曜會
hyŏksin 革新
hyŏngmyŏng 革命

in 仁
innaech'ŏn 人乃天
iyong husaeng 利用厚生

Kabo kyŏngjang 甲午更張
Kaebyŏk 開闢
Kaebyŏksa 開闢社
Kaehwadang 開化黨
kaejo 改造
kaejo undong 改造運動
kaejojuŭi 改造主義
Kaejoron 改造論
Kaihō 開放
Kaizō 改造

Kakp'a yuji yŏnmaeng
各派有志聯盟
Kapsin chŏngbyŏn 甲申政變
Kiho hakhoe 畿湖學會
kokugo 國語
kongnoe 共腦
Kong'yŏng 公榮
Koryŏ kongsandang
高麗共產黨
Kōtō keisatsu 高等警察
Kukch'ae posang undong
國債報償運動
Kungmin kyoyukhoe
國民教育會
kwahakchŏk ŭisik
科學的意識
kwijok 貴族
Kwinong undong
歸農運動
"Kyehae wa kapcha"
癸亥와甲子
malhyŏp 末洽
manse 萬歲
minjok 民族
minjokchuŭi 民族主義
"Minjok kaejoron"
民族改造論
minjoksŏng 民族性
"Minjokchŏk kyŏngnyun"
民族的經綸
minjung 民衆
Minnip taehak kisŏng chunbihoe
民立大學期成準備會

minnip taehakkyo
民立大學校
munhwa undong 文化運動
munhwajuŭi 文化主義
munhwap'a 文化派
Mujŏng 無情
Musanja 無産者
Musanja tongmaenghoe
無産者同盟會
nissen dōka 日鮮同化
nissen yūwa 日鮮宥和
nonch'on chach'i 農村自治
nodong munje 勞動問題
Nonong kongjehoe
勞農共濟會
Paekcho 白湖
Puksŏnghoe 北星會
pup'ye 腐弊
P'yeho 廢墟

sadae 事大
sadae ŭisik 事大意識
sadaejuŭi 事大主義
Sahoejuŭi tongmaeng
社會主義同盟
sain yŏch'ŏn 事人如天
San'ŏpkye 産業界
sasang t'ongil 思想統一
Seoul ch'ŏngnyŏnhoe
서울(Seoul)青年會
Sidae ilbo 時代日報
Shinjinkai 新人會
shuyō 收養

Silhak 實學
sijo 時調
Silla 新羅
Sin sasang yŏn'guhoe
新思想研究會
Sinch'ŏnji 新天地
Sin'ganhoe 新幹會
sinmin 新民
Sinminhoe 新民會
Sinsaenghwal 新生活
Sinsaenghwalsa 新生活社
Sŏbuk hakhoe 西北學會
sŏdang 書堂
sŏhak 西學
sŏn'gakja 先覺者
Sonyŏn 少年
suhak tongmaeng 修學同盟
suyang 收養
suyang tongmaeng 收養同盟

tae kyŏlsa 大結社
Taedong hakhoe 大東學會
T'aeguk sŏgwan 太國書館
Taehan cha'ganghoe
大韓自強會
Taehan cha'ganghoe wŏlbo
大韓自強會月報
Taehan cheguk 大韓帝國
Taehan hŭnghakhoe
大韓興學會
Taehan kurakbu 大韓俱樂部
Taehan maeil sinbo
大韓每日申報

T'aepy'ŏngyang hoeŭi
太平洋會議
Taewŏngun 大院君
Tan'gun 檀君
ti-yung 體用
to 道
tŏk 德
tong'in chapchi 同人雜誌
Tonga ilbo 東亞日報
Tonghak 東學
Tongmyŏng 東明
T'ongni'gimu amun
統理機務衙門
tongnip 獨立
T'ongnipdang 獨立黨
Tongnip sinmun 獨立新聞
Tong'u 同友
Tong'uhoe 同友會

T'osan aeyong puinhoe
土産愛用婦人會
Toshoka 圖書課
tosi chungsimjuŭi
都市中心主義
T'oyohoe 土曜會

udŭng injong 優等人種
ŭi 義
Ŭibyŏng 義兵
Ŭiryŏldan 義烈團

wang 王
wijŏng ch'oksa 衛正斥邪
yangban 兩班
yeŭi 禮儀
yŏldŭng injong 劣等人種
Yŏnjŏnghoe 研政會
yusanja 遺産者

Bibliography

In Korean and Japanese

Aogi Nammei. *Chōsen tōchiron* [Treatise on the governance of Korea]. Keijō: Chōsen kenkyūsha, 1923.

Chang Tŏksu. "Saesidae ŭi saesaram" [A new man for a new age]. *Kaebyŏk* 3, no. 1 (Jan. 1922): 31–35.

Cho Kijun. *Han'guk chabonjuŭi sŏngnip saron* [The history of the origins of Korean capitalism]. 1973. Seoul: Taewangsa, 1982.

_____, ed. *Ilcheha ŭi minjok saenghwalsa* [A history of national life under Japanese rule]. Seoul: Minjung sŏgwang, 1971.

_____. "Chosŏn mulsan changnyŏ undong ŭi chŏn'gae kwajŏng kwa ku yŏksajŏk sŏnggyŏk" [The development and character of the Korean production movement]. In An Pyongjik, ed., *Han'guk kŭndae saron III* [Papers on modern Korean history], pp. 62–91. Seoul: Chisik san'ŏpsa, 1977.

_____. *Han'guk ŭi minjok kiŏp* [Korean national entrepreneurship]. Seoul: Han'guk ilbosa, 1975.

Cho Yongman. "Ilcheha ŭi uri sinmunhwa undong" [The new culture movement under Japanese rule]. In Cho Yongman et al., eds. *Ilcheha ŭi munhwa undongsa* [History of the new culture movements under the Japanese], pp. 1–208. Seoul: Asea munje yŏn'guso, Minjung sŏgwang, 1970.

Ch'oe Ch'un. *Han'guk sinmunsa* [The history of Korean newspapers]. Seoul: Ilchogak, 1968.

_____. "Han'guk ŭi ch'ulp'an yŏn'gu: 1910 ŭrobut'ŏ 1923 kkaji" [Studies on Korean publishing: 1910–1923]. *Seouldae sinmun yŏn'gu hakbo* 1 (1964): 11–20.

_____. "Kyop'o sinmun kwa ilbon ŭi ch'imnak chŏngch'aek" [Korean newspapers in exile and Japanese repression]. *Chung'ang taehak pŏpchŏng nonjip*, no. 15 (n.d.), pp. 15–33.

Ch'oe Chunggap. "Kŭm'il Chosŏn ŭi noja kwan'gye" [Relations between labor and capital]. *Kaebyŏk* 2, no. 9 (Sept. 1921): 28–38.

Ch'oe Hyŏnbae. *Chosŏn kaengsaeng ŭi to* [A way for the rebirth of the nation]. 1926. Seoul: Chŏng'ŭmsa, 1962.

_____. *Han'gŭl ŭi parŭnkil* [The correct path for Han'gul]. 1937. Seoul: Chŏng'ŭmsa, 1945.

197

Ch'oe Minji and Kim Minju, eds. *Ilcheha minjok ŏllon saron* [Studies on the history of Korean media under Japanese rule]. Seoul: Ilwŏn sŏgak, 1978.

Ch'oe Yonghŭi et al., eds. *Ilcheha ŭi minjok undongsa* [A history of the nationalist movement under Japanese rule]. Seoul: Minjung sŏgwang, 1971.

Chŏng Paek. "Chisik kyegŭp ŭi mimang" [The delusion of the intellectual class]. *Sinsaenghwal*, vol. 1, no. 3 (May 1922).

————. "Minjung chŏngsin ŭi il koch'al" [An analysis of the spirit of the masses]. *Sinsaenghwal* 1, no. 1 (March 1922): 29–33.

Chŏng Chinsŏk. *Han'guk ŏllonsa yŏn'gu* [Studies on the history of Korean journalism]. Seoul: Ilchogak, 1983.

————. *Han'guk ŏllon t'ujaengsa* [A history of the struggle of the Korean press]. Seoul: Chŏng'ŭm mungo, 1975.

————. "Ilcheha Han'guk ŭi ŏllon ch'ulp'an yŏn'gu" [Studies of the press and publishing in Korea under Japanese rule]. *Sinmun yŏn'gu* (1978).

————. "Nōhon ken'etsu" [Manuscript censorship]. *Asea kōron*, vol. 3, no. 10 (Oct. 1974).

Chŏng Sehyŏng. *Hang'il haksaeng minjok undongsa yŏn'gu* [Studies on the history of the anti-Japanese student movement]. Seoul: Ilchisa, 1975.

"Chŏngch'ijŏk kyŏlsa wa undong e taehayŏ" [On political associations and movements]. *Tonga ilbo*, Jan. 29, 1924.

"Ch'ŏngnyŏndang taehoe haech'oe" [The opening of the conference of Korean youth groups]. *Tonga ilbo*, Jan. 30, 1923.

Chōsen sōtokufu. *Chōsen hōrei shuran* [Compilation of laws in Korea]. Keijō: Chōsen sōtokufu, 1915.

————. *Shisei nijugonenshi* [A twenty-five year history of the administration of Korea]. Keijō: Chōsen sōtokufu, 1935.

————, Hōanka. *Kōtō keisatsu gaiyō* [Survey of the high police]. Keijō: Keimukyoku, hōanka, 1930.

————, Kamboka. *Chōsenjin no shisō to seikaku* [The thought and character of Koreans]. Keijō: Kamboka, 1927.

————, Keimukyoku. *Chōsen chian jōkyo* [Conditions of public order in Korea]. Keijō: Chōsen sōtokufu, 1922.

————. *Chōsen ni okeru shuppanbutsu gaiyō* [Survey of publications in Korea]. Keijō: Keimukyoku, 1930.

————. *Chōsen shuppan keisatsu gaiyō* [Survey of the Korean publication police]. Keijō: Keimukyoku, Toshoka, 1939.

————, Keimukyoku, Hōanka. "Chōsen shisō undō no gaikyō" [Conditions in Korean thought movements]. *Kōtō keisatsubō*, no. 2 (n.d.), pp. 1–27.

————, Mombusho gakuseibu. *Chōsen tokuritsu undō to kyōsanshugi undō no kankei gaiyō* [A survey of Korean independence and Communist movements]. Keijō: Mombusho, 1932.

"Chosŏn ch'ŏngnyŏn yŏnhaphoe ch'wijisŏ" [Prospectus of the All Korea Youth League]. *Tonga ilbo*, July 15, 1920.

Chosŏn ilbo ch'ulp'anguk. *Chosŏn ilbo myŏng sasŏl obaeksŏn* [500 famous editorials from the *Chosŏn ilbo*]. Seoul: Chosŏn ilbosa, 1972.

"Chosŏn minnip taehak p'algi e ch'wihayŏ" [On establishing a Korean national university]. *Chosŏn ilbo*, Dec. 1–2, 1922.

"Chosŏn mulsan ch'angnyŏ ch'wijisŏ" [Prospectus on promoting Korean industries]. *San'ŏpkye* 1, no. 1 (March 1923): 55–56.

"Chosŏn ŭi t'ŭki han ch'ŏji wa iedaehan t'ŭki han kujech'aek" [A special plan for the special conditions in Korea]. *Kaebyŏk* 3, no. 1 (Jan. 1923):2–32.

Chu Chonggŏn. "Musan kyegŭp kwa mulsan changnyŏ" [The propertyless class and the buy Korean movement]. *Tonga ilbo*, April 6–17, 1923.

Chu Sigyŏng. "Kungmunnon" [Treatise on the national language]. *Tongnip sinmun*, April 24, 1897.

Han Yong'u. *Chosŏn chŏngi ŭi sahoe sasang* [Early Korean social thought]. Seoul: Han'guk ilbosa, 1975.

Han'gŭl hakhoe. *Han'gŭl hakhoe 50 nyŏnsa* [The fifty-year history of the Korean Language Society]. Seoul: Han'gŭl hakhoe, 1971.

Hong Isŏp. "Sin Ch'aeho maemol toen yŏksa ŭi palgulja" [Sin Ch'aeho, excavator of buried history]. *Han'guk in'gansang* 4 (1965): 490–506.

Hong Ir'u. "Pandong munhwa ŭi choyak" [The rise of reactionary literature]. *Singyedan* 1 (Oct. 1932): 1–3.

Hōrei shuran [Compilation of laws]. Tokyo: Naikaku Kanbō kirokuka, 1929.

Hyŏn Sangyun. "Kŏdŭm naja" [Let's be reborn]. *Kaebyŏk* 3, no. 1 (Jan. 1922): 20–30.

Hyŏng'amsaeng [pseud.]. "Kaksŏng hara singsang ŭl" [Awake to new ideas]. *Sinsaenghwal* 1, no. 1 (March 1922): 39–41.

"Ilchu'nyŏn ki'nyŏm ŭl tanghayŏ" [Looking back at the first year]. *San'ŏpkye* (March 1924).

Kajimura Hideki. "Sin Ch'aeho no keimō shisō" [The enlightenment thought of Sin Ch'aeho]. *Sansenri*, no. 9 (Feb. 1977), pp. 54–61.

Kang Chaeon. *Kindai Chōsen no shisōshi* [An intellectual history of modern Korea]. Tokyo: Kinokuniya shinsho, 1970.

Kang Ha. "Chosŏn sinmun paldalsa: sasang p'yŏnch'ŏn ŭl chungsim ŭro" [The development of Korean newspapers from the standpoint of intellectual transition]. *Sindonga* 4, no. 5 (May 1934): 52–59.

Kang Mae. "*Sinsaenghwal* ŭl sin kiwŏn cheilnyŏn cheilil ŭi na ŭl somang" [My wishes on the beginning of *New Life*]. *Sinsaenghwal* 1, no. 1 (March 1922): 10–13.

Kang Tŏksan. "Yi Tonghwi no shisō to kōdō" [The thought and action of Yi Tonghwi]. *Sansenri*, no. 9 (Feb. 1977), pp. 70–80.

Kang Tongjin. *Ilche ŭi Han'guk ch'imnyak chŏngch'aeksa* [History of Japanese imperialist policy in Korea]. Seoul: Han'gilsa, 1980.

Keimukyoku. *Keimu ihō* [Police gazette], vol. 288 (April 1930). Seoul: Chōsen sōtokufu.

Kil Chinhyŏn. *Yŏksa e tasi mut'nŭnda: panmin t'ŭkwi wa ch'in'ilp'a* [Asking again of history: The antinational crimes committee and the pro-Japanese group]. Seoul: Samminsa, 1984.

Kim Chunyŏp and Kim Ch'angsun, eds. *Han'guk kongsanjuŭi undongsa 1–5*

[The history of the Korean Communist movement, vols. 1–5]. Seoul: Aseamunje yŏn'guso, 1967.

Kim Kŭnsu. *Ilche ch'iha ŏllon ch'ulp'an ŭi silt'ae* [The Korean press under Japanese rule]. Seoul: Han'gukhak yŏn'guso, 1974.

_____. *Han'guk chapchi kaegwang mit hobyŏl mokch'ajip* [General survey and index of Korean magazines]. Seoul: Han'gukhak yŏn'guso, 1973.

Kim Myŏngsik. "Ku'munhwa wa sinmunhwa" [Old and new culture]. *Sinsaenghwal* 1, no. 2 (March 1922): 2–6.

Kim Nakchung. *Han'guk nodong undongsa* [The history of the Korean labor movement]. Seoul: Ch'ongsa, 1982.

Kim Sangman, ed. *Tonga ilbosa 50 nyŏn sa* [A fifty-year history of the *Tonga ilbo*]. Seoul: Tonga ilbosa, 1975.

Kim Tong'in. "Chi'nan shijŏl ŭl ch'ulp'anmul kŏm'yŏl" [Censorship of publications in recent times]. In *Tong'in chŏnjip* [The collected works of Kim Tong'in], pp. 318–28. Seoul: Saja ch'ulp'ansa, 1964.

_____. *Han'guk kŭn sosŏl ko* [Studies on the modern Korean novel]. Seoul, 1950.

Kondo Tsuneno. "Shuppanbutsu yori mitaru Chōsen" [Seeing Korea through its publications]. *Chōsen* (Jan. 1927), pp. 34–40.

Koryoku [pseud.]. "Chōsen ni okeru shuppanbutsu no kosatsu" [An analysis of publishing in Korea]. *Keimu ihō*, nos. 293–99 (Oct. 1930–March 1931).

Kunwŏn [pseud.]. "Puin munje ŭi chongjŏn" [Various women's questions]. *Sinsaenghwal* 1, no. 1 (March 1922): 42–45.

"Kusidae wa sinsidae" [The old and new ages]. *Sinsaenghwal*, vol. 1, no. 2 (March 1922): 1.

"Kyehae wa kapcha" [1923 and 1924]. *Kaebyŏk* 5, no. 1 (Jan. 1924): 2–12.

"Kyoyuk'yong ilbon'ŏ e taehayŏ" [On Japanese use in the schools]. *Chosŏn ilbo*, May 19, 1920.

Lee Hyunhi. *Taehan minguk imsi chŏngbusa* [A history of the provisional government of the Republic of Korea]. Seoul: Chimmundang, 1982.

Maruyama Tsurukichi. *Chōsen chian no genjō oyobi shōrai* [Public peace and order in Korea, today and in the future]. Keijō: Chōsen sōtokufu, Jimukan, 1922.

Min [pseud.]. "Sasang ŭi ch'ase wa undong ŭi panghyang" [The condition of thought and direction of movements]. *Kaebyŏk* 5, no. 3 (March 1924): 41–48.

"Minjok ilch'i taedong tan'gyŏl ŭl unwi hanŭn i ege" [To those who advocate mass organizations and national unity]. *Kaebyŏk* 4, no. 3 (May 1923): 13–20.

"Minnip taehak p'algi ch'wijisŏ" [Prospectus for establishing a national university]. In *Tok kŭndae myŏng nonsŏljip* [A collection of famous modern Korean essays]. Seoul: Sindonga, 1967.

Nak Nak Cha [pseud.]. "Chi'gŭm ch'angdo toenŭn kyouk ŭi mokjŏk" [Goals for education today]. *Ch'ŏngch'un* 15 (Oct. 1918): 39–41.

O Taehwan. "Kuppyŏn hayaganŭn sin'gu sasang ŭi ch'ungdol" [The current clash of old and new ideas]. *Kaebyŏk* 1, no. 1 (June 1920): 80–84.

Oka Shigematsu. "Chōsen ni okeru eiga no ken'etsu ni tsuite" [On film censorship in Korea]. *Chōsen* (March 1931), pp. 128–40.

Okudaira Yasuhiro. "Ken'etsu seido" [The censorship system]. *Kōza nihon kindai hō hattatsushi* 11 (May 1967): 3–73.

Paek Sunjae. *Chosŏn sinmunhak sajosa* [An intellectual history of modern Korean literature]. Seoul: Susŏnsa, 1948.

———. "Chapchi rŭl t'onghae pon ilchesidae ŭl kŭndaehwa undong" [The modernization movement under Japanese rule as seen through magazines]. *Sindonga*, vols. 18–23 (Jan.–June 1966).

Pak Chesun. "Ŭmyang sulsŏ" [Book of conjury based on yin-yang cosmology]. *Taehan chagang wŏlbo*, no. 2 (Sept. 1906).

Pak Ch'unja. "Chosŏn sasang undongja tŭrŭl kyegŭpjŏk chosŏn ŭl ch'ugu hamyŏnsŏ" [An analysis of the class structure of the Korean intellectual movement]. *Kaebyŏk* 7, no. 7 (July 1926): 2–13.

Pak Kyŏng-ja. "20 segi ch'ogi ŭi Han'guk minjokjuŭi ilsaeng: Ch'unwŏn ŭi minjok kaejoron chungsim ŭro" [Thoughts on early twentieth-century Korean nationalism: Considering Yi Kwangsu's *Kaejoron*]. *Sukdae saron*, no. 7 (Dec. 1972), pp. 169–85.

Pak Sajik. "Chosŏn sahoe ŭi suyang munje" [The problem of cultivation in Korean society]. *Kaebyŏk* 1, no. 2 (July 1920): 45–49.

Pak Ŭnsik. "Taehan chŏngsin" [The spirit of Korea]. *Sŏbuk hakhoe wŏlbo*, vol. 3, no. 16 (n.d.). In *Pak Ŭn-sik*, pp. 26–27. Seoul: Han'gilsa, 1980.

———. "Taehan chŏngsin ŭi hyŏlsŏ" [Writing the spirit of Korea in blood]. *Taehan maeil sinbo*, Sept. 25–26, 1907.

———. *Han'guk t'ongsa* [The bitter history of Korea]. Seoul, 1910.

Pak Yŏnghyo. "*Kaebyŏk* ŭi ch'anggan ŭl munhago" [Upon reading the first edition of *Kaebyŏk*]. *Kaebyŏk* 1, no. 1 (June 1920): 30–31.

"Pŏm'inganjŏk minjokjuŭi" [Pan-humanist nationalism]. *Kaebyŏk* 3, no. 12 (Dec. 1922): 2–10.

"P'yŏng'an pukdo ŏttohan ch'ingu ŭi kul" [Notes from a friend from P'yŏng'an pukdo]. *Tongnip sinmun*, Mar. 12, 1898.

"P'yŏnjip ŭl mach'igo" [Upon finishing compilation]. *Sinsaenghwal*, vol. 1, no. 1 (March 1922).

"Sahoein i pon Chosŏn ŏllongye" [The Korean press as seen by leading social figures]. *Sindonga* 4, no. 5 (May 1934): 66–67.

"Segye rŭl alla" [Know the world]. *Kaebyŏk*, no. 1 (June 1920): 3–12.

"Segye sam taemunje ŭi p'agŭp kwa Chosŏn'in ŭi kag'o yŏha" [The three great world problems and Koreans' understanding thereof]. *Kaebyŏk* 1, no. 1 (June 1920): 2–17.

Sin Ch'aeho. *Tanje Sin Ch'aeho chŏnjip* [The collected works of Sin Ch'aeho]. Seoul: Ulso munhwasa, 1972.

———. "Nonsŏl" [Editorial]. *Taehan maeil sinbo*, Aug. 10, 1909.

——. "Todŏk" [Morals]. In *Tanje Sin Ch'aeho chŏnjip* 3: 60–68. Seoul: Hyŏngu Ch'ulp'ansa, 1977.

——. "20 segi tongguk ŭi sin yong'ung" [A new valor in twentieth-century Asia]. In *Tanje Sin Ch'aeho chŏnjip* (1977) 3:13–19.

Sin Ilch'ŏl. *Sin Ch'ae-ho ŭi yŏksa sasang yŏn'gu* [Studies on the historical thought of Sin Ch'aeho]. Seoul: Koryŏ taehakkyo ch'ulp'anbu, 1981.

Sin Ilyong. "Ch'unwŏn ŭi minjok kaejoron ŭl p'yŏng ham" [A critique of Yi Kwangsu's treatise on reconstruction]. *Sinsaenghwal* 1, no. 7 (June 1922): 2–18.

Sin Paeg'u. "Saehoe undong ŭl sŏn'guja ch'ullae rŭl ch'ok hanora" [A call for leaders of social movements to step forward]. *Sinsaenghwal*, vol. 1, nos. 2–3 (April, May 1922).

Sin Sang'u. "Ch'unwŏn ŭi minjok kaejoron" [Yi Kwangsu's *Kaejoron*]. *Sinsaenghwal* 1, no. 6 (June 1922): 73–77.

Sin Yongha. *Tongnip hyŏphoe yŏn'gu* [Studies on the Independence Club]. Seoul: Ilchogak, 1976.

——. "Chu Sigyŏng ŭi aeguk kyemong sasang" [The patriotic enlightenment thought of Chu Sigyŏng]. *Han'guk sahoehak yŏn'gu cheilchip pyŏlswe*, no. 1 (Jan. 1977), pp. 13–58.

——. "Pak Ŭnsik ŭi kyoyuk ku'gak sasang e taehayŏ" [The enlightenment thought of Pak Ŭnsik]. *Han'guk hakbo* 1, no. 1 (Fall 1975): 50–75.

Sinsaenghwalsa. "Ch'wijisŏ kŭp chojik" [Prospectus and organization]. *Sinsaenghwal* 1, no. 1 (March 1922): 1.

So Chaep'il. "Sosŏl" [Editorial]. *Tongnip sinmun*, Sept. 3, 1896.

"Sobi chohap ŭi naeryŏk kwa kyŏng'yŏng" [The history and management of a consumer cooperative]. *San'ŏpkye* 1, no. 1 (March 1923): 59–61.

Sŏl Hwasa. "Se'gŭn simnyŏn p'ilhwa" [Journalistic controversies in the last ten years]. *Samchŏlli* 5, no. 14 (May 1931): 13–15.

Song Kŏnho. "Sin'ganhoe" [The new Korea society]. In An Pyongjik, ed., *Han'guk kŭndae saron* [Studies on modern Korean history] 2: 439–72. Seoul: Ch'ongsa, 1977.

Song Minbo. "Ilcheha ŭi Han'guk chohang munhak" [Resistance literature under Japanese imperialism]. In Cho Yongman, ed., *Ilcheha ŭi munhwa undongsa* [The history of cultural movements under Japanese imperialism]. Seoul: Minjung sŏgwang, 1970.

Song Uk. "Han'guk chisig'in kwa yŏksajŏk hyŏnsil" [Korean intellectuals and historical reality]. *Sasanggye*, no. 145 (April 1965), pp. 206–27.

Sonyŏnsa. "Kungmin sahaeng ŭi p'yojŏn" [A standard of action for the people]. *Sonyŏn* 3, no. 5 (May 1910): 6–20.

——. "Sonyŏn sion" [Miscellany]. *Sonyŏn* 3, no. 4 (April 1910): 6–19.

Tonga ilbosasa: 1920–1945 [A history of the *East Asia Daily*: 1920–1945]. Seoul: Tonga ilbosa, 1975.

XY Saeng [pseud.]. "Hyŏnha sinmun chapchi e taehan pip'an" [Critique of contemporary magazines and newspapers]. *Kaebyŏk* 6, no. 10 (Dec. 1925): 45–56.

XYZ [pseud.]. "Minjokchŏk cheundong ŭi hoego kwa pi'pan" [Reflections on and criticism of various national movements]. *Tonga ilbo*, Jan. 1, 1924.

_____. "Cheundong ŭi hoe'ŏk kwa pip'an" [Reflections and criticism of several movements]. *Tonga ilbo*, Jan. 1, 1924.

Yi Chŏngsu. "Chosŏn chapchi paldalsa" [A history of the development of Korean magazines]. *Sindonga* 4, no. 5 (May 1934): 60–64.

Yi Hŭisŭng, ed. *Han'guk inmyŏng taesajŏn* [Biographical dictionary of Korea]. Seoul: Han'guk inmyŏng taesajŏn p'yŏnch'ansil, 1967.

Yi Kibaek. *Han'guksa sillon* [A new history of Korea]. Seoul: Ilchogak, 1975.

_____. "Minjok sahak ŭi munje" [Problems in nationalist history]. *Sasanggye*, no. 156 (Feb. 1966), pp. 244–51.

Yi Kwangnin [Lee Kwangrin]. *Han'guk kaehwa sasang yŏn'gu* [Studies on Korean enlightenment thought]. Seoul: Ilchogak, 1979.

_____. *Kaehwasa yŏn'gu* [Studies on the history of the Korean enlightenment]. Seoul: Ilchogak, 1960.

Yi Kwangsu. *Minjok kaejoron: Ch'unwŏn ŭi myŏngjak nonmunjip* [Treatise on reconstructing the nation: Selected writings of Yi Kwangsu]. Seoul: Usinsa, 1981.

_____. "Chanyŏ chungsimnon" [Treatise on children]. *Ch'ŏngch'un*, no. 15 (Sept. 1918), pp. 9–17.

_____. "Chosŏn minjoknon" [Treatise on the Korean people]. *Tonggwang ch'ongsŏ* (June 1933), pp. 2–6.

_____. "Minjok kaejoron" [Treatise on the reconstruction of the nation]. *Kaebyŏk* 3, no. 5 (May 1922): 18–72.

_____. "Minjŏkchok kyŏngnyun" [Treatise on national statecraft]. *Tonga ilbo*, Jan. 1–5, 1924.

_____. "Na ŭi kobaek" [My confessions]. In *Yi kwangsu sonjip* [Selected works of Yi Kwangsu]. 1948. Seoul: O'mungak, 1979.

_____. "P'alchasŏl ŭl kijorohan Chosŏn minjok ŭi insaenggwan" [The life view of Koreans based on fatalism]. *Kaebyŏk* 2, no. 8 (Aug. 1921): 35–45.

_____. *Ch'unwŏn ŭi myŏngjak nonmunjip: Minjok kaejoron* [Collection of important writings of Yi Kwangsu: Treatise on reconstructing the nation]. Seoul: Usinsa, 1981.

_____. "Sonyŏn ege" [To youth]. *Kaebyŏk*, vol. 2, no. 11—vol. 3, no. 3 (Nov. 1921—March 1922).

Yi Myŏngjae. "Ilche ŭi kŏm'yŏl i sinmunhak e kich'in yŏnghyang" [The influence of censorship on the new literature during the Japanese period]. *Ŏnmun yŏn'gu* 3, nos. 1–2 (May 1975): 250–68.

Yi Sŏn'gŭn. "Ilche ch'ongdokbu ŭi hŏnp'yŏng chŏngch'aek wa sasang t'anap" [The Japanese colonial military police policy and thought repression]. *Han'guk sasang*, no. 8 (June 1966), pp. 7–42.

Yi Sŏngt'ae. "Chungsan kyegŭp ŭi igijŏk undong" [The self-serving movement of the middle class]. *Tonga ilbo*, Mar. 20, 1923.

_____. "Hyŏndae munhwa ŭi panghyang" [The direction of modern culture]. *Sinsaenghwal*, vol. 1, no. 9 (Nov. 1922).

_____. "Sanghwal ŭi pullan" [Uncertainties of life]. *Sinsaenghwal* 1 (March 1922): 24–38.

Yi Tonhwa. "Chosŏn sinmunhwa kŏnsŏl e taehan t'oan" [A plan for building a new Korean culture]. *Kaebyŏk* 1, no. 4 (Oct. 1920): 9–16.

_____. "Saenghwal ŭi chokkŏn ŭi ponwirohan Chosŏn ŭi kaejo saŏp" [Rebuilding Korea from the basic conditions of life]. *Kaebyŏk* 2, no. 10 (Oct. 1921): 2–27.

Yi Tuhyon, ed. *Han'guk minsŏnghak taesŏng* [A survey of Korean folk customs]. Seoul: Minjung sogwan, 1974.

Yun Pyŏngsŏk, Sin Yongha, and An Pyongjik, eds. *Han'guk kŭndae saron 1–3* [Studies on modern Korean history, vols. 1–3]. Seoul: Chisik san'ŏpsa, 1977.

In English

Ahn, Paul. "Education as an Instrument of National Assimilation: A Study of Japan in Korea." Ph.D. diss., Columbia University, 1931.

Apter, David E. *The Politics of Modernization*. Chicago: University of Chicago Press, 1965.

Baldwin, Frank, Jr. "The March First Movement: Korean Challenge and Japanese Response." Ph.D. diss., Columbia University, 1969.

Beasley, W. B. *The Meiji Restoration*. Stanford, Calif.: Stanford University Press, 1972.

Bianco, Lucien. *Origins of the Chinese Revolution*. Stanford, Calif.: Stanford University Press, 1971.

Borkenau, Franz. *World Communism: A History of the Communist International*. Ann Arbor: University of Michigan Press, 1962.

Bottomore, Tom, ed. *A Dictionary of Marxist Thought*. Cambridge: Harvard University Press, 1983.

Brandt, Conrad. "Stalin's Failure in China, 1924–1927." Cambridge: Harvard University Press, 1958.

Brass, Paul R. *Language, Religion and Politics in North India*. London: Cambridge University Press, 1975.

Chandra, Vipan. "The Independence Club and Korea's First Proposal for a National Legislative Assembly." *Occasional Papers on Korea*, no. 4 (Sept. 1975), pp. 19–35.

_____. "Nationalism and Popular Participation in Government in Late 19th Century Korea: The Contribution of the Independence Club (1896–1898)." Ph.D. diss., Harvard University, 1977.

Chang, Hao. *Liang Ch'i-ch'ao and Intellectual Transition in China, 1890–1907*. Cambridge: Harvard University Press, 1971.

Chen, I-te. "Japanese Colonialism in Korea and Formosa: A Comparison of Its Effects upon the Development of Nationalism." Ph.D. diss., University of Pennsylvania, 1968.

Ch'oe, Ching-young. *The Rule of the Taewŏngun 1864–1873: Restoration in Yi Korea.* Cambridge: Harvard East Asian Institute, 1972.

Ch'oe, Yong-ho. "The Kapsin Coup of 1884: A Reassessment." *Korean Studies* 6 (1982): 105–24.

Chow Tse-tung. *The May Fourth Movement: Intellectual Revolution in Modern China.* Cambridge: Harvard University Press, 1960.

Clark, Allen. *Religions of Old Korea.* Seoul: Christian Literature Society of Korea, 1961.

Clark, Donald. "Autonomy, Legitimacy, and Tributary Politics: Sino-Korean Relations in the Fall of Koryŏ and the Founding of the Yi." Ph.D. diss., Harvard University, 1978.

_____. *Christianity in Modern Korea.* New York: University Press of America, 1986.

Coleman, J. S. *Nigeria, Background to Nationalism.* Berkeley and Los Angeles: University of California Press, 1958.

Conroy, Hilary. *The Japanese Seizure of Korea 1868–1910: A Study of Realism and Idealism in International Relations.* Philadelphia: University of Pennsylvania Press, 1960.

Cook, Harold. "Kim Ok-kyun and the Background of the 1884 Emeute." Ph.D. diss., Harvard University, 1968.

Craig, Albert. "Fukuzawa Yukichi: The Philosophical Foundations of Meiji Nationalism." In Robert Ward, ed., *Political Development in Modern Japan.* Princeton, N.J.: Princeton University Press, 1968.

Cumings, Bruce. *The Origins of the Korean War.* Princeton, N.J.: Princeton University Press, 1981.

_____. "Kim's Korean Communism." *Problems of Communism,* no. 23 (March–April 1974), pp. 27–41.

Dahrendorf, Ralf. *Essays in the Theory of Society.* Stanford, Calif.: Stanford University Press, 1968.

De Bary, Wm. Theodore, Wing-tsit Chan, and Burton Watson, eds. *Sources of Chinese Tradition.* 2 vols. New York: Columbia University Press, 1960.

Deuchler, Martina. *Confucian Gentlemen and Barbarian Envoys: The Opening of Korea, 1875–1885.* Seattle: University of Washington Press, 1977.

Deutsch, Karl W. *Nationalism and Social Communication.* Cambridge, Mass: MIT Press, 1977.

_____. "Social Mobilization and Political Development." *American Political Science Review,* vol. 55, no. 3.

Dong, Wonmo. "Japanese Colonial Policy and Practice in Korea, 1905–1945: A Study in Assimilation." Ph.D. diss., Georgetown University, 1965.

Eckert, Carter J. "The Origins of Korean Capitalism: The Koch'ang Kims and the Kyŏngsŏng Spinning and Weaving Company, 1871–1945." Ph.D. diss., University of Washington, 1986.

Emerson, Rupert. *From Empire to Nation.* Cambridge: Harvard University Press, 1962.

206 *Bibliography*

Eisenstadt, S. N. *Modernization, Protest, and Change.* Englewood Cliffs, N.J.: Prentice Hall, 1966.

Esherick, Joseph W. *Reform and Revolution in China.* Berkeley and Los Angeles: University of California Press, 1976.

Fairbank, John K., ed. *The Chinese World Order.* Cambridge: Harvard University Press, 1968.

_____and S. Y. Teng, eds. "On the Ch'ing Tributary System." In *Ch'ing Administration: Three Studies.* Harvard-Yenching Institute Studies, no. 19. Cambridge: Harvard University Press, 1961.

Furth, Charlotte, ed. *The Limits of Change: Essays on Conservative Alternatives in Republican China.* Cambridge: Harvard University Press, 1976.

Gardner, Arthur. "The Korean Nationalist Movement and An Ch'angho, Advocate of Gradualism." Ph.D. diss., University of Hawaii, 1979.

Geertz, Clifford, ed. *Old Societies and New States.* New York: Free Press, 1963.

_____. "The Integrative Revolution." In Clifford Geertz, ed., *Old Societies and New States.*

Gellner, Ernst. *Thought and Change.* Chicago: University of Chicago Press, 1964.

Ghose, Sankar. *Political Ideas and Movements in India.* Bombay: Allied Publishers, 1975.

Gleason, Abbott. *Young Russia: The Genesis of Russian Radicalism in the 1860s.* New York: Viking Press, 1980.

Government General of Chōsen. *Annual Reports on Reforms and Progress in Chōsen 1914–1930.* Keijō: Government General of Chōsen, 1914–30.

_____. *Results of Three Years Administration of Chōsen Since Annexation.* Keijō: Government General of Chōsen, 1914.

Gragert, Edwin. "Landownership Change in Korea under Japanese Colonial Rule: 1900–1935." Ph.D. diss., Columbia University, 1982.

Grajdanzev, Andrew. *Modern Korea.* New York: John Day Co., 1944.

Greider, Jerome. *Hu Shih and the Chinese Renaissance.* Cambridge: Harvard University Press, 1970.

Hayes, Carlton. *The Historical Evolution of Modern Nationalism.* New York: Richard Smith, 1931.

Henderson, Gregory. *Korea: The Politics of the Vortex.* Cambridge: Harvard University Press, 1968.

Hsiao, Kung-chuan. *A Modern China and a New World: K'ang Yu-wei, Reformer and Utopian, 1858–1927.* Seattle: University of Washington Press, 1975.

Hutchins, Francis G. *India's Revolution: Gandhi and the Quit India Movement.* Cambridge: Harvard University Press, 1973.

Isaacs, Harold R. *Idols of the Tribe: Group Identity and Political Change.* New York: Harper and Row, 1975.

Janelli, Roger. "The Origins of Korean Folklore Scholarship." *Journal of American Folklore* 99 (1986): 24–49.

Jansen, Marius B. "Changing Japanese Attitudes Toward Modernization." In Marius Jansen, ed., *Changing Japanese Attitudes Toward Modernization*. Princeton, N.J.: Princeton University Press, 1965.

Juhn, Daniel S. "Nationalism and Korean Businessmen under Japanese Colonial Rule." *Korea Journal* 17 (Jan. 1977): 4–12.

Kalton, Michael. "The Neo-Confucian World View and Value System of Yi Dynasty Korea." Ph.D. diss. Harvard University, 1977.

Karl, Hongkee. "A Critical Evaluation of Modern Social Trends in Korea." Ph.D. diss., University of Chicago, 1934.

Kautsky, J. H., ed. *Political Change in Underdeveloped Countries*. New York: Wiley, 1962.

Kedourie, Elie. *Nationalism*. London: Hutchinson, 1960.

Kendall, Laurel. "Caught Between Ancestors and Spirits: Field Report of a Korean Mansin's Healing Kŭt." *Korea Journal* 17, no. 8 (Aug. 1977): 8–23.

———. and Mark Peterson, eds. *Korean Women: A View from the Inner Room*. New Haven, N.J.: East Rock Press, 1984.

Kim, C. I. Eugene, and Han-kyo Kim. *Korea and the Politics of Imperialism, 1876–1910*. Berkeley and Los Angeles: University of California Press, 1967.

———. and Doretha E. Mortimore, eds. *Korean's Response to Japan: The Colonial Period, 1910–1945*. Kalamazoo: Western Michigan University, 1977.

Kim, Joungwon. *Divided Korea: The Politics of Development*. Cambridge, Mass.: East Asian Research Center, 1975.

Kim, Key-hiuk. *The Last Phase of the East Asian World Order*. Berkeley and Los Angeles: University of California Press, 1980.

Ko, Seong-kyun. "The March First Movement: A Study of the Rise of Korean Nationalism under the Japanese Colonialism." *Korean Quarterly*, vol. 14 (1972).

Kohn, Hahns. *The Idea of Nationalism*. New York: Macmillan, 1967.

Ku, Dae-yeol. *Korea Under Colonialism: The March First Movement and Anglo-Japanese Relations*. Seoul: Royal Asiatic Society, Korea Branch, 1985.

Ledyard, Gari. "The Korean Language Reform of 1446: The Origin, Background, and Early History of the Korean Alphabet." Ph.D. diss., University of California, Berkeley, 1966.

Lee, Chong-sik. *The Politics of Korean Nationalism*. Berkeley and Los Angeles: University of California Press, 1964.

Lee, Grant S. "A Philosophical Appraisal of Yi Kwang-su: Man and Writer." *Korea Journal* 17, no. 1 (Jan. 1977): 40–56.

Lee, Hoon K. *Land Utilization and Rural Economy in Korea*. Shanghai: Kelly and Walsh, 1936.

Lee, Kwang-rin [Yi Kwangnin]. "Korea's Response to Social Darwinism." *Korea Journal*, vol. 18 (April, May, 1978).

Lee, Hi-seung. "Recollections of the Korean Language Society Incident." In Marshall Pihl, ed., *Listening to Korea*. New York: Praeger, 1973.

Levenson, Joseph R. *Confucian China and Its Modern Fate: A Trilogy.* Berkeley and Los Angeles: University of California Press, 1970.

_____. *Liang Ch'i-ch'ao and the Mind of Modern China.* Berkeley and Los Angeles: University of California Press, 1970.

Lew, Young-ick. "The Kabo Reform Movement: Korean and Japanese Reform Efforts in Korea, 1894." Ph.D. diss., Harvard University, 1972.

_____. "An Analysis of Reform Documents of the Kabo Reform Movement." *Journal of Social Science and Humanities*, vol. 40 (Dec. 1974).

_____. "Korean-Japanese Politics behind the Kabo-Ulmi Reform Movement, 1894 to 1896." *Journal of Korean Studies* 3 (1981): 39–82.

_____. "Yüan Shih-k'ai's Residency and the Korean Enlightenment Movement, 1885–94." *Journal of Korean Studies* 5 (1984): 63–108.

Lin, Yü-sheng. *The Crisis of Chinese Consciousness: Radical Antitraditionalism in the May Fourth Era.* Madison: University of Wisconsin Press, 1979.

_____. "Radical Iconoclasm in the May Fourth Period and the Future of Chinese Liberalism." In Benjamin Schwartz, ed., *Reflections on the May Fourth Movement*, pp. 23–58. Cambridge: Harvard University Press, 1973.

Maruyama, Masao. *Thought and Behaviour in Modern Japanese Politics.* London: Oxford University Press, 1963.

McCann, David. "Arirang: The National Folksong of Korea." In David McCann, ed., *Studies on Korea in Transition*. Honolulu: Center for Korean Studies, University of Hawaii, 1980.

McNamara, Dennis. "Cultural Autonomy: The Righteous Armies." *Korean Studies*, vol. 10 (1986).

Meisner, Maurice. *Li Ta-chao and the Origins of Chinese Marxism.* New York: Atheneum, 1970.

_____. "Leninism and Maoism: Some Populist Perspectives in Marxist-Leninism in China." *China Quarterly*, vol. 45 (Jan.–Mar. 1971).

_____. "Cultural Iconoclasm, Nationalism, and Internationalism in the May Fourth Movement." In Benjamin Schwartz, ed., *Reflections on the May Fourth Movement*, pp. 14–22. Cambridge: Harvard University Press, 1973.

_____. "Utopian Socialist Themes in Maoism." In J. W. Lewis, ed., *Peasant Rebellion and Communist Revolution in Asia*. Stanford, Calif.: Stanford University Press, 1974.

Metzger, Thomas A. *Escape from Predicament: Neo-Confucianism and China's Evolving Political Culture.* New York: Columbia University Press, 1977.

Moore, Barrington. *Social Origins of Dictatorship and Democracy.* Boston: Beacon Press, 1966.

Morris, Ivan. *Nationalism and the Right Wing in Japan.* London: Oxford University Press, 1960.

Moskowitz, Karl. "The Creation of the Oriental Development Company:

Japanese Illusions Meet Korean Reality." *Occasional Papers on Korea*, no. 2 (March 1974), pp. 73–121.

_____. "Current Assets: Employees of Japanese Banks in Colonial Korea." Ph.D. diss., Harvard University, 1979.

Nahm, Andrew D., ed. *Korea under Japanese Colonial Rule*. Kalamazoo: Western Michigan University, 1973.

Nelson, M. Fredrick. *Korea and the Old Orders in Eastern Asia*. Baton Rouge: Louisiana State University Press, 1946.

North, Robert C. *M. N. Roy's Mission to China*. Berkeley and Los Angeles: University of California Press, 1963.

Paik, George L. *The History of Protestant Missions in Korea, 1832–1910*. Seoul: Yonsei University Press, 1971.

Palais, James B. *Politics and Policy in Traditional Korea*. Cambridge: Harvard University Press, 1975.

_____. "Political Participation in Traditional Korea." *Journal of Korean Studies* 1 (1979): 73–121.

_____. "Confucianism and the Aristocratic/Bureaucratic Balance in Korea." *Harvard Journal of Asiatic Studies* 44, no. 2 (1984): 427–68.

_____. "Han Yongu's Studies of Early Chosŏn Intellectual History." *Journal of Korean Studies* 2 (1980): 199–224.

Power, Paul F. *The Meanings of Gandhi*. Honolulu: University Press of Hawaii, 1971.

Pyle, Kenneth B. *The New Generation in Meiji Japan*. Stanford, Calif.: Stanford University Press, 1969.

_____. *The Making of Modern Japan*. Lexington, Mass.: D. C. Heath and Co., 1978.

Redfield, Robert. *Peasant Society and Culture*. Chicago: Chicago University Press, 1956.

Rew, Joung Yole. "A Study of the Government-General of Korea, with an Emphasis on the Period Between 1919 and 1931." Ph.D. diss., American University, 1962.

Robinson, Michael. "Ch'oe Hyŏn-bae and Korean Nationalism: Language, Culture, and National Development." *Occasional Papers on Korea*, no. 3 (June 1975), pp. 19–33.

_____. "The Origins and Development of Korean Nationalist Ideology, 1920–1926: Culture, Identity, National Development and Political Schism." Ph.D. diss., University of Washington, 1979.

_____. "Colonial Publication Policy and the Korean Nationalist Movement." In Ramon H. Myers and Mark R. Peattie, eds., *The Japanese Colonial Empire*, pp. 312–46. Princeton, N.J.: Princeton University Press, 1984.

_____. "Ideological Schism in the Korean Nationalist Movement, 1920–1930: Cultural Nationalism and the Radical Critique." *Journal of Korean Studies* 4 (1982–83): 241–68.

_____. "National Identity and the Thought of Sin Ch'ae-ho: *Sadaejuŭi* and *chuch'e* in History and Politics." *Journal of Korean Studies* 5 (1984): 121–42.

———. "Nationalism and the Korean Tradition, 1896–1920: Iconoclasm, Reform, and National Identity." *Korean Studies*, vol. 10 (1987).

Scalapino, Robert A. *The Japanese Communist Movement, 1920–1966.* Berkeley and Los Angeles: University of California Press, 1967.

———. and Chong-sik Lee. *Communism in Korea.* 2 vols. Berkeley and Los Angeles: University of California Press, 1972.

Schram, Stuart R. *The Political Thought of Mao Tse-tung.* New York: Praeger, 1963.

Schwartz, Benjamin. "Introduction." In Benjamin Schwartz, ed., *Reflections on the May Fourth Movement*, pp. 1–13. Cambridge: Harvard University Press, 1973.

———. *In Search of Wealth and Power: Yen Fu and the West.* Cambridge: Harvard University Press, 1964.

Seton-Watson, Hugh. *Nations and States.* Boulder, Colo.: Westview, 1977.

Shafer, Boyd C. *Nationalism: Myth and Reality.* New York: Harcourt, Brace and Co., 1955.

Shively, Donald H. "Nishimura Shigeki: A Confucian View of Modernization." In Marius Jansen, ed., *Changing Japanese Attitudes Toward Modernization.* Princeton, N.J.: Princeton University Press, 1965.

Smith, Anthony D. *Theories of Nationalism.* New York: Harper and Row, 1971.

Smith, Henry, II. *Japan's First Student Radicals.* Cambridge: Harvard University Press, 1972.

Struve, Walter. *Elites Against Democracy.* Princeton, N.J.: Princeton University Press, 1973.

Suh, Dae-sook. *Documents of Korean Communism, 1918–1948.* Princeton, N.J.: Princeton University Press, 1967.

———. *The Korean Communist Movement, 1918–1948.* Princeton, N.J.: Princeton University Press, 1967.

———. and Chae-jin Lee, eds. *Political Leadership in Korea.* Seattle: University of Washington Press, 1976.

Suh, Doo Soo. *Korean Literary Reader.* Seoul: Donga Publishing Co., 1965.

Suh, Sang Chul. *Growth and Structural Change in the Korean Economy, 1910–1945.* Cambridge: Council on East Asian Studies. Dist. by Harvard University Press, 1978.

Van Slyke, Lyman P. *Enemies and Friends: The United Front in Chinese Communist History.* Stanford, Calif.: Stanford University Press, 1967.

Wakemen, Frederic, Jr. *History and Will: Philosophical Perspectives of Mao Tse-tung's Thought.* Berkeley and Los Angeles: University of California Press, 1973.

Waldron, Arthur N. "Theories of Nationalism and Historical Explanation." *World Politics* 37, no. 3 (April 1985): 416–31.

Wallace, Anthony F. C. "Revitalization Movements." In W. A. Lessa, ed.,

Reader in Comparative Religion: An Anthropological Approach. New York: Harper and Row, 1972.

Weems, Benjamin B. *Reform, Rebellion, and the Heavenly Way.* Tucson: University of Arizona Press, 1964.

Wells, Kenneth M. "Civic Morality in the Nationalist Thought of Yun Ch'i-ho, 1881–1911." *Papers on Far Eastern History* (A.N.U.), no. 28 (1983), pp. 107–51.

———. "The Rationale of Korean Economic Nationalism under Japanese Colonial Rule, 1922–1932: The Case of Cho Man-sik's Products Promotion Society." *Modern Asian Studies* 19, no. 4 (October 1985): 823–60.

Wright, Mary C. *The Last Stand of Chinese Conservatism: The T'ung-chih Restoration, 1862–1874.* Stanford, Calif.: Stanford University Press, 1962.

Yoo, Sae Hee. "The Communist Movement and the Peasants: The Case of Korea." In J. W. Lewis, ed., *Peasant Rebellion and Communist Revolution in Asia.* Stanford, Calif.: Stanford University Press, 1974.

———. "The Korean Communist Movement and the Peasantry Under Japanese Rule." Ph.D. diss., Columbia University, 1974.

Index

Abe Mitsuka, 102, 116
Alexeyevsk incident, 109
Alphabet, phonetic. *See Han'gŭl*
All Korea Youth League, 111
All Parties Local Notables Association, 103, 142
An Ch'angho: in exile government, 48; and gradualism, 66, 94; mentioned, 41, 71, 121
Anglo-Japanese Alliance, 37
Aoyagi Nammei, 116
Assimilation, 40, 50

Bethell, Ernest, 38
Bolsheviks, 63
Budan seiji. *See* Military Dictatorship Government
Bunka seiji. *See* Cultural policy

Cadastral survey. *See* Land survey
Censorship: system of, 5, 51–52; and *Kaebyŏk*, 63; relaxation of, 115; standards of, 51, 122, 142; risks under, 151, 153
Chach'i undong. *See* Self-rule
Chajakhoe. *See* Self-Production Association
Ch'a Kŭmbong, 112
Chang Chiyŏn, 29, 31, 54, 80
Chang Tŏksu: ideas of, 60–61; and youth league leadership, 84–85, 111; mentioned, 57
Chemulp'o, Treaty of, 20
Cho Mansik: forms Chajakhoe, 95; in production movement, 97
Chinbodang. *See* Progressive party
Ch'oe Cheu, 23
Ch'oe Hyŏnbae, 91
Ch'oe Namsŏn: early studies, 56; and youth magazines, 54, 65–66; and cultural nationalism, 73; and folklore, 81; relations with GGK, 102
Ch'oe Rin, 142, 144. *See also* Self-rule

Choe Tonggyŏng Chosŏnin yuhaksaeng hag'uhoe. *See* Tokyo Korean Students' Friends of Learning Society
Chŏn Chosŏn ch'ŏngnyŏndan taehoe. *See* Conference of Korean Youth Groups
Ch'ŏndogyo: origins of, 24, 43; and independence movement, 55; and morality, 60; influence on Yi Kwangsu, 65; pan-humanism, 115. *See also* Yi Tonhwa
Ch'ŏndogyo ch'ŏngnyŏnhoe. *See* Ch'ŏndogyo Youth Association
Ch'ŏndogyo Youth Association, 55
Ch'ŏndogyo Youth Department for the Study of Doctrine, 61
Ch'ŏngch'un (Youth), 54
Ch'ŏngnyŏn hag'uhoe. *See* Student Youth Association
Chŏng Paek, 120–24, 131
Chŏng Yag'yong, 68
Chōsen sangyō keizai chōsakai. *See* Industrial Economic Investigation Committee for Korea
Chosŏn chigwang (Light of Korea), 55, 115
Chosŏn ch'ŏngnyŏn yŏnhaphoe. *See* Korean Youth League
Chosŏn hakhoe. *See* Korea Study Society
Chosŏn ilbo (Korea Daily), 46, 52, 86, 90, 114
Chosŏn kyoyuk hyŏphoe. *See* Korean Education Association
Chosŏn mulsan changnyŏhoe. *See* Society for the Promotion of Native Products
Chosŏn nodong kongjehoe. *See* Korean Fraternal Labor Federation
Chosŏn nonong ch'ong tongmaeng. *See* Korean Labor-Farmer Organization
Chosŏn yŏja hŭnghakhoe. *See* Korean